Radicalism, Cooperation and Socialism:
Leicester working-class politics 1860–1906

Radicalism, Cooperation and Socialism:

Leicester working-class politics 1860–1906

Bill Lancaster

1987
Leicester University Press

First published in 1987 by Leicester University Press

Distributed in North America by
Humanities Press, Inc.,
Atlantic Highlands, NJ 07716

Designed by Geoffrey Wadsley
Photoset in 10 on 12 point Galliard
Printed and bound in Great Britain by
Biddles Ltd, Guildford
and King's Lynn

The publication of this book has been assisted by a grant from the Twenty-Seven Foundation

British Library Cataloguing in Publication Data
Lancaster, Bill
Radicalism, cooperation and socialism:
Leicester working-class politics 1860–1906.
1. Labour and labouring classes – England
– Leicester (Leicestershire) –
History – 19th century   2. Socialism
– England – Leicester (Leicestershire)
– History – 19th century   3. Leicester
(Leicestershire) – History
I. Title
322'.2'0942542   HD8400.L4

ISBN 0–7185–1286–3

Contents

List of Illustrations

Figures

Plates

between pages 42–3

List of Tables

Abbreviations

ASE	Amalgamated Society of Engineers
BFC	British Federal Council
BSU	British Secular Union
BUSMC	British United Shoe Machinery Company
CAS	Citizens' Aid Society
CWS	Cooperative Wholesale Society
FWK	framework knitter
IISH	International Institute of Social History
ILP	Independent Labour Party
LAHU	Leicester Amalgamated Hosiery Union
LHMA	Leicester Hosiery Manufacturers' Association
LRC	Labour Representation Committee
NAC	National Administrative Council
NSS	National Secular Society
NUBSO	National Union of Boot and Shoe Operatives
NUORF	National Union of Operative Rivetters and Finishers
PP	Parliamentary Papers
RC	Royal Commission
SC	Select Committee
SDF	Social Democratic Federation
SL	Socialist League
TUC	Trades Union Congress
USMC	United Shoe Machinery Company

Acknowledgments

I am deeply grateful for the help I have received during the production of this book from the staff of numerous libraries and archives. In particular those at the University Libraries of Warwick and Leicester, the Birmingham Reference Library, Leicester Reference Library, the British Library of Political Science and Economy, the British Library at Bloomsbury and the newspaper collection at Colindale, have cheerfully complied with my many demands. The staff at the Leicestershire Records Office provided efficient service, indispensable advice and much helpful guidance. Richard Storey at the Modern Records Centre, University of Warwick, has supplied many references for which I am most thankful. The General Secretary and staff at the National Union of Leather, Footwear and Allied Trades at Earls Barton, Northampton, gave access to the union's excellent archive collection and made my stay with them extremely comfortable, as well as rewarding. Miss M. W. H. Schreudner of the International Institute of Social History, Amsterdam deserves special mention for her expert guidance through the complexities of the Institute's holdings. Lord Brockway kindly discussed with me his knowledge and recollections of Leicester secularism and socialism in the early years of the present century.

Many colleagues and friends have cheerfully put up with my Leicester obsession over the years and provided helpful criticism, advice and encouragement. Professor Royden Harrison, the staff and students at the Centre for the Study of Social History at the University of Warwick provided an intellectual home; while Mr J. L. Halstead of Sheffield University and an honorary member of the Centre discussed much of this book with me and provided many useful comments. Dr Fred Reid gave helpful and enthusiastic supervision over the doctoral research that forms the basis for much of this book. Dr Tony Mason, Director of Studies at the Centre, advised me on how to turn my thesis into a book in between the more important business of following the fortunes of Coventry City Football Club. Amanda Noble, amongst many other things, helped me prepare the manuscript. Mrs D. Hewitt typed this work without complaint at my often illegible handwriting. Needless to say, any faults or inaccuracies are entirely my responsibility.

Let us go to the king, he is young, and shew him what servage [servitude] we be in, and shew him how we will have it otherwise, or else we will provide us of some remedy; and if we go together, all manner of people that be now in any bondage will follow us to the intent to be made free; and when the king seeth us, we shall have some remedy, either by fairness or otherwise.

John Ball 1381

'To His Most Gracious Majesty King Edward VII

'May it please Your Majesty – We, your most dutiful and loyal subjects of Leicester unemployed workmen, beg to acquaint Your Majesty of our great sufferings, through want of employment.

'We have suffered long and patiently, and as there are no immediate signs of our sufferings being lessened, we make bold to present our complaints to Your Majesty in person, knowing how deeply you have been interested in the housing question, and other matters concerning the welfare of the poor.

'Many of us are old soldiers and took an active part in the late South African war. We are reduced to the extreme of misery and want. We are unable to fulfil one of the first duties of husbands and fathers, namely to provide food for our wives and children.

'In our sorrow we turn to Your Majesty, as father of your people, and humbly ask you to receive us and to use your kindly and powerful influence on our behalf.

'I am Your Majesty's most dutiful and humble servant.'

Signed on behalf of the unemployed by George White.
June 1905

Introduction

This work had its origins in an attempt to answer a somewhat simple question during the third year of an undergraduate degree. A course on British Labour History in the years before 1914 had highlighted the strains and tensions that existed in the early Labour Party, but left me dissatisfied with orthodox explanations of its early problems. These accounts, which had concentrated on the parliamentary relationship between Liberal and Labour and the apparently conflicting concerns of trade unionists and socialists in the formation of political objectives, were not fundamentally wrong, but seemed to lack a certain important dimension. A clue to what this missing dimension might be was furnished by Ross McKibbin's monograph on the history of the party after 1910. It was not so much McKibbin's overall interpretation that was appealing but rather his short chapter on constituency unrest in the years immediately before the outbreak of war in 1914.[1] Why, for example, was the most potent challenge to the stability of the Parliamentary Labour Party and the major threat to the electoral arrangements between the party and the Liberals arising not from the often tension-ridden elements that formed the party nationally but from the grass-roots activists in the constituencies? Was this unrest at local level the beginnings of what was often to be that stormy relationship between Constituency Labour Parties and the national leadership?

On re-reading McKibbin it was noticed that perhaps the major event in this early expression of local unrest was the threat by the Leicester Labour Party to field a candidate in the 1913 parliamentary by-election, in direct contravention of the 1903 electoral agreement. It seemed an apparent motion of censure against the performance of the parliamentary party. This incident was given extra significance by the fact that the sitting member for this double constituency was none other than James Ramsay MacDonald, the leader of the party in Parliament and the co-author of the 1903 electoral pact.

Subsequent work on the subject for a short M.A. dissertation led in the opposite direction to that of my initial interest.[2] My concern to examine a significant instance of early grass-roots unrest in the Labour Party became subordinate to a growing interest in the continuities between the Leicester

Labour movement in the first years of the present century and previous forms of local working-class political activities. Research suggested that the Leicester Labour Party was partly the product of a tenacious local working-class culture that stretched back deep into the nineteenth century. This appeared to answer more fully the original question and at the same time presented a more complete picture of the early Labour Party. The early Leicester Labour Party possessed a Janus face: on the one side the party with MacDonald at the helm appeared to prefigure the future process of bureaucratizing and centralizing Labour politics; on the other the Leicester movement manifests itself as a product of a specific local political tradition deeply entrenched in, and taking direction from, issues rooted in the local community.

Such a characterization sets this study apart from previous interpretations of the early Labour Party. The emphasis upon the continuing importance of the local dimension in the political activites of the working class during the Edwardian period challenges the argument of P. F. Clarke that 'the whole ambit of politics had changed from the local to the national'.[3] The attention given to local economic and social issues and their role as generating forces in the emergence of independent Labour politics is, of course, diametrically opposite to the organizational interpretation offered by McKibbin.[4] Similarly this focus on issues and their effect on the local community differs somewhat from the arguments of Henry Pelling. In his classic study *Origins of the Labour Party* Pelling emphasizes the failure of Liberals to allot adequate offices of representation to 'labour men' in his explanation of why the working class formed independent political institutions.[5]

It could be argued that Leicester was not representative and that the findings of this research should not be extrapolated as a general explanation of Labour politics. There is much to commend this argument, but in defence of any wider claims that emerge in this study it should be pointed out that as yet we have very few works on local Labour movements on which to base firm judgments. Thus, unlike Clarke, no claim will be made that the arguments presented here can be writ large over working-class politics nationally. Indeed a central theme of this study is that up to 1906 Labour and socialist politics were essentially local. Where distinct, independent, working-class institutions occur they tended to be the product of specific struggles within individual communities. Therefore to understand the emergence of independent Labour as a political force it is necessary to study the movement's origins in individual localities. Once this exercise has been undertaken the historian will perhaps not be too startled to find that the early Labour Party did not present a crystallization of the movement nationally but rather an attempt to form a gel out of stubborn ingredients, the most obdurate one being an intense sense of parochialism amongst the rank and file.

In order to demonstrate the parochialism of a specific Labour movement it is necessary to pursue two themes. First, a thorough understanding of the structure of the working class has to be achieved in order to grasp the complexities of the relationship between material forces and the Labour movement. Thus close attention has to be paid to the world of work, its organization and the changing relations of production during a period when work, or the lack of it, was the dominant feature of working-class life. Important as this theme is, too great a reliance upon its explanatory powers leads to a somewhat mechanistic analysis of working-class political action. Moreover, such an analysis would be crucially flawed as it would fail to take account of other important aspects of working-class life that are not directly linked to the world of work yet can still play determinant roles in the politics of the Labour movement. This point can be underlined if we pose the question, why do apparently similar communities, with similar economic structures, produce radically different forms of working-class political action? The key to answering such a question lies in grasping the unique world of working-class culture and political traditions that exist in specific places. In short, working-class communities possess both a structure and a nature. These two components, however, never exist in isolation from each other; they have to be seen as constantly interacting and reshaping each other.

To understand the dynamics of these two factors in shaping Leicester politics and creating the ambiguity that was so apparent to the local Labour movement in the early years of the present century, it is necessary to shift the focus from regarding local working-class politics as prefacing twentieth-century trends. Instead it will be argued that the early years of the Labour Party in Leicester displayed all the tensions that existed in a political movement that looked back to the world of Victorian working-class radicalism while at the same time taking its first hesitant steps towards the social reformism which was to characterize the modern Labour Party.

Leicester was a unique and distinct place. It does, however, have a strong general claim to significance in terms of English nineteenth-century working-class history. For example, continuity can be detected which links the world of the Hampden Clubs, Owenism and Chartism, through to the era of the First International, working-class republicanism and secularism, early forms of socialism, and Independent Labour Party (ILP) and the Labour Party itself. Indeed there are few provincial towns that ranked as prominently as Leicester did in all these movements. Similarly, Leicester's major industries, especially hosiery and shoemaking, were trades that either figured in, or provided activists for, major episodes of working-class upheaval.

The industries of Leicester played a major role both in generating issues that fed into these working-class movements and by providing an industrial and social milieu in which traditions and political cultures could persist. An important theme to be explored is the longevity of the putting-out system of industrial organization in both hosiery and footwear production. Indeed this theme cannot be stressed too strongly, because the outwork system dominated many aspects of working-class life, and not only those directly concerned with production. Thus when mechanization and centralization gathered pace in hosiery during the 1870s and 1880s its effects upon working-class life were manifold, and an even more dramatic change was created when the larger footwear industry embarked on a similar process during the early 1890s.

It will be argued that the longevity of outwork in Leicester as the dominant mode of industrial organization nurtured working-class cultural traditions that are usually associated with artisan forms of production. Furthermore, the persistence of outwork, by imbuing the working class with a strong sense of independence, produced much of the vitality that was so characteristic of the Leicester Labour movement. Indeed it will be shown that early socialist movements, the ILP and even the Labour Party were born out of the social and economic tension created by the centralization of local industry. Such a portrayal of working-class life and politics is radically different from other studies of the period which focus upon the factory community during the second half of the nineteenth century. Yet given the reiteration by a new generation of scholars of Sir John Clapham's reminder of the slow growth of the factory system in England, how far was Leicester from the norm?[6]

This study begins in 1860. Leicester was then, at long last, entering a period of economic prosperity that was to last for three decades. The 'lean hungry stockinger' who worked in what was still the major local industry, was losing his deep association with poverty as living standards rose to levels unknown for two generations. The rising prosperity of the stockinger was produced by the rise in demand of Leicester hosiery, a rise in line with demand for consumer goods nationally.[7] It was also aided by the easing of the local labour market thanks to the rapid growth of the town's new ready-made footwear trade. This new industry, which had been growing since the early 1850s, was soon to enter a period of spectacular growth, increasing the size of its workforce nineteen-fold in the half century up to 1901. It contributed greatly to the three-and-a-half-fold increase in the town's population during the same period.[8] By 1891 the workers in hosiery and footwear constituted 62.5 per cent of Leicester's industrial workforce.

We have noted that both these industries were based on outwork production late into the nineteenth century. Despite this atomization of the work process, both industries possessed strong trade union traditions which were to play an important part in Liberal and Labour politics throughout the period. Outwork and its tendency to underpin an independent artisan-type culture ensured, however, that working-class politics were never totally subsumed within liberalism. Similarly, old forms of working-class organization from earlier in the century continued unhindered by the marching decades. Owenism and its subsequent transformation to organized secularism was particularly important in Leicester.

This persistence of an independent artisan culture was further assisted by the growing stream of immigrant workers into Leicester's expanding number of workshops. The majority of the migrants, coming from the countryside, released from the communal bonds of rural life, found few constraints in their new urban surroundings. Fitting comfortably into the informal world of the workshops, where St Monday was still honoured, they indeed found that 'city air breathes free'.

This world of work and all its communal and cultural manifestations became increasingly challenged during the 1880s and 1890s, by new machines and working practices as Leicester manufacturers undertook a far-reaching programme of industrial restructuring. This was in response to the growing threat of foreign competition, tariff barriers and a slump in demand. The turmoil created by these changes saw a shift in the local working-class political culture away from extreme forms of radicalism and towards the new doctrine of socialism. Yet this shift was far from being clear-cut, and a distinct sense of direction failed to emerge. Rather socialism was modified to meet the needs of workers still steeped in the artisan notion of the independent self-regulating workman. One result of this was that, during the 1890s, cooperative production became intermingled and bound up with socialism as hosiery and footwear workers attempted to escape from the increasing vicissitudes of capitalist production and preserve their autonomy at work.

The socialist commonwealth became coterminous with the cooperative commonwealth for many in the Leicester Labour movement during these years. It was an ideology that looked forward to the communal ownership of the instruments of production and back to the old workshops. They had never been entirely self-governing but they had at least enjoyed a high degree of informality of organization. The 1895 boot and shoe lock-out signalled the victory of the manufacturers in both hosiery and footwear in their campaign to achieve centralized mechanized production. It also meant the waning of the cooperative ideal. Just to survive, cooperatives now had to compete with mechanized capitalist enterprises, a task which dictated not only similar machines but also similar relationships of production.

Mechanized production entailed an element of de-skilling, with handworkers being turned into semi-skilled machine operatives. Moreover, competition in both the home and international markets was so intense that manufacturers increasingly resorted to cutting labour costs still further by substituting young, unskilled for old, skilled workers. Thus by 1900 Leicester was beginning to experience the ravages of long-term structural unemployment, particularly amongst adult male footwear workers. With such changing social circumstances Leicester socialism had to reshape itself and in particular to develop concern and to formulate remedies for the growth of local poverty. It is in this period that a distinct programme of municipal socialism emerges designed to alleviate poverty locally. It is also in this period that belief grew in the ability of independent Labour representation at Westminster to provide the most potent long-term solution to the problems caused by unemployment.

Yet in 1900 the Leicester labour movement still had one foot in each century. It is true that locally the need for the palliatives of welfare reform were gaining expression, but many still clung to older solutions, especially land reform and agricultural colonies. It was into these circumstances that MacDonald stepped and by both stealth and populism was able to square the circle of apparently contradictory pressures. Despite this ambiguity the Leicester Labour Representation Committee (LRC) with MacDonald as the figurehead was able to capitalize on growing concern over unemployment. By 1905 the new party had achieved a solid political base in local elections and liberalism was suffering organizational decline in many working-class wards. The election of MacDonald to Parliament in 1906 sealed the consolidation of class-based, Labour politics in Leicester: it did not, however, eradicate its ambiguities.

1 The Leicester Hosiery Industry in the Nineteenth Century: A Survey

Hosiery was the single most important industry in Leicester until the final quarter of the nineteenth century. In 1851 it was the largest single source of employment, accounting for 38.5 per cent of Leicester's industrial workforce and in 1891 it still provided 21.5 per cent of the town's industrial employment. Moreover, the pattern of industrial organization in the Leicester hosiery trade for a large part of this period, the putting-out system, served as a model for the new industry of mass-produced footwear, introduced to the town in 1851. By 1891 Leicester was the undisputed capital of British hosiery and footwear production, the two trades employing 62.5 per cent of the workers in the town.

The hosiery industry has generally been overlooked by labour historians which is unfortunate for labour historiography in general, as the trade in Leicester offers a tangible link between the world of Thomas Cooper's Chartists, Edward Miall's Liberation Society and, arguably, the first British trade union to possess a socialist leadership. The experience of the Leicester hosiery trade between the ending of Chartist hostilities and the emergence of socialism also carries implications for those accounts of mid-century class harmony, usually based on Lancashire sources, that on the one hand stress the importance of status divisions within the working class, created by the labour process, and on the other focus upon 'employer hegemony' as a product of communal deference based upon close employer–employee relationships.[1]

The origins of the hosiery industry in Leicester lie deep in the seventeenth century and have been well documented by Wells in his study of the trade.[2] In 1850 hosiery was still a handicraft industry based largely on the hand frame invented by William Lee in the 1580s. The 'putting-out' system was still the main form of industrial organization which over the years had developed a complex network of hosier merchant capitalists, middlemen, bag men, frame renters, stockingers and ancillary trades. The location of the industry was also becoming more complex. Some workers still laboured at home, while others were increasingly moving into workshops and in a few instances into the hosiers' warehouses. Factories, however, were absent at the mid-century. It was to take another three decades before hosiery finally abandoned the home and the workshop in favour of the factory.

Generally speaking the main stimulants to factory production in hosiery were a general upturn of demand after 1850, increased competition from mechanized factories in Saxony, alternative employment opportunities in the new boot industry, and various legislative measures. Taken collectively these factors provided both the economic imperatives and the change in attitudes that were necessary for factory production. This process, however, did not occur overnight and the old system was far from extinct in 1880.

Before we survey the emergence of the Leicester hosiery factory a note of qualification on the limitations of statistical information is required. Apart from Gravenor Henson's early history of the hosiery industry,[3] William Felkin's account, produced in 1845, is the most useful early work on our period and above all it is the first history of the trade that contains reliable statistical information.[4] Felkin, a former framesmith and hosier from Nottingham turned statistician, was fired by a philosophy of industrial 'Malthusianism' in his writings. Believing that the major cause of the industry's stagnation was an over-abundance of both men and frames, he undertook his statistical survey as part of his evidence to the 1845 Commission. Felkin's highly detailed enumerations were presented as part of the commissioner's report and received wide publicity throughout the trade; most importantly from the historian's viewpoint, they were never challenged by any of the witnesses. This numerical snapshot of Leicester in 1844 does, however, lack detail in certain crucial areas. While Felkin's tables display the number, types and products of all the frames in the town they do not show where the frames are located. We therefore cannot with accuracy state the size of the 'workshop' and 'domestic' sectors. Felkin also failed to furnish data on the crucially important issue of frame ownership, and therefore the changing relationships between hosier, middlemen, and stockingers remains highly impressionistic.

Official statistics are even more elusive and frustrating than Felkin's. Hosiery was included with other textile industries in the 1833 Factory Act, but the statistical emphasis of the early inspectorate was largely directed towards the Lancashire cotton mills. No figures at all on the hosiery trade appeared in the 'factory inspectors' returns' until 1862, and these tables are of little utility as they enumerate the industry on county divisions and it is impossible to disentangle Leicester from Leicestershire in any meaningful way.[5]

The two sets of 'returns' that were published before the 1867 Workshops Act, that contain information on hosiery, those of 1862 and 1867, do list the number of factories in Leicestershire and the number of hand and steam-powered frames that they employed, but given the Factory Act's loose definition of a factory – any establishment employing over 50 people – it is impossible to differentiate between large workshops and genuine steam-powered factories. The two 'returns' do show a small rise in steam horsepower in the five years between 1862 and 1867, from 305 hp to 330 hp, but Felkin's 1844 survey shows that Leicester did not possess a monopoly of steam over the county; the town of Loughborough, for instance, employed 84 steam frames in comparison to Leicester's 24.[6]

One of the few hard pieces of statistical evidence furnished by official returns is contained in the return of 1870 showing those 'boroughs enforcing the Workshops Acts'. In this return Sergeant Wright, the Leicester Borough Sanitary Inspector responsible for enforcing the Workshops Act, claimed that the town possessed 714 workshops which were mainly employed in hosiery and footwear production.[7] Unfortunately, this figure is not broken down into its component industries and is only useful as an indicator of the overall industrial organization of the town in 1870.

The potentially fruitful returns of 1871 which attempted to incorporate data from both the factory and workshop sectors for the first time were crucial for Musson's work.[8] The tables on Leicester, however, were incomplete with the local inspector admitting that the workshop returns were only 'partially received'.[9] Furthermore, the major section of this volume is tabulated in county divisions, which roughly accorded with the individual inspector's area of authority. Leicester town failed to appear in the lists of tables from selected boroughs at the rear of the volume.

After 1871 the quality of the returns improved with figures from the hosiery trade enumerated collectively under the heading of 'The Three Midland Counties', i.e. Nottingham, Derby and Leicester. Separate statistics do not reappear until 1887 in the returns relating to 'Factory Inspectors Salaries etc.' Again, unfortunately, these figures are based on Leicestershire, but they do, however, show the decline of the workshop with less than 50 employees, and the domination of the factory employing more than 50, with 893 of the former and 1,118 of the latter.[10]

The most reliable sources on the developments of the Leicester hosiery industry during the second half of the nineteenth century are the various royal commissions and parliamentary inquiries that sat between 1845 and 1892. Numbers, of course, only appear spasmodically and are difficult to tabulate into an orderly list or graph, but nevertheless the wealth of impressionistic evidence, occasionally anchored in quantitative data, that appear in these reports makes this source the most comprehensive available.

Perhaps the main consideration uppermost in the mind of Richard Muggeridge, the commissioner who sat in 1844 to consider the hosiery trade, was to find the answer to the failure of the factory system to develop in the industry. The plight of the Midland stockinger had received widespread national publicity and the actions of Thomas Cooper's Chartist followers were still fresh in the minds of concerned contemporaries. The solution to the ills of the hosiery trade was largely dictated by the ideology of Utilitarianism which perceived the emergence of regulated factories as the best method of overcoming the abuses and disorder of the apparently anarchic methods of organization that existed in the hosiery industry.

Muggeridge, in his report, concluded that the stagnation of the trade was caused primarily by overpriced products which were the result of outdated methods of production. When an employee of T. Collins, the pioneer of the steam-powered hosiery production in Leicester, informed the commissioner about the easy application of steam power to hand-operated rotary frames, Muggeridge gave his statement an enthusiastic endorsement.[11] Collins, however, was the only manufacturer in Leicester applying steam in the 1840s and was undoubtedly the owner of the 24 steam rotaries listed by Felkin.[12]

Despite the obvious stagnation of the trade some changes were taking place. Of the 65 working stockingers interviewed in 1844, 46 were employed in shops, the majority of which belonged to middlemen. The largest of these employed some 50 or 60 workers.[13] In 1840 none of the six most important hosiers in the town had shops of their own, but those entering the trade in the next few years established their own workshops from the start. Thus by 1844 hosiers' workshops, as well as those owned by middlemen, were competing with, and in many cases, emptying the small shops adjacent to, and often inside, the stockinger's home. Thomas Winters told the commissioner that 'Now there are many men who have to walk a mile from their homes, to work in large shops holding 40–50 frames or more.'[14] The major spur to this process of centralization was the increasing use of wide frames. Felkin's figures suggest that two-thirds of all the frames in Leicester were of the wide variety in 1844. These machines, which required considerable strength to operate, were generally used in garment production.[15] Each frame would produce a particular part so that production under one roof, especially if the seaming was also carried out within the building, was often seen to be desirable.

By 1855, however, only slight change can be discerned. The Report of the Select Committee on Stoppage of Wages (Hosiery) 1855 noted that there were only 200 power frames in Leicester that year. There was also a slight drift away from the tendency to concentrate frames in workshops, which was caused by a revival in the fancy sector where hosiers needed to keep tight control on quality and thus preferred to deal direct with the knitter.[16] The workers, of course, favoured this development as it freed them from the middleman and assured them the full warehouse price. Nevertheless, in 1855 most of the hosiers of whom we have specific knowledge worked mainly through middlemen. R. Mitchell employed all his 700 to 800 outside frames via 'undertakers'.[17] The 4,000 frames of John Biggs depended mainly on middlemen, and Biggs claimed that all the major hosiers did likewise.[18] Bilson, Baines, Walker and even Corah, who was rapidly overtaking Biggs as Leicester's largest hosier, all confirmed that they depended on middlemen.[19] Clearly the wide frames owned by large hosiers were increasing the activities of the 'undertakers', while the return of fortune to the fancy trade gave a boost to the small hosiers working the narrow frames.

A few major hosiers were reported to have attempted centralized production inside their own warehouses, but Baines told the committee that 'a few hosiers, having failed to make a workshop pay, because of the workers' opposition, were forced to return to putting-out through middlemen'.[20] At least two manufacturers, however, had made positive steps towards factory production, and these two hosiers accounted for the 200 power frames recorded in 1855.[21]

Between 1855 and the 1871 Royal Commission on the Truck System our sources largely dry up. All we have are the crude bench-marks supplied by the returns of the Factory Inspectorate, the inadequacy of which has already been noticed. These returns, however, if nothing else, confirm the slow growth of steam. In 1871 the County and Town of Leicester possessed only 389 hp of steam in comparison to 305 hp in 1862. The reasons for this slow progress can easily be discerned from the reports of the truck commissioners.

Corah's informed the commissioners that they had finally abandoned the rent system in 1866 with the opening of their St Margaret's works.[22] Corah's, however, were an exception. Their success was based on an elaborate network of regional warehouses which tended to iron out the fluctuations of seasonal demand.[23] Indeed, the most striking feature that emerges from the pages of the 1871 report is its similarity to that of 1845. J. Brindley, a stockinger and leader of the local knitters union, described a mode of industrial organization that still clung to frame rent and ancillary charges, was dominated by middlemen and was susceptible to severe seasonal fluctuations.[24] 'Spreading' of work amongst frames in times of poor trade still continued and one manufacturer had even given it a novel form. Brindley, when questioned on 'spreading', related how Sam Odams, a hosier employing 200 to 300 men, owned far too many frames for the amount of work available. Brindley claimed that in order to overcome this problem:

> He has instituted a system of lending money; it is called a bank there, and there is a cry on Mondays that the bank is open. In a factory of 200 or 300 men, there is always a number that will embrace the opportunity of borrowing money and getting drunk with it; and he calculates on a lot of the men going to drink with the bank money ... You have not to ask for the money; you walk into the warehouse, and show your face; there is a crowd about and it is quite well known what you want. The book-keeper looks round and puts the names down on the list; he places a couple of sovereigns on the table and then he reads the names out for 2s. each.[25]

When questioned by the commissioners Odams admitted that he did practise the 'bank system', but only for indoor men. When asked 'Is the rent you receive for your frames a very profitable part of the business of manufacture in Leicester?' Odams replied, 'We do depend on it being a profitable part.'[26] So profitable, in fact, that even those manufacturers employing steam were still charging factory operatives machine rent which was often as high as 13 shillings per week.[27]

A major technological breakthrough occurred in 1864 when William Cotton of Leicester invented his 'Cotton's patent' frame. This was a flat frame driven by a rotary mechanism which finally solved the problem of 'fashioning' by power. It followed the same principles as Lee's original frame but carried them out with different motions, introducing a needle bar which moved vertically. Moreover, its adaptability enabled all kinds of fashioned work to be produced, and soon improved models were making a dozen or more hose at once. The early 'rotaries' which appeared in the 1840s and were the first generation of steam-powered machines in the industry were not superseded by the 'Cotton's patent', as both types of frame continued to produce their own specialities. The flat machinery usually made garments or their separate parts and the circulars turned out large amounts of fabric as well as seamless stockings.[28]

Cotton was employed by a Loughborough hosier when he perfected his invention, but it was the Nottingham trade that was first to utilize the new technology when Mundella and Morley entered into an agreement with Cotton for the latter to build machines for their exclusive use. It was not until 1878, when Cotton started business on his own account, that his machines became generally available.[29] The contract between Cotton, Mundella and Morley was obviously an important factor in the slow growth of the factory in Leicester, since the Leicester trade, increasingly based on garment manufacture, produced on wide flat frames, stood to gain most from the new technology.[30]

As we have already seen, it is impossible to gauge with precision the genesis and development of the steam-powered factory in Leicester. Much of the evidence contained in the reports of the Royal Commission on the Depression of Trade and Industry relates rather impressionistically the quickening pace of the introduction of steam-powered frames in the late 1870s.[31] Daniel Merrick, the founder of Leicester Trades Council, and leader of the local hand frame knitters' union, The Sock and Top Society, told the 1886 Commission that employment had been good up to 1875 and then fell away, and by 1885 was totally depressed. Out of 1,100 skilled male workers and 100 others, in that branch of the industry, 700 were wholly unemployed and 'new modes-of-production' were blamed.[32]

Apart from the availability of new technology, other factors assisted the rise of factory production. Increased foreign competition undoubtedly acted as a spur to innovation. The yearbooks of the Leicester Chamber of Commerce are full of references to the urgent need for technical education throughout the 1880s, as a means of challenging the mechanical superiority of the Saxony trade based in the factory town of Chemnitz. When a technical school was opened in 1885 W. T. Rowlett, a major local hosier, set to work on translating Gustav Willkomm's college textbook

Technology of Frame-Work Knitting for the Leicester students.[33] The threat from the Chemnitz factories was indeed serious with the export value of woollen hose falling from £348,000 in the year 1861 to £288,000 in 1875.[34]

The industry faced other problems besides foreign competition. Perhaps the major obstacle to factory production was the deeply rooted structure of the putting-out system with its multitude of social and economic aspects. Professor Wells has argued that the most significant event in the decline of outwork was the passing of the Education Act in 1870.[35] He claims that the old method of organization was highly dependent on child labour. The boy who from an early age carried out his father's winding, became socialized into the stockinger's milieu and soon developed his father's attitudes and independence. Similarly young girls were trained by their mothers in the art of seaming. With the arrival of the board school, especially after 1876 when attendance was made compulsory by local by-law, children were removed from the workshops into the classrooms where new horizons and attitudes were instilled, and this vital area of recruitment to the putting-out system was closed.

There is much evidence to support this thesis. Angrave and Harris, the representatives of the Leicester Hosiery Manufacturers' Association (LHMA), told the commissioners investigating the workings of the Factories and Workshops Acts in 1876 that they wanted all child labour under 13 years of age abolished, as Leicester manufacturers found it extremely difficult to recruit the young and female labour already in workshops into factories.[36] When asked 'How is it then with very much less wages in workshops you find any difficulty in getting them in factories where you are giving higher wages?' they replied, 'There are many circumstances that lead to that. There are family connexions, persons where they have been in the habit of working for a certain place continue to do so; they are brought up to work at that place and they remain there.'[37]

It is interesting to note the emergence of this manufacturers' society, and the formulation of corporate policies, which contrasts strongly with the diversity of opinion expressed by hosiers at the 1871 Truck Acts Commission.[38] A major stimulus to the formation of this association and the changing attitudes of hosiers towards technology must have come from the abolition of frame rent in 1874, the legislative outcome of the 1871 Commission. Wells claims that frame rent was virtually moribund by 1874 and the effect of the legislation was unimportant. This may have been the case in Nottingham, where Mundella and Morley pioneered factory production in the 1860s, but the hostility expressed by the Leicester knitters over frame rent to the 1871 Commission and the evidence of Odams suggests that rent was still a major component in the Leicester trade in the early 1870s. Thus increased foreign competition, the rise of the board school and the abolition of frame rent all helped to diminish the antipathy of the Leicester hosiers towards factory production.

The new technology was to prove expensive. Each 'Cotton's Patent' cost £200 plus a considerable further investment in steam plant. It is easy to imagine the reluctance of manufacturers to scrap the old system. With the high costs of installation hosiers endeavoured to maximize output. Night-shift working became the norm, and as the 'Cotton's patent' shared many characteristics with the hand frame, skilled hand frame knitters were recruited to operate the new machinery. Hand frame knitters also possessed maintenance skills, vital to the smooth running of the expensive machines, and unlike women they could work at night.[39]

With the spread of steam-powered factories in the late 1870s the trade began to rationalize its ancillary processes. Improved sewing machines, capable of being powered by steam, facilitated centralized production. This development, however, was somewhat tardy. Among the early sewing machines there was only one type that rivalled hand work in the quality of its stitching. This was the 'linking' or 'turning-off' machine, invented by Campion of Nottingham in 1858, which joined the selvedged fashion fabric loop by loop with a chain stitch. For cut-work, however, with no selvedge, the 'linker' could not be used, and in any case it was too slow for the production of cheap garments.[40] In the early period of steam factories there was an expansion of putting-out to the seaming sector. The introduction, however, of a machine which neatly trimmed the edge of the fabric as it seamed gave a boost to the cut-out trade, but it was not until 1887 that the 'overlock', a machine that not only trimmed but also covered the raw edge, finally solved the problem of seaming cut-out garments. Cut-work now began to rival the fashioned article for quality and was so much cheaper in production as to have serious effects on the fashioned trades. The concentration of female stitchers in factories now continued more rapidly as did that of 'menders' and 'cutters'. Although their work was done by hand, it was so closely allied with the other processes of manufacture that it could most conveniently be carried on in the same building.

Other mechanical changes were also affecting the sexual composition of the hosiery factories. Although some women were employed on mechanically driven circular frames from the beginning,[41] the demand, at first, was mainly for skilled men to operate the steam rotaries such as the 'Cotton's patent'. We have already noted the advantages in employing male operatives on the rotaries, but as machines were improved and became more automatic in operation female substitution became possible, especially on the new 'Lamb's' and 'Griswold' machines.[42] The machine, however, that did more than any other to increase the numbers of women knitters was the automatic seamless hose and half-hose frame. Not only did it provide a new field for female employment, it also severely affected the demand for fully fashioned goods made on rotaries.[43] The prevailing desire throughout the trade was for cheaper and cheaper goods and the seamless automatic frame cheapened production in two ways: it made possible the turning out of hose in one operation, and its operation only required semi-skilled labour.[44] Table 1 clearly shows the increasing employment of women in Leicester hosiery.

Table 1.   Numbers employed in Leicester hosiery, 1871–1901.

	1871	1881	1891	1901
Males	3,037	3,391	4,286	3,282
Females	1,886	5,308	8,381	9,107

Source: Census reports, 1871–1901

This trend brought repeated complaints from the Leicester Amalgamated Hosiery Union (LAHU), whose policy of one man, one frame was being seriously undermined.[45] However, the most ominous threat to the standard of living of the town workers came from the country districts. All through the history of the trade we can trace the interplay of centralizing and decentralizing forces. In the early years of the steam factory the town was dominant, but during the last decade of the century this was reversed. One cause of the 'flight to the periphery' was the introduction of automatic frames whose operatives could be trained quickly. Another was the marketing practice of selling by sample through travelling salesmen, which resulted in factories in the 'trade centre' losing their marketing advantage.[46]

Although country labour was less efficient, wage rates were often 30 to 50 per cent below trade union prices. Country competition forced the LAHU to make concessions but the migration of work continued.[47] Employers would select a poverty-stricken area, where almost any wage would be accepted, in which to establish a factory. The LAHU would respond by reducing Leicester wage rates, to enable the town manufacturers to compete effectively, and to prevent a further migration of machinery. The country employers would then retaliate with even lower wages, and so the struggle went on. The last 15 years of the nineteenth century witnessed a growth in hostilities between capital and labour which dominated the trade, and to understand more fully the nature of these disputes it is necessary to examine in closer detail the world of labour organization in hosiery.

Labour Organizations in Leicester Hosiery 1858–1900

There had been many instances of trade unionism amongst Leicester hosiery workers before our period. Indeed the Webbs, in their classic history, identified the eighteenth-century East Midlands stockingers' combinations as the pioneers of the British trade union movement.[48] These early associations were, however, to say the least, mercurial, often being formed solely for the advocacy of the enforcement of the laws of the old guild system.[49] The 'seven-year union' of 1819–26 was perhaps the first really permanent combination in Leicester. This union operated under the cloak of a friendly society during the era of the Combination Acts. It was headed by Robert Hall, the minister of the Harvey Lane Baptist Chapel. Hall, who is widely regarded as Leicester's finest ever preacher, showed a remarkable talent in bringing together workers, hosiers, the Tory corporation and large county landowners to support the union. The main policy of the union was to maintain the statement of prices in Leicester. It used the device of paying the relatively large unemployment benefit of 6s. 6d. per week to those workers who refused to work at less than the statement.[50] The scheme was of course a grandoise strike fund carried out under the guise of a friendly society which was designed to impose a town-based 'producers' cartel'. The main target of the 'union'[51] were those renegade employers who attempted to gain competitive advantage by paying below the statement. It was also aimed at the bagman described by Hall as 'that reptile race who with a mixture of cruelty and rapacity, at once snatch bread from the worker and fair profits from the hands of the regular and honest manufacturer'.[52]

At its peak Hall's union represented 8,000 members who contributed 6d. per week to the fund which was supplemented by large cash payments from nonconformist hosiers, members of the landed aristocracy, such as the Duke of Rutland and the Earl of Stamford, and the Tory corporation. The parish authorities also made frequent contributions to match the savings on local poor relief that resulted from the fund's operation. This alliance of the usually warring factions of local society was probably the product of those troubled times. Luddism may not have appeared in Leicester but it was certainly abroad in the county, and this was also an era when revolutionary ideas were being expressed. A political battle between the largely Unitarian hosiers and the Tory corporation, however, dominated the local scene. The frameworkers, with their freeman's franchise which gave them nearly 20 per cent of the electorate, were obviously a section of local society that could not be alienated by either side.[53] The involvement of the aristocracy in the fund is more ambiguous as they could have been motivated either by a desire to extend Tory paternalism into the town during a troubled era or by a wish to assist their political colleagues in the corporation.

The outcome of the community-based alliance was industrial peace for over a decade. The seven-year union ceased its activities in 1826 after the repeal of the Combinations Acts, which also coincided with an upturn in trade. The idea of a union of all classes still continued to receive a periodic airing. William Jackson, a stockinger, one of the leaders of the seven-year union and a popular local figure, attempted to revive Hall's union when hard times again returned in 1833.[54] Jackson's initiative appears to have failed by 1834,[55] but the idea of a union of all classes was again taken up by J. P. Mursell, Robert Hall's successor at the Harvey Street Chapel. Despite support from some large hosiers including Biggs, Harris and Coltman, Mursell's plan was doomed to failure. It proved impossible to recruit the 'large bagmen', which made the formation of a 'producers' cartel', the central feature of the scheme, impossible.[56] The following ten years of framework knitters' organization are closely linked to Leicester's famous Chartist period, an episode that has been the subject of two stimulating histories. Little use would be served by going over this well-known period.[57]

While Chartism attracted the energy and talents of the stockingers' leaders, major developments were occurring within the world of Leicester trade unionism. The emergence of a society exclusively for 'fine glove hands' in the early 1840s marks a distinct discontinuity in the history of hosiery workers' organizations. Unlike the 'industrial', 'open' unions of previous decades the 'glove society' was of an 'exclusive' type, ignoring their less fortunate colleagues in the 'common' branches.[58] Glove hands had traditionally been the most skilled and highly paid members of the Leicester trade and the use of elastic web helped to keep this section of the industry buoyant. In 1844 John Biggs employed 300 frames in the glove trade and nearly 30 per cent of Leicester's 1,200 frames worked in the glove branch.[59] The glove union claimed to represent 1,200 members, subscriptions were 3d. per week and strike pay was fixed at 8s. 0d. per week.[60] Did the glove workers constitute an 'aristocratic' stratum amongst the Leicester framework knitters? This question is difficult to answer owing to the lack of precise data on those aspects of the 'labour aristocracy' identified by Hobsbawm.[61] William Biggs claimed that earnings in the glove branch were as high as £3 and occasionally £5 per week during the early years of the trade, but by 1841 the wages of glove hands averaged 20s. 0d. per week.[62] Felkin noted in 1844 that glove workers averaged between 14s. 0d. and 17s. 8d. per week while one exceptional worker earned 38s. 0d. in one particular week. Felkin also pointed out that even glove hands had to seek parochial relief during slack periods.[63]

Glove hands may not have been 'labour aristrocrats' but several important features set them apart from the rest of the trade. As we have seen, there was a marked differential between their wages and those of other stockingers, but of even more importance was the mode of organization in the glove sector. Worsted gloves, being a fashion product, necessitated the gathering together of men and frames into relatively large workshops. This facilitated the trade's quick response to the vagaries of demand. Thomas Winter, the secretary of the glove union, reported to the commissioner in 1844 that glove hands generally worked in large shops, often containing as many as 60 frames, and none of the men used the labour of their own families for winding and seaming.[64] When questioned on the success of his union and the failure of other sectors of the hosiery trade to emulate the glove hands' organization, Winters pointed to two factors that aided the unionization of the glove trade: high wages, and the centralization of workers into large shops.[65]

'The men in the glove branch have many more privileges than in the stocking branch', A. Caple, a glove worker, told the commissioner. We can, of course, isolate the material advantages of glove workers relative to the stocking trade: higher wages, trade union organization, a domestic life uncluttered by frames and the attendant family labour. Another important feature that distinguished the glove branch was the reliance upon narrow frames in glove manufacture. Virtually every glove worker interviewed in 1844 had previously been employed in the narrow frame fancy hose sector. Thus while their colleagues in the stocking trade had, increasingly, to suffer the heavy toil of wide frames producing fabric for 'cut-outs' and the spurious trade, the glove workers were able to retain the 'genuine skill' that was essential to the production of fashioned garments on narrow frames.

The emergence of 'sectionalism' in the organization of Leicester hosiery workers in the 1840s has interesting implications for the debate on the general rise of 'exclusive' unions during this period. The previous forms of trade unionism amongst Leicester hosiery workers were 'open' and usually involved other parts of the community, especially hosiers and the town corporation, in their efforts to impose a 'producers' cartel'. This strategy, however, was peculiar to the predominantly home-based stockinger of the 1820s, whose main strength lay in his 'freeman's vote'. As we saw earlier, in 1826 framework knitters constituted nearly 20 per cent of the electorate and it is not surprising that both radical hosiers and the Tory corporation were eager to assist in Robert Hall's union.[66] However, the proportion of enfranchised stockingers declined after 1826 and by 1857 they accounted for only 8.6 per cent of votes.[67]

The arrival of the glove union, therefore, was a distinct break from previous forms of trade unionism in Leicester. This organization was firmly based in the new larger workshops, the majority of which were owned by former middlemen.[68] Although the glove union declined, as the trade became depressed in the 1870s, its emergence in the 1840s was to herald the imminent arrival of other sectional hosiery organizations as the industry increasingly became based on workshops producing for particular branches of the trade.

During the 1850s the clouds of depression that had overshadowed the Leicester hosiery trade for more than 40 years began to clear. The general rise of living standards gave a boost to the market and with the arrival of the boot industry in 1853 employment prospects brightened. This improvement was reflected in the growing confidence of the stockingers and it was during the 1850s that permanent trade unions appeared in other branches of the trade. The Hose, Shirt, and Drawer Union and the Sock and Top Union were both formed in 1858, and as their names suggest they, like the glove hands, were primarily concerned with their own particular sectors rather than the trade in general. Both unions enjoyed a certain measure of success. Advances gained in the prosperous years of 1858–61 were maintained and by 1873 skilled rates had climbed to 24s. 0d. per week, in comparison with 19s. 0d. in 1859. In 1860 the Hose, Shirt, and Drawer Union represented 800 members in the town and 200 in the surrounding villages and by 1870 membership had increased to 1,000 in the town and 1,000 in the country. The smaller Sock and Top Union represented 800 workers in 1870 when its membership reached its peak.[69]

Trade union organization along product divisions was a consequence of the increasing number of large workshops specializing in particular branches of the trade and the marked variations in demand between the various sectors. In 1844 the glove hands pointed out to the commissioner that despite their higher wages and 'privileges' the glove trade suffered from extreme fluctuations in demand in comparison to the stocking trade.[70] The Hose, Shirt, and Drawer Union organized workers who were enjoying the fruits of the Victorian fad for woollen underwear, but this sector, like the glove trade, could often find itself victim to the fickleness of fashion.[71] Another outcome of this work differentiation was the emergence and institutionalization of complex wage structures that were peculiar to each particular branch. The hosiery trade in Leicester had always produced a variety of products that commanded different levels of remuneration based on such factors as demand, labour supply and skill. With the arrival of separate trade unions these variations became fixed and embodied in the various wage agreements negotiated by the individual unions. Furthermore, these differentials appear to have been successfully maintained for many years.[72]

Despite their undoubted success these sectional trade unions failed to increase their influence in the country districts. The Leicester trade was therefore always susceptible to damaging competition from country entrepreneurs whose wages and costs were well below those in Leicester. Access to frames was still unrestricted and certain branches of the trade were faced with the problem of female labour working narrow frames. It is therefore not surprising to find these unions somewhat inclined to pragmatism and afraid of confronting major issues. Robert Brindley, the leader of the Hose, Shirt, and Drawer Union, explained to the commissioners investigating the truck system why his union had not struck against frame rents and shop charges.

> There is a union among frame-work knitters in Leicester, and there is no rule laid down in that union to strike against charges – not for their total abolition ... It is too formidable a question for us. It would be more than we would be able to overcome ... When we strike it is generally an isolated case; it is some unprincipled manufacturer who wants to get his work cheaper than the rest, and when we have one or two in hand we can overcome them, but if we had

the whole body coming with their capital against us at once we should have no chance.[73]

As would be expected under these circumstances, subscriptions to both unions were very low. The Hose, Shirt, and Drawer Union charged 3d. per week when payment was first introduced in the early 1860s. Little is known of the early years of the Sock and Top Union but in the early 1870s their leader, Daniel Merrick, fixed subscriptions at 6d. per week for men and 4d. for women and boys. Neither organization paid friendly society benefits nor employed full-time officials.[74] Despite these shortcomings the Leicester knitters were fairly successful, wages rose steadily up to the late 1870s and they avoided being drawn into an arbitration agreement on the lines of Mundella's Nottingham scheme.[75] The diversity of products manufactured in the Leicester trade also acted as an obstacle to an arbitration scheme as uniform 'statements' were virtually impossible to formulate. A board of arbitration was set up in the town in 1866 but its meetings were infrequent. Mundella informed the commissioners investigating the truck system that the 'The Leicester Board was not a very lively thing. It has not been carried out very well.'[76]

The slow introduction of steam-powered frames in the late 1860s had no detrimental effects on the knitters' unions. If anything, the concentration of work into larger units, both factories and workshops, probably assisted the growth of the two unions, and by 1885 the majority of the power frame workers in Leicester were organized by the Leicester and Leicestershire Framework Knitters' Union, a product of the federation of the two societies in 1872 designed to coordinate their campaign against frame rent.[77] During the 1860s and 1870s increased product demand and the slow development of steam technology produced an Indian summer for the hand frame knitters. The early steam machines displaced the broader gauge narrow frames, traditionally operated by young learners and women,[78] but created no disruption to the fancy sector, while the wide frames, producing garments and 'cut-ups', were improved to such an extent that they were able to match the early steam rotaries in performance.[79]

Increased productivity led to a parallel increase in demand for seaming work. So great was the expansion of the domestic seaming sector, an area dominated by female workers paid incredibly low wages, that 'Some town councillors and other gentlemen of the neighbourhood, seeing with concern the depressed conditions of female labour in the Leicester hosiery trade appealed to the "Women's Trade Union League" for assistance.' A meeting was held in the Town Hall where the seamers formed a union. Negotiations with employers secured an advance of 25 per cent on wages and members threw themselves with extraordinary vigour into the movement, conducting the whole of the business themselves. The Society of Seamers and Stitchers was governed by an executive committee composed of 'middle-aged and elderly married women' whose members would often walk 10 or 20 miles to collect subscriptions or to interview employers.[80] Their secretary, Mrs Mason, a colourful local personality, described to delegates at the fourth annual meeting of the Women's Trade Union League their efforts to recruit workers in the surrounding villages in the first winter of the union's existence. 'The ground was covered with snow and we had to go all through the snow and frost. We were over our shoe tops in snow and our clothes froze on us, but we did not care for that, we were in earnest and determined to find them out.'[81] The valiant efforts of these pioneers were soon rewarded when membership climbed to 3,000 by 1876.[82]

Mrs Mason represented her union at the TUC of 1877, crossing swords with Henry Broadhurst over her oppositon to the cotton union's resolution which called for greater restrictions on female labour. She was also the first woman to serve on a local Trades Council. The Society of Seamers and Stitchers was obviously the League's major success and represents a remarkable achievement in the history of organization amongst female outworkers. This success, however, was to prove short-lived. Mrs Mason died in 1880, and the society, in many ways a product of her hard work and considerable personality, lost nearly 2,000 members soon after her death, and the organization became insolvent. The secretary of the framework knitters' union reported to the League that 'the women have become indifferent to their union', adding that the long distances to be covered by homeworkers in order to pay contributions hampered the society. By 1882 the Society of Seamers and Stitchers were forced to take refuge in the men's union.[83]

The hard work of Mrs Mason and her friends was obviously a major factor in the rapid growth of the seamers' union, yet despite their efforts the society's decline was inevitable. Although the growth of factory production was particularly slow in the worsted hosiery trade, by 1876 the trend towards centralized production units can be seen. When Mrs Mathews, a member of the seamers' executive committee, was asked by the commissioners investigating the workings of the Factories and Workshops Acts in 1876 if the numbers of hand seamers were declining, she replied that her trade was increasingly being affected by the growth of factory-based machine seaming.[84] Clearly the growth of factories was encouraging the adoption of Campion's linking machine. This was an ominous development for the seamers as the machine was only suitable for the better-paid fancy trade. The seamers, therefore, were left with poorly remunerated cut-up work until 1887 when the arrival of the overlock stitcher ended the hand-seaming industry.[85] The meteoric rise and decline of the Society of Seamers and Stitchers can be accounted for by a unique conjunction of circumstances: middle-class propaganda from the League, genuine grievances, the appearance of a strong local leadership, and above all a high demand for the women's labour. It is therefore not surprising that female workers in Leicester, apart from sporadic outbursts such as the 1886 riots, remained quiescent, generally leaving it to the men to 'do the fighting', until a remarkably similar set of circumstances appeared in the footwear trade in 1911.[86]

The 1870s saw the organization of other groups of women workers in the hosiery trade. Barbara Drake had noted the formation of a small 'menders'' society who followed the example of the seamers' organization in 1874.[87] The menders worked inside the hosier's warehouse alongside the 'aristocratic' warehousemen. These formidable ladies had for many years been a constant irritant to the Leicester hosiers. As the warehouses were classified as factories under the Factories Acts, the women were not allowed to work after 7 p.m.[88] Moreover, their refusal to start work until after breakfast gave them the benefit of a relatively short working day. The mending ladies considered themselves superior to other female hosiery workers. Mundella even went so far as to compare their status with that of milliners.[89] The 'Menders' Society' succeeded in obtaining wage rises of up to 5s. per week, and was finally absorbed into the LAHU in 1885.

The growth of a factory-based labour force led to tensions between the factory workers and their predominantly workshop-based union. Competition from factories, constant changes in design and fashion, together with the depression of the early 1880s, all served to undermine the wages of the factory knitters and to challenge their rule of one man, one frame.[90] The hand knitters themselves were suffering from similar forces and with their lower wages they could hardly be expected to look favourably upon the factory workers' repeated request for union funds to maintain their higher rates.[91] The outcome of this tension was the formation in 1885 of the Leicester Amalgamated Hosiery Union for the exclusive organization of factory workers.

Unlike the older unions, LAHU was an industrial union from the outset. The male power knitters were always aware of the threat from female factory labour and the recruitment of women into the union was obviously a sensible strategy, especially as women were entering the factories in large numbers as the ancillary processes became centralized. Moreover, as many of the new factories produced a host of different products under one roof the LAHU never faced the problem of sectionalism. Corah's, for example, produced in their Leicester factory virtually every type of knitwear imaginable, marketed under their 'St Margaret's' label.[92] R. Walker's factories in Charles Street and Abbey Park Mills produced a diversity of products including their market leader of 'Wolsey' natural woollen underclothes.[93] Above all, the shared experience of operating the same type of power-driven machine employed in the production of different items helped to develop a craft homogeneity amongst the male power machine knitters.

The emergence of the LAHU was to prove a distinct departure from the previous forms of hosiery societies. The secretary of the new organization,

Jimmy Holmes, 1850–1911, was the first full-time paid official in the hosiery trade since Gravenor Henson. Holmes's background was typical of the men that he led. He had entered the trade as a winding boy, progressing to hand frames before moving to the steam-powered machines. His knowledge of the industry was vast and he could claim with some justice to have operated almost every type of knitting machine in existence.[94] He had been elected to the executive of the Leicestershire Framework Knitters' Union in the mid-1870s and soon afterwards became the unofficial leader of the power machine men. Holmes was both an exceptional organizer and a powerful orator. His links with the local Labour movement were, to say the least, extensive: a secularist lecturer in the 1870s,[95] a leading member of the Leicester Socialist League in the 1880s,[96] a prominent ILP member in the 1890s and shareholder in the Leicester Pioneer Press in the 1900s.[97] He also had connections with the national Labour movement through his membership of the TUC parliamentary committee in the late 1880s, and he became a founder member of the General Federation of Trade Unions in 1899. His life, however, ended in disgrace when it was discovered, as he lay dying of cancer in 1911, that he had embezzled union funds on a grand scale, investing them in property in and around Leicester.[98]

The LAHU, unlike the old hand frame society, possessed permanent offices in Horsefair Street and began to issue monthly reports in 1886. Members' subscriptions were the same as those charged by the old society, 6d. per week for men and 3d. for women. By 1886 membership had reached 1,800 and grew steadily to a peak of 12,000 by 1914.[99] Throughout these early years two major issues were to dominate the LAHU: competition from the country, and the fight to retain male exclusiveness over the operation of power-driven frames.

The process of removing work from the 'centre' to the 'periphery' in search of lower costs and higher profit was as old as the trade itself. In 1870 Robert Walker, a Scottish hosier, opened a steam-powered factory in the Leicestershire village of Fleckney and began the trend towards village factory production.[100] By 1886 at least 30 firms were to be found in 11 nearby villages, most of which had populations of under 5,000 inhabitants,[101] and in 1889 the Fair Wages Committee reported that over the previous 15 years one firm per year had been leaving Leicester for the rural districts. It is not surprising that the Leicester workers occasionally became desperate in their attempts to stop this exodus, and in 1884 they even struck for a *reduction* in wages in their efforts to stop an employer removing his plant.[102] The 'General Strike' of February 1886, caused by the LAHU's campaign to unify wages in the town, led to riots and the stoning of hosiery factories and hosiers' homes, and also increased the pace of machine removal.[103] Soon after the strike was settled, James Hearth and Co. left Leicester for Burbage and Wigston Magna, while Robert Rowley moved to Syston and Fleckney, and Taberer and Lorrimer to

Foleshill, Warwickshire. In the following year there were reports of small steam hosiery factories being built in the villages of Rothley and Hathern.[104]

The obvious strategy for the union to follow under these circumstances was to recruit the country workers. This policy was in fact adopted at an early date when immediately after the 1886 strike the union, although virtually bankrupt, sent a delegation, led by Holmes, to organize the Hinckley workers. This small town was the largest of the 'country villages' and most of the male workforce were old members of the moribund Frameworkers' Union. Wages in Hinckley were amongst the lowest in the trade. The adult male rate, for example, at 16s. 0d. per week was less than two-thirds of the Leicester average. Furthermore, women and youths were freely employed on the smaller and more automatic machines. After several meetings, Holmes was able to recruit the 120 male knitters employed in Hinckley's two largest factories. The employers, however, threatened to sack all trade unionists and all but two employees relinquished their membership.[105] Keen to preserve their low cost advantage, the country hosiers battled against the Amalgamated wherever and whenever it appeared. The Nottingham trade was also experiencing similar developments and in order to fight the common enemy the LAHU joined forces with the Nottingham Rotary Union in 1888 to form the Midland Counties Hosiery Federation. The Federation saw their role as that of a protector of small village societies while the very existence of the Federation, it was hoped, would encourage local organization.[106]

The Federation certainly had appeal in some country districts, and by 1890 the LAHU was able to open a branch in Hinckley, with nearly 400 members, after a vigorous recruitment campaign by the Federation.[107] 1,800 workers were called out on strike in Hinckley in 1892. The successful outcome of this action won wage increases of up to 40 per cent. This victory was repeated at Earl Shilton, near Hinckley, where the LAHU were able after a recruitment rally to impose the Hinckley list on the village employers.[108] The fortunes of the union in the Hinckley area, however, soon deteriorated. In 1895, an extremely poor year for the trade, the LAHU in Leicester was forced to accept reductions of between 15 and 20 per cent in the existing lists in order to meet the acute competition from country manufacturers. The Hinckley workers, fearing competition from Leicester, followed the Loughborough branch and seceded from the union.[109]

Throughout the 1880s and 1890s the vast majority of the country workers remained indifferent to union organization, an indifference often reinforced by the hosiers' tight paternalistic control over village life. Walker, whose large works dominated the village of Fleckney, was particularly notorious. After an unsuccessful recruitment campaign in 1889, Holmes was convinced that Walker had 'blinded his workers with benefactions of tracts, soup, and blankets'. In 1890, perhaps because of the

Hinckley victory, the Fleckney workers called on the LAHU for assistance. Walker replied by imposing fines of 1½d. in the shilling on those employees who were brave enough to take out membership.[110] Holmes broadened his campaign by attempting to organize another of Walker's factories in the village of Kirkby. The policy turned out to be quite successful and Holmes was able to call out the Kirkby workers in order to gain an advance in wages. Walker, ever determined to defeat the LAHU removed his machines from Kirkby to Nailsworth, a small village near Stroud in Gloucestershire. Holmes, indefatigable in his feud with Walker, organized and led a Labour League deputation to Nailsworth and tried to hold a meeting with a view to organizing the district. But Walker

> had packed the meeting, and did ... [his] best to make the meeting a failure. The ignorant, benighted people of Nailsworth howled, sung, groaned, and yelled to such an extent that we are bound to say that for ignorance, cowardice, meanness, and rowdyism, England has not a place to compare with Nailsworth, Gloucestershire. It is veritably 'Darkest England' and the best way we found was the way out.[111]

The country recruitment campaign of 1886–94 was conducted against a background of both small and middle-sized firms leaving the town, and an open threat from Leicester's largest hosier that failure to unionize the villages would result in the ending of the 1886 list.[112] The revision of the Leicester list in 1895 underlines the failure of the LAHU to recruit the country workers. Nevertheless, in many respects Jimmy Holmes achieved a great deal. The workers of Hinckley, Earl Shilton, Loughborough, Fleckney and Kirkby were briefly brought into the union. This was no mean achievement considering the centuries-old antipathy between the country workers and the Leicester trade, the grinding poverty that existed within the villages, where the only alternative employment was agriculture, and the determined tactics of the employers to maintain their low cost advantage.

The policy of 'one man, one machine' had been central to the power knitters' defensive tactics since the beginning of steam-powered knitting. These men, recruited from the ranks of skilled male wide frame operatives, carried their craft tradition into the new steam factories. This point is substantiated by several pieces of evidence from the 1890s. Jimmy Holmes, in his questionnaire returned to the Webbs in 1894, stressed the importance of the heavy maintenance and repair tasks performed by 'Cotton's Patents' operators.[113] This remark was more than a justification for sexual wage differentials; the consistent policy of the Leicester hosiers throughout this period was to turn the male 'Cotton's' operators into 'overlookers' and maintenance men.[114] Those members of the LAHU who accepted offers from hosiers, usually in the villages, to leave Leicester and take up positions as 'overlookers' could expect the full wrath of the union. The monthly reports during this period printed the photograph and personal details of members, in mock obituary form, who had become overlookers (see fig. 1) an honour usually reserved for 'blacklegs' and 'scabs'.[115]

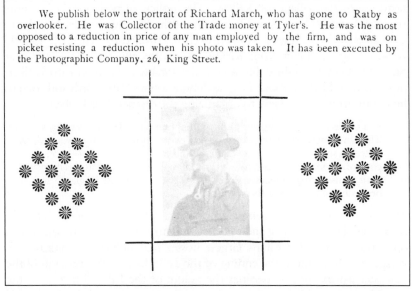

We publish below the portrait of Richard March, who has gone to Ratby as overlooker. He was Collector of the Trade money at Tyler's. He was the most opposed to a reduction in price of any man employed by the firm, and was on picket resisting a reduction when his photo was taken. It has been executed by the Photographic Company, 26, King Street.

Fig. 1 Portrait of a Cotton's Patent operative on accepting promotion (LAHU Monthly Reports: photograph courtesy London School of Economics and Political Science Library)

'Cotton's Patents' were by no means the only steam-powered machines in use during this period. The early rotaries that predated the 'Cotton's' in Leicester by 30 years were often operated by women,[116] and employers repeatedly attempted to place women on the new generation of machines that appeared in the 1880s. The 'Lamb's' flat knitting machine, introduced into Leicester in the early 1880s, posed a major threat to the male operatives because its simplified needle technology, speed and lightness of operation, and productive versatility made it ideal for female operation.[117] It is not surprising that the 'Lamb's' was at the centre of one of the first major disputes faced by the LAHU, when in 1886 J. Taberer, the director of Taberer and Lorrimer, defied the union by placing women on his new batch of 'Lamb's' machines. After a particularly bitter dispute Taberer removed his plant to Foleshill near Coventry, where he stubbornly refused to employ a single trade unionist.[118]

An improved version of the 'Lamb's' appeared in 1888. Called the 'Rothwell', this machine was particularly adaptable to the circular rib branch of the trade and Holmes complained that the first factory to utilize the 'Rothwell' employed only 10 men to 140 women. When the union tried to alter this situation they found that the women, in a rare display of union activity, voted against the advice of the executive. Holmes, annoyed

20

at this defeat, tried to lift the men's spirits by pointing out that an improved 'Cotton's' soon to appear would probably make the 'Rothwells' redundant.[119] The following year, however, he complained that the new 'Griswold' and 'Royal Knitter's' machines were competing with the 'Cotton's' and warned that this competition would probably increase as the pedal-powered 'Griswold' was ideal for domestic use.[120]

The 'Griswold' appears to have remained a threat to the factory workers for a number of years, since Holmes expressed his fears on domestically based 'Griswolds' to the Webbs in 1894.[121] By February 1890, however, the improved 'Cotton's' were replacing the older rotaries and a distinct sexual division of machine operation appeared to have emerged: men on Cotton's, women on the new automatics, and some domestically based women operating the manual Griswolds.[122]

The men were able to retain operation of the 'Cotton's' until 1914,[123] but they were often challenged and occasionally they had to accept the role of 'overlookers' while the frames were operated by youths. Yet despite this achievement the clear underlying trend of the hosiery trade was towards the ascendancy of female labour. This is well illustrated in Table 1.1 printed above which shows a dramatic fall of 25 per cent male employment during the ten years between 1891 and 1901. This decline from 4,286 men in 1891 to 3,282 underestimates the fall in numbers of adult male knitters, given the increasing tendency to employ unskilled youths on frame operation. In the monthly report of February 1890 Holmes noted, with an element of despair, that the slightest drop in demand led to firms stopping the night shift, the main preserve of male exclusiveness. This caused the LAHU much concern as, more often than not, men who were laid off found great difficulty in regaining employment, a situation that was exacerbated following the implementation of the McKinley tariff in the USA which caused the collapse of Leicester's major export market.[124]

In the late 1880s and throughout the 1890s Holmes found his organization threatened on virtually every front. The country question appeared insoluble, while the problem of female substitution was, to say the least, extremely delicate in a union in which women formed the majority.[125] The union made repeated complaints throughout the period over the difficulty experienced in recruiting the growing number of female workers. In 1885 Holmes informed the Women's Trade Union League that 'it is impossible to get a woman to serve on the Executive Committee, so accustomed are they to have everything done for them.'[126] A separate women's committee was started in 1886 to manage women's affairs, but was soon abandoned and was later described by the union's president, Jabez Chaplin, as 'an expensive farce'.[127] After the collapse of the American trade the production of worsted hosiery became increasingly seasonal and by March 1895 the LAHU was complaining that only 10 per cent of their members were in full-time employment.[128]

Holmes and the executive responded in various ways to these worrying

21

circumstances. A scheme was started which employed out-of-work members on the chopping and selling of firewood.[129] On a more grandiose scale the LAHU was firmly committed to cooperative production schemes as an answer to the distress caused by the recklessness of capitalist competition.[130] Solutions to the problem of female labour required sensitive handling and it is not surprising that the monthly reports, distributed free to both male and female members, though often chastising women for being poor trade unionists, rarely mentioned the subject of sexual demarcation. Indeed, Holmes only referred to the problem once, during the 1888 dispute over women operating the new 'Rothwells', when he noted, with a touch of exasperation, 'how can a society fight its own members without committing suicide?'[131] The women, however, were not entirely at fault. The union, whose offices were too small for meetings and other functions, usually held their elections, general meetings and social gatherings in pubs and working men's clubs, hardly the best venues to attract female participation.[132] Outside the pages of the reports Holmes could be more outspoken in expressing his desire to see a reduction in female labour, especially amongst married women.[133] His support for Henry Broadhurst during the late 1880s may have been partly based on Holmes's endorsement of Broadhurst's campaign to increase legislation against female labour.[134]

Holmes and his executive were far from blind to the underlying forces generated by capitalist competition that were creating the problems experienced by the hosiery workers. His recruitment speech to the Hinckley workers in November 1890 contained a discussion on the virtues of cooperative production. The leading article in the reports often expounded Holmes's thoughts on the 'Labour Theory of Value'.[135] On 18 March 1888 Holmes, together with Warner, a member of the LAHU executive, Barclay, who had briefly been general secretary in 1886, and Robson, an LAHU activist, met with 18 others at a house in King Street. The party sat down to have tea in honour of the Paris Commune, and in the discussion that followed it was resolved to form a Socialist Club and subscriptions were taken.[136] The club, which became known as the Leicester Labour Club, was to provide a home for local socialists during the early 1890s, a period which was to witness a growing interest by trade unionists in socialism.

By the late 1880s the Leicester hosiery industry had been thoroughly transformed. A few stubborn pockets of the old hand trade still survived in the countryside, but overall the steam-powered factory was now dominant.[137] The manufacture of hosiery had also become centralized with the removal of ancillary processes from the home and workshops into the new factories. Yet despite this belated modernization hosiery was of diminishing importance in the local economy. Employment in the trade had increased by less than 50 per cent in the decades between 1851 and 1891, while the local industrial workforce had expanded by over 150 per cent.[138]

Most of this increase in employment is accounted for by the rise of the local footwear industry after 1851, a trade which by 1891 was dominating the local economy, having increased its number of workers seventeen-fold in the preceding four decades. Although hosiery was shrinking in local importance it was, however, a more prosperous trade in the 1890s than it had been in the mid-century. The 'lean hungry stockinger' was now happily a phenomenon of the recent past although his ghost was still to haunt the more conscious members of the workforce.[139] The trade was also more highly capitalized, expensive power-driven machines now being the norm. Yet continuities were to persist between the old and new modes of production, particularly in labour relations. The male 'Cotton's' frame–operative still possessed the stockinger's sense of independence and their deep commitment to trade unionism, a point which is demonstrated by the refusal of the 'Cotton's' operatives to be divided by the manufacturers' attempts to transform at least some of them into a stratum of junior supervisors. Indeed it was this conflict that was at the heart of the employers' renewed tactic to remove parts of the industry to the country villages, a conflict which also impelled the LAHU to widen its political horizons and pay serious attention to the new doctrines of socialism.

2   The Footwear Industry in Leicester

The arrival of the mass production ready-made shoe industry in Leicester in the 1850s heralded a new era in the economic and social life of the town. Leicester's century-old dependence on hosiery as the main source of employment was at last broken and the town entered a period of unprecedented prosperity. As the new trade flourished jobs were created in abundance and Leicester became a magnet for migrant workers attracted by the profusion of work in the semi- and unskilled sectors of the shoe industry. This boom in the Leicester economy was reflected in the growth of the town's population from 60,584 in 1851 to 211,579 in 1901, the highest rate of expansion amongst towns of a similar size recorded in the United Kingdom during the period.[1] The role of boots and shoes in the multiplication of the town's population during the second half of the nineteenth century is highlighted by the growing numbers employed in the trade and the increasing importance of the industry as Leicester's major source of employment. Footwear employed 2,741 workers in 1861 and nearly 27,000 in 1901, and by 1891 the industry accounted for 41 per cent of all industrially employed workers in the town.[2]

It might seem that footwear constituted a new social force, large-scale production replacing the old domestic system which, as we have seen, was so characteristic of the Leicester hoisery industry down to the 1880s. This picture of thorough transformation, though accurate in the long run, requires some modification. As we shall see, footwear was not entirely distinct from hosiery. Many Leicester hosiers sank capital and other resources into the new trade during the 1850s and 1860s. Moreover, in the decades after the industry's arrival in Leicester, production methods were still quite primitive and ideally suited to the putting-out system of production that already existed in the town.

The Anatomy of the Leicester Footwear Industry

Local historians have offered several accounts of the growth and development of the Leicester footwear industry. Patterson has drawn attention to the influx of village shoemakers in 1851, who specialized in making boots for navvies, after the completion of the Syston to Peterborough railway and the arrival of a Northampton firm to employ these workers on government contracts. This modest beginning was boosted in 1853 when Thomas Crick, a local shoemaker, invented the riveting process for attaching soles to uppers, a method which announced the era of factory-produced footwear.[3] Both Jack Simmons and V. W. Hogg have emphasized the importance of the previous existence of a small (by Northampton standards), but nevertheless vital, local wholesale trade.[4]

In the first half of the nineteenth century Leicester could not be called a shoe town. In 1831, for instance, Leicester contained 21 shoemakers per 1,000 inhabitants. Set against the Northampton figure of 88 shoemakers per 1,000 population the Leicester footwear industry appears rather small, but when compared to an industrial town such as Newcastle, which contained only 14 shoemakers per 1,000 inhabitants, it is clear that the Leicester trade was above average size.[5] During the 1830s several shoemakers in the town began to specialize in the production of cheap, brightly coloured strap-on sandals and boots for children, known locally as cacks, which were sold in large numbers to the country villages.[6] By 1835 the town contained two wholesale manufacturers, T. Crick of Peacock Lane and J. Dilkes of Loseby Lane.[7] Dilkes was also a hosiery manufacturer and his early involvement in the footwear industry was to set a precedent followed by many of his fellow hosiers.

In 1843, 36 of the town's shoemakers owned their own 'show shops' for the sale of ready-made boots and shoes but the main recruits to the ranks of the wholesalers, that is, firms producing goods for retail outlets other than their own, came from the hosiery trade.[8] The notable exception to this pattern of recruitment of wholesale manufacturers was Thomas Crick. The firm of T. Crick first appeared in the town's directories in 1835 and continued to produce from the same premises for the next twenty years, which suggests that business was steady if not spectacular. In 1853 Crick invented, or rather rediscovered, the method of attaching soles to uppers by means of metal rivets inserted by a mechanical press.[9] This device undoubtedly revolutionized the trade as it rendered unnecessary that vital aspect of the cordwainer's work, the sewing, by hand, of the sole on to the upper. A division of labour was then possible in the production of footwear. The labour process of the old cordwainer, who typically performed all the operations in shoe manufacture, became divided into four distinct areas. 'Clicking', where the leather was cut and shaped prior to assembly, was the first. This was followed by 'closing', where the various pieces of upper leather were stitched together. The completed upper then passed to the 'making' sector where the upper was shaped on to a last and the sole attached. Finally the shoe would then pass into the hands of the finisher who trimmed off excess leather, and burnished and polished the shoe ready for marketing.

Previous accounts of Crick's invention tend to focus primarily on the mechanical aspects of his new method. A more important question is why did he innovate when he did? Perhaps we can go some way towards an answer by looking at the type of product made by Crick. In the 1840s Crick was known locally as a 'translator', that is, he was in the business of collecting and buying worn-out shoes and boots and renovating them by attaching new soles to the old uppers.[10] This service must have been in great demand among the impoverished working classes of Leicester in the 1840s. When the new process was applied to the more discerning new boot market Crick experienced a degree of consumer resistance, and was forced, for a time, to dispose of his products via a chimney sweep who operated a stall in the weekly market.[11] This early setback was soon overcome and by 1855 Crick had moved to more extensive premises in Highcross Street in which steam power was used in the operation of the riveting machines.[12]

Crick's removal to Highcross Street saw the beginning of a period of spectacular growth in the firm's productivity. By 1863 Crick employed 420 females aged between 15 and 23, and 300 men and boys, all of whom worked inside the Highcross Street premises. Steam power was applied to a series of different processes. The firm was the first to employ steam-powered sewing machines and steam was also used to power pricking and cutting machines. A year later the factory achieved the distinction of being the first to employ 1,000 workers in the British shoe trade.[13]

Owing to the lack of company records, caused by the high rate of bankruptcy in the trade and the take-over activities of the late Sir Charles Clore in the 1950s and 1960s, it is extremely difficult to document precisely the growth of individual firms in the Leicester shoe trade.[14] Other source material, such as directories, commercial guides and snippets culled from official publications, help to establish a broad pattern of development. Several distinct groups of entrepreneurs joined Crick in the mass production of footwear during the 1850s and 1860s. The largest source of capital and personnel undoubtedly came from local hosiery interests. As we have already seen, Crick's associate in the wholesale trade during the 1830s and 1840s was the hosier J. Dilkes. By 1861 many of the major hosiery firms were also engaged in footwear manufacture including J. Biggs and Sons, J. Lanham and Sons, Pool and Lorrimer, and Corah's.[15] J. Preston and Son and Walker and Kempson even went so far as to cease hosiery production and to concentrate entirely on footwear.[16]

The precise details of the decisions by individual hosiery firms to enter the shoe trade will never be known. At best the historian can only suggest what appear to have been the major attractions of footwear manufacture to hosiery firms. The major asset which hosiery possessed during this period was its vast and intricate network of labour organization. When Crick's invention had dispensed with the cordwainer's needle for sole attachment a division of labour was possible, and most of the new processes could be quickly learned by hosiery workers.[17] A more detailed analysis of skills will be given below. At this stage it is only necessary to point out that the majority of recruits to the new trade could be trained within weeks to perform the new simplified forms of shoe manufacture. Furthermore, a system of leasing of shoe machines was employed early on by the manufacturers that was strikingly similar to frame rent.[18] Many other aspects of footwear manufacture had a close relationship with hosiery. The elastic web trade, for instance, was at first an ancillary division of hosiery, but during the 1860s the fashion for elastic gusseted boots gave the industry a major new outlet. Did this development push John Biggs, with his elastic web interests, into shoe manufacturing? Were female hosiery workers, skilled in stitching, recruited to the shoe trade to operate the 800 sewing machines reported in the Leicester shoe trade in 1864?[19] How useful were the marketing networks developed by hosiers during the nineteenth century to the sale of Leicester-made shoes?[20] These questions can, of course, never be satisfactorily answered, but, nevertheless, the very fact that they can be put is suggestive.

Other recruits to the ranks of early Leicester footwear entrepreneurs came from a variety of different backgrounds. The firm of Stead and Simpson were already established in footwear manufacture in Leeds before they removed their business to Leicester in 1853 in order to escape from the labour difficulties they had experienced in Yorkshire.[21] This company was to play an innovative role in the Leicester trade with their early introduction of American technology. The 'Blake' sewer, which stitched the insole, already attached to the upper, to the outer sole, was first used by Stead and Simpson in 1858. It proved to be even more important than Crick's riveting device which it eventually displaced.[22] This method vastly improved the quality of mass-produced footwear and at the same time facilitated a massive expansion in productivity. For example, one man and a boy assistant could last and rivet 18 pairs of shoes per day using the rivet method; one operative on a treadle-powered Blake could turn out 200 pairs in a ten-hour day and 300 if powered by steam.[23] In America this machine is reputed to have reduced sole-sewing costs from 75 cents to 3 cents per pair.[24] Stead and Simpson remained at the forefront of the Leicester trade for the rest of the century. Their future managing director, J. Griffin Ward, became president of the Leicester Boot Manufacturers' Association in 1890 and a leading advocate of mechanization.[25]

The firm of S. Hilton is an interesting example of the rags to riches type of shoe entrepreneur so often cited in historical accounts of the Leicester trade. Sam Hilton's father owned a small tannery in Leicester. This business was a small-scale family affair and in 1876 Sam, with the aid of a building society mortgage, opened a small shoe factory in Wharf Street. The original workforce comprised Sam, his sister, her friend, and one other. Hilton's did, however, give work to outside labour based in small workshops. Hilton's pioneered the factory-owned High Street retail multiple shoe shops when they opened their first outlet in 1883. By 1889 Hilton's possessed 25 branches.[26]

The rise of the foreman and clicker to the ranks of the entrepreneurs is another aspect of local economic mythology that does have some factual basis. Sam Hilton, increasingly disgruntled by labour problems, sold out his manufacturing interests in 1895 to two clickers, Tom Howard and Richard Hallam.[27] Crick's foreman, J. Thornton, set up on his own account in 1866, and by 1891 Thornton owned a 'modest establishment' employing 150 workers and was 'favoured by well known wholesalers who draw upon him'.[28] The major factor that assisted such humble men to become factory owners was undoubtedly the leasing method employed by machinery manufacturers, which allowed businesses to be set up with the minimum of capital outlay.

The origins of the leasing system are, to say the least, veiled in obscurity. The connection between frame rent in hosiery and the leasing of shoe machines is of course obvious, especially so when the frame owner was also the owner of sewing machines which must have been the case amongst those entrepreneurs who had both hosiery and footwear interests. Before we can investigate this connection, however, we need to ask why the early entrepreneurs failed to follow Crick's example and set up factory-based production units where manufacture was centralized, the capitalist owned the instruments of production outright, and paid his employees by the piece without the encumbrance of rent and other deductions. Because of a lack of documentation no precise answer can be given but several factors peculiar to the early shoe entrepreneurs are suggestive. As we have seen, the majority of newcomers to the trade in the 1850s already possessed hosiery interests. What footwear manufacture offered to the mid-century hosier was essentially a supplementary activity that neatly fitted into his existing organization. Thus the few skilled clickers necessary to the labour process could be recruited from Northampton and accommodated within the hosier's warehouse,[29] while the 'closing' process could be performed by female sewing machine operatives either inside the warehouse or in an outside workshop, or even inside their own homes. Similarly the lasting operation could easily be performed by male operatives inside small workshops, the making process being suitable to the workshop sector since both the riveter and 'Blake' sewer could be manually operated.[30]

The early sewing machine, vital to large-scale production in the closing process, provides a useful illustration of the interconnections between hosiery and footwear. Mr Stanyon, a hosier and footwear manufacturer whose warehouse was in Belvoir Street, reported:

> I have had as many as 120 machines on my premises, but I now much prefer to give my work out ... I let out my machines at a fixed rent of 1s. a week; some have two and a few three of them. The cost of a machine is £11 or £12, and reckoning that they get knocked to pieces in two or three years, still it

answers my purpose ... I would not go back to the old system, for I get by this means a better class of girls, whose parents would not like them to work in a factory.[31]

Walker, of the Walker and Kempson hosiery and footwear business, reported to the Royal Commission in 1864 that 'We have some young women from a country village in the neighbourhood learning the use of the machine; when they are proficient they will be able to have their work at home, and bring, or send in every week or so',[32] which indicates that this firm in particular was exploiting its network of country workers for the new trade.

The 'Blake' sewer proved very suitable to the outwork system. The treadle-operated 'Blake' was capable of extremely high productivity rates. The steam-powered Blake was, of course, even more productive but it must be remembered that three of the treadle machines in an outdoor workshop could produce the same amount of work as two steam-powered machines. Considering the high investment costs required to establish a steam-powered factory, and the legacy of conservatism from the hosiery trade, it is not surprising that most entrepreneurs in footwear opted for the continuation of the outdoor system.

The Blake machine was manufactured in the USA, imported into Britain and sold through showrooms that were established in the leading centres of the trade.[33] The leasing system of shoe machinery has traditionally been regarded as an evil forced upon the industry by unscrupulous Americans. Day, the editor of the trade journal the *Shoe and Leather Record*, noted in his 1903 essay that the manufacturers paid Blake's a premium of £100 and a royalty of one penny for every pair of boots sewn by the machine even though the machine cost only £30 to build. Profits for the machine companies were therefore considerable and Day commented bitterly that 'every yankee inventor began to turn his attention to the shoe machinery as the easiest way to fame and fortune'.[34] Precisely when leasing began, however, is difficult to establish. David Schloss's research for Booth's London survey in 1889 contains references to some early 'Blake's being owned outright by the Manufacturer'.[35] By 1871, however, it appears that it was the policy of the American company to make their machines available only on the leasing system. This policy is not really very surprising. Internationally, footwear production was carried out by outworkers.[36] Moreover, these workers had often traditionally paid rent for certain relatively expensive forms of machinery. The leasing system was, therefore, in many ways a continuation of past practice with the important difference that the machine manufacturer, rather than the merchant capitalist, received the rent.

In Britain in the 1860s there were only two steam-powered footwear factories, and a survey of these two plants shows how the machine manufacturer retarded centralized production. Crick's in Leicester were able to start factory production in the early 1850s because Thomas Crick was utilizing a technology, the riveting process, that was largely of his own making. Similarly, Clarks of Street in Somerset were able to bypass the American machine companies thanks to the inventiveness of their employee William Keats, who designed a series of machines that allowed the Somerset firm to mass produce footwear without recourse to American technology.[37]

The Leicester footwear industry in the 1860s was largely carried out in small workshops or inside the workers' homes. How was this trade organized? What were the social relations of production? What was the social composition of the workforce and what were their working conditions? Again, owing to gaps in the source of material available, these questions are difficult to answer. But if we follow the process of manufacture from a piece of leather on the clicker's table to the completed shoe on the finisher's bench some light will be thrown on them.

The clicker was the undisputed aristocrat of the labour force. The price of leather accounted for between 50 and 60 per cent of total production costs.[38] The skill of the clicker was therefore vital to the manufacturer's profitability. The clicker, in assessing the way a hide was to be divided, and therefore maximizing the number of uppers from the raw material, required dexterity with scissors, a good sense of geometry and a keen understanding of the variations in different types of leather.[39] The craft involved a lengthy apprenticeship which survived while apprenticeship in other areas of mass-produced shoemaking declined. The clickers were, in many ways, a real and tangible link with the old hand-sewn industry. '... the steady clicker was the "Gentleman John" of the trade, not a few went to work and from their work in tall beaver hats'. Similar to the old cordwainer, the clicker continued to work inside the employers' premises. Clickers were also paid by the day rather than by the piece, which was the norm for other workers in the mass production trade. Face-to-face relationships with the employer also facilitated a harmony of interest between the clickers and their masters.[40] As we have seen, in later years it was not unusual for clickers to become manufacturers in their own right.

The apprentice clickers in the early years of the Leicester trade were normally employed on the less demanding task of cutting out the lining leather. As the division of labour in the trade became more organized and speed-ups in the closing and making departments became possible the labour process in the clicking room came under scrutiny. To meet this new demand the clicker's work was broken down into smaller, less demanding tasks. Machinery could not be used as no two pieces of leather were the same and the demands of economy in the use of material made the clicker's eyes a major asset that could not be mechanized. The solution to the problem of productivity therefore lay in restricting the clicker's work to those tasks that only he could perform. Under this system the clicker would mark out the leather and leave the cutting to apprentices who were specially trained to work on one particular type of leather. This development in turn led to the decline of apprenticeships in the clicking rooms. The young apprentice became what was known in the trade as 'boy labour' performing repetitive tasks that could be learnt in a few months.[41]

The clicking room which contained these aristocrats of the labour force was also the location of the 'rough stuff cutter', the worker with the least status in the trade. These workers cut out the soles and heels from tanned leather and, like the clicker, were paid by the day. Their wages, however, were generally acknowledged to be the lowest male rates in the trade. In 1866, for instance, rough stuff cutters received 20s. 0d. per week in comparison to 27s. 6d. which was the average wage paid to males in the Leicester trade.[42] By the early 1880s the rough stuff cutting process became mechanized with the arrival of the cutting press and after this the workers in this branch became known as 'pressmen'. The low wages of the rough stuff cutters corresponded to their low status: 'of uncouth manners and untidy aspect ... he shambles in and shuffles out of the factory as though no man cared for his soul'.[43] Collectively the workers in the clicker's room accounted for 10 per cent of the workforce, although the number of skilled clickers employed was often small.[44]

Once the leather had been cut out by the clickers' department the jigsaw pieces of material that formed the shoe upper had to be stitched together or 'closed', as the process was termed in the trade. In the old hand-sewn industry this task had been performed by the cordwainer's awl but with the emergence of the sewing machine in the 1850s it became an ideal area of female employment. Despite the undoubted technological break-through created by the arrival of a sewing machine capable of stitching leather, the early machine required several operations to perform the task of stitching pieces of leather together. The machinist, usually a girl in her late teens or a young woman, who would have spent several weeks train-ing in the methods of sewing machine operation, was assisted by one or two younger girls known as 'fitters'. This latter group of workers were employed in the task of positioning and holding the pieces of material in the machine while the machinist performed the stitching. In 1863 one Leicester manufacturer estimated that between 2,000 and 3,000 women and girls were employed in operating the 800 sewing machines which were 'tolerably well known' to exist in the town.[45] The same manufacturer claimed that the majority of these machines were to be found in the 'larger factories', but this early trend towards centralized production was checked during the 1860s as manufacturers increasingly resorted to employing their sewing machines on the outwork system.[46]

As we have seen, one dividend in putting out work was access to higher-quality labour than those who were prepared to endure factory work. There were, however, other advantages to manufacturers in the outdoor system apart from raising the standard of employees. The small workshops in which the sewing machines were located enjoyed much laxer regula-tions than the factories. W. H. Walker, of Walker and Kempson, when asked by the commissioners investigating the workings of the Factories Act in 1876 if he thought that 'the latitude allowed by the Workshops Act has tended to stimulate a number of small workshops competing with factories' he replied, 'Yes, decidedly, and the result has been that as far as may be the work has got done out of factories, and is sent into the workshops.'[47]

The status of the machninists and fitters was never very high in the Leicester trade. In 1866 female machinists received 12s. 0d. per week for 60 hours' work and the young fitters 11s. 0d. for similar hours. By 1879 the category of 'fitter' had disappeared from official sources on wages, which suggests that improved machines had rendered their services obsolete. The machinists' wages on the other hand had risen to 16s. 0d. for 56 hours' work in 1879 but this was still 4s. 0d. lower than the rate paid to the rough stuff cutter.[48]

The availability in Leicester of this large source of cheap, young, female labour was undoubtedly a major factor in the location of the footwear trade in the town. The two principal centres of English footwear manufacture, Northampton and Stafford, experienced major strikes in the 1850s against the introduction of sewing machines.[49] Leicester therefore was able to capitalize on the productive potential of the sewing machine at the expense of the traditional shoe centres and at the same time utilize the skilled male labour which was forced into the 'tramping system' by the troubles in Northampton and Stafford during the 1850s.

Once the uppers had been closed they returned to the manufacturers' warehouse to be distributed to the lasters, riveters and stitchers who peformed the tasks in the 'making' process. The distinction between these three groups of workers is often blurred, as it was common practice in Leicester at least for lasters to continue the making process by riveting or stitching the sole to the lasted upper. The workshops in which the making tasks were carried out were described by an assistant commissioner in 1864: 'In one of the former 13 men were working, and in another 10; in each case there were children of 11 or 12 years old.' One room was 'tolerably ventilated and not very dirty' but 'the other three were in all respects detestable; the ceilings and walls black with gas soot; the faces of the workpeople, men and boys alike, colourless and grimy; the children literally in rags of the dirtiest description, the heat of the atmosphere almost unbearable'.[50]

The workers employed in the making process certainly brought much colour to Leicester life. Many of these men in the early years were recruited from the ranks of the itinerant shoemakers and they carried with them many of the traditions of that most radical of crafts. 'Your ... rivetter and finisher must keep "St. Monday" sacred; he must attend race meetings, rabbit coursings, trotting, bicycling, and foot racing handicaps and if he is not able to make up a little for lost time in a few extra hours at night in his own home, he and his family must suffer.'[51] Dare of the Unitarian

Domestic Mission noted in a similar vein the arrival of the riotous St Crispin's day festival in 1860.[52]

It is notoriously difficult to document precisely the ebb and flow of itinerant workers into a particular locality. Recruits into the making trade were mainly composed of lasters and these workers invariably came from outside Leicester. Virtually all the lasters of whom we have specific knowledge, mostly trade union officials, came from older footwear centres.[53] Again, similar to the clickers, the lasters possessed a high element of skill and most appear to have served some form of apprenticeship.[54] The task of mounting the upper on to the last, stretching and shaping the leather without creasing, required skilful manipulation. Different qualities of leather and footwear styles demanded the types of skill that could not be picked up after a few weeks on the job. Because of the close proximity in the labour process between lasting and sole attachment, the lasters in the making shops also operated the various types of stitching and riveting machines.

Finally the shoe, complete with sole, would travel from the making shop back to the warehouse to be redistributed, this time to the finishing sector. Generally speaking, finishing entailed the trimming of surplus leather from the edge of the sole, burnishing the edges, inserting socks and eyelets and touching up any marks on the shoe. Little skill was required for any of these menial tasks and the finishing workshops were often staffed entirely by youths where 'they are packed as close as they can sit, on each side of a large table, on which are several broad gas flames, always burning to heat their burnishing and other irons'.[55]

Finishers, according to official wage data, were usually amongst the highest paid in the Leicester trade, receiving 28s. per week in 1879, the same rate as that paid to clickers.[56] This figure, however, is deceptive. The finishers described in this official return were probably young men in their late teens, who, according to Dare, were themselves small-scale employers usually employing two or three younger boys or 'sweaters' as they were known in the trade.[57] Apart from his sweaters' wages the finisher also had to buy from his employer eyelets, rivets and other materials, normally referred to as 'grindery'. Furthermore, the finisher would also have to pay rent for his use of the workshop, and gas charges, known locally as blue light, and extensively used in the burnishing process.[58]

The finishing sector of the Leicester footwear industry during the 1860s and 1870s was extremely labour intensive. The local factory inspector reported a scarcity of labour in the shoe trade in 1863 and by 1865 Dare was expressing concern at the rapid influx of youths from country villages into the finishing workshops.[59] Finishing was undoubtedly the first access point for potential shoeworkers. After a year or so the young finisher would be both old enough and possibly have accumulated enough money to pay the apprentice laster's premium,[60] he himself being replaced in the finishing shop by one of his 'sweaters'. Dare, as the head of an agency whose aim was the moral uplift of the lower classes, not surprisingly viewed the immigrant youths with concern. '... the vast number of youths of a certain grade who have passed the school age [and therefore received no Board School education] will continue to darken the skirts of society. They have in a great measure been created by immigration. Raw from the country they are intoxicated with town life and intensify its worse manifestations.'[61]

Thus by the 1870s the footwear industry was well established in Leicester. The mode of organization in the industry followed traditional patterns established by the hosiery trade with the notable exception that middlemen were usually absent from the network of production relationships.[62] Workers were recruited both locally and from other footwear towns according to skill. Furthermore, the industry was beginning to experience dramatic growth, employing 21.6 per cent of the local workforce in 1871 and 33.4 per cent in 1881.[63] For the first time in living memory work for all was in abundance and the trade was even able to draw unskilled labour from the surrounding countryside.

The Economic Development of the Footwear Industry in Leicester

In the preceding section the emergence and establishment of the footwear industry in Leicester was traced from its origins in the 1830s up to 1870. This present section continues the analysis of economic developments within the trade up to the late 1880s.

Table 2. Number of wholesale footwear manufacturers in Leicester, 1861–77.

1861	...	21
1864	...	80
1876	...	117
1877	...	193

Sources: 1861 Drake's *Directory of Leicestershire*
1864 Wright's *Midland Directory*
1876 Harrod's *Directory of Leicestershire and Rutland*
1877 White's *Directory of Leicester*

Table 2, which is compiled from local directories, gives some idea of the scale of expansion of the footwear industry in the decades up to 1880. This table, of course, only consists of firms manufacturing for the wholesale trade and does not account for those firms producing exclusively for their own retail outlets. Furthermore, it offers no indication as to the scale and extent of the workshop sector, the area where the major part of the production process was carried out. The reservations expressed about official statistics in the chapter on the hosiery industry apply equally to footwear. There is no extant, reliable data avaliable to the historian on the scale and composition of the Leicester footwear industry. The census returns (see Table 3) offer a rough bench-mark to the numbers employed in the trade but the proportion of the workforce employed in either factory or workshop can only be obtained from non-numerical, often impressionistic, sources.[64] The membership figures of the workers' trade union, the National Union of Boot and Shoe Operatives (NUBSO), given in Table 4, may offer a rather tentative comparison with Table 3 as the union had more success in recruiting in factories and larger workshops.

Table 3.   Numbers employed in footwear in Leicester, 1851–1901.

1851	1861	1871	1881	1891	1901
1,396	2,741	5,103	13,056	24,159	26,561

Source: Census returns

Table 4.   NUBSO membership in Leicester, 1874–1901.

1874	1881	1891	1901
1,397	2,129	11,965	10,933

Source: NUBSO Annual Register[65]

The larger manufacturers, when questioned by various commissioners investigating the industry during our period, invariably admitted that the growth of large factories usually entailed an equal growth in the workshop sector. In 1876, at the Royal Commission investigating the workings of the Factories and Workshop Acts, John Butcher, the manager of the large Cooperative Wholesale Society works in Leicester and a leading advocate of factory production, confessed to Lord Balfour that even his plant relied almost totally on the workshop sector to perform the finishing processes. W. H. Walker of the firm Walker and Kempson, when questioned in his capacity as a school board member, on the scale of the half-time system, informed the commissioners that the factories accounted for 331 half-timers in comparison with 931 from the workshops.

A major problem facing the school board, according to Walker, was that many workshops were 'back kitchens and small rooms in private houses where a man works with two or three lads under him at some branch of the trade'. Hence it proved extremely difficult to ensure that all eligible children attended school, a situation compounded by the vast influx of children from the country districts.[66]

Walker's evidence is also interesting in that while, as a member of the school board, he was obviously concerned about truancy, he did not, like Angrave and Harris of the Leicester Hosiery Manufacturers' Association, advocate a total ban on child labour. Walker, of course, was a member of the local Unitarian congregation,[67] and also possessed interests in the hosiery trade, but increasingly his firm's fortunes were tied to footwear production. As we have seen, by 1876 hosiers were firmly committed to factory production and they were extremely anxious to see the demise of the workshop sector in order to assist factory recruitment and discipline, but shoe manufacturers on the other hand were still highly dependent on workshops. Sergeant Buxton, a local policeman, who also carried out the function of sanitary inspector responsible for workshops, informed the commissioners that in 1876 the 800 workshops were 'chiefly populated by boot finishers and boot riveters'.[68]

There were clearly marked differences in the patterns of development of the two major local industries. Hosiers by 1876 perceived quite clearly that their future lay in steam-powered 'Cotton's patent' frames which in turn entailed centralized production, but what was the position of technology in footwear and to what extent did technology encourage rather than curtail workshop production?

In the preceding section the arrival of two different machines (Crick's riveter and the Blake sole sewer) and their effect on the Leicester industry during the 1850s was discussed. This technological survey will be continued up until the late 1880s. It will go beyond a mere classification of new technology, however, by exploring the economic and social consequences of the introduction of new machinery.

The main input of improved technology undoubtedly came from the American machine manufacturers. John Day, the editor of the *Shoe and Leather Record* from 1886 until early in the present century, expressed the feelings of the shoe manufacturers towards the machine firms in an essay published in 1903. Day criticized the high profits made by the machine companies, denounced their monopolistic practices and noted that the leasing system began with the Blake company, whose profits were extremely large.[69] The Blake was followed by an improved version called the Blake-McKay in 1867, and in 1872 the Goodyear welt-sewing machine and chain stitcher was introduced. This was claimed to be 54 times faster than sewing by awl and thread and produced the first exact replica of the hand-sewn boot.[70] All of these machines were capable of operation by treadle. Essentially they improved the quality of the ready-made product, but did not affect the method of industrial organization. If anything, the improved quality of Leicester shoes helped to expand the market for the town's products which in turn stimulated an expansion of outwork. In 1872 Dare noted that 'numerous workshops, factories and dwelling houses ... have been built and others are being erected'.[71]

In the United States, on the other hand, factory production proper was becoming the norm. Stimulated by demand for army boots during the Civil War the Massachusetts manufacturers centralized production in large factories. Machinery was widely employed and those areas of production which had not as yet been affected by mechanical innovation – closing, lasting and finishing – were subjected to a highly detailed division of labour, in which the component tasks were broken down into simplified hand operations. This manual division of labour, known as the hand-team system, worked alongside the sewing and stitching machines to facilitate assembly line manufacture. In the Massachusetts shoe town of Marlboro, for instance, there were only five remaining outworkers in 1875.[72] Clark's of Street in Somerset had similarly perfected the team system by 1880. This firm did of course enjoy the benefits of geographical isolation which, together with a strong ethos of paternalism, produced a workforce which was compliant by British standards.[73]

Another important factor aiding the continuation of the workshop system was the tendency towards regional specialization in footwear manufacture during the latter half of the nineteenth century. Leicester's speciality was ladies' lightweight fashion shoes, children's footwear, some men's fashion products and novelty items such as football boots.[74] Northampton, the traditional centre for the production of men's hand-sewn boots, continued to concentrate on that sector after the introduction of machinery. Stafford produced heavy welted ladies' shoes, but increasingly after the 1870s this town's trade declined as consumers began to favour the lighter Leicester product. Norwich produced high-quality fancy ladies' shoes, while Bristol was famous for its heavy quality protective boots.[75] Street in Somerset produced quality men's boots and a rivalry existed between that town and Northampton.[76]

This marked regionalization was largely the product of local specialities. Northampton's renown as the centre of quality men's boots rested on the town's reputation as an army supplier, while Leicester's position as a major manufacturer of children's (known locally as 'cacks') and women's shoes can be attributed to the development by local entrepreneurs of the market first opened up by the 'cacks' producers in the 1820s. Another important factor that contributed to local product specialization was the diversity of products in the footwear trade. A manufacturer who wished to produce both male and female footwear would be faced with considerable extra investment in lasts, machinery and warehouse capacity. Women's dress shoes could not be manufactured by a production unit specializing in men's boots. Furthermore, skilled labour experienced in working on a particular style of shoe usually found great difficulty in adapting to another type of footwear.[77]

This regionalism carried important consequences for the economic development of the industry. Between 1860 and 1885 Leicester enjoyed an expanding market both at home and abroad with virtually no competition. Indeed so great was the demand from both the Empire and South America for British footwear that it was often exported unpriced to be sold by auction on arrival, a marketing method which realized enormous profits for British manufacturers.[78] By 1881 the industry employed just over one-third of the town's workforce and in the previous year the local directory proudly noted that 'Leicester has suffered less than almost any other town from the stagnation that has affected English industry, this applies especially to the boot and shoe trade.'[79]

This era of prosperity and lack of competition, which facilitated the survival and indeed the expansion of the workshop system of industrial organization, did not, however, continue unchecked during the 1880s. This decade witnessed a massive expansion in the numbers employed in the industry in Leicester from 13,056 in 1881 to over 24,000 in 1891, but this growth was increasingly punctuated by short-time working and lay-offs.[80] This was partly caused by an inherent weakness in the nature of Leicester's market: women and children bought their footwear at particular times of the year, especially at Whitsun. It is extremely difficult to chart the ebb and flow of demand for Leicester footwear. The best source available, the *Labour Gazette* of the Board of Trade, which began in 1893, indicates that the months of April, May and June were invariably the busiest. The remainder of the year tended to be uniformly flat.[81] Other factors, however, were also at work, the most important being the encroachment of competition into Leicester's traditional export market. Canadians, for instance, were by the early 1880s predominantly wearers of shoes made in Massachusetts and the country was no longer the third largest export market for British footwear. Similarly, Australians were turning to both non-British shoes and increasingly to footwear manufactured by local industry.[82]

These changes in the industry's market brought several responses among Leicester shoe manufacturers. As we have already noted the Leicester industry was based on a mixture of factory and workshop production, individual firms typically relying on both methods. The entrepreneurs, therefore, in an effort to cut costs and increase competititiveness, undertook measures that affected both areas of production. Inside the factory, new second-generation technology imported from the USA was increasingly used. Those firms with the necessary capital slowly began to centralize production, a process that was aided by the arrival during the 1880s of machines capable of carrying out tasks in the finishing department, such as edge paring, edge burnishing, sole levelling and buffing, and edge levelling. Another important technological breakthrough occurred with the development of machines which revolutionized the heeling department. The emergence of the heel-building, moulding, attaching, breasting and finishing machines, many of which were capable of operation by boys, made deep inroads into the area of hand work that still existed in the making departments.[83]

Finally, the most important breakthrough came in the late 1880s with the development of the lasting machine. The clickers apart, the lasters had traditionally considered themselves the elite of the trade. In some centres lasting was still the subject of apprenticeship, while in Leicester the more informal method of spending three or four years as a laster's boy was needed to master the craft. The calculated pulls and tensions upon the upper performed by the laster, while seemingly simple to the eye, was a genuine skill that took several years to master. Hence the Bed lasting machine and the Consolidated type removed from the labour process the operation which required skilled and therefore expensive labour and facilitated a subdivision of labour in which the component tasks could be performed by relatively unskilled and often young workers. Of even more far-reaching consequence was the fact that the lasting machine filled the technological gap that had previously existed in the production process. It was now possible to produce a shoe, from closing to finishing, in which all the major operations were mechanized. The trade union expressed much consternation at this development and noted 'the tendency these machines have to introduce the team system, as without it ... they will not pay'.[84]

Mechanization, however, was only one response to increased international competition. Contemporary literature, particularly the trade journal, the *Shoe and Leather Record*, noted that the new machines were largely being used by the 'more progressive houses'.[85] Although it is impossible to be precise, most of the evidence suggests that the majority of the Leicester trade was anything but progressive.[86] The workshop sector, in theory, was severely curtailed by the passing of the 1878 Factory Act, which supposedly brought the workshops into line with factories. In practice, however, the workshops continued unchecked. One reason for this may have been that the traditional response of the Leicester entrepreneur to increased competition, particularly those with a background in hosiery, was to seek out cheaper sources of labour. The country workshops were to prove especially attractive.

As we have seen, some entrepreneurs exploited Leicester's traditional connection with outworkers from the surrounding countryside. Throughout the 1870s and 1880s the network of 'country' workers continued to expand. In 1876 the evidence suggests that virtually all of the 'finishing' was still carried on outdoors[87] and in 1881 the trade union reported a 'mushrooming of small shops in out of the way places'.[88] A major factor in this continuous development was, of course, the failure of the factory inspectorate to enforce the legislation. H. Thornhill, the inspector whose district covered Leicester, Leicestershire and part of Derbyshire,[89] admitted to the 1876 Commission that legislation 'was a dead letter in country villages'.[90] By 1883 the union was noting with concern the tendency for redundant bag-hosiers to enter the footwear trade and their increasing use by even the large employers.[91]

Paradoxically the workshop sector received a further boost during the 1880s from increased mechanization. New machines and work methods produced widespread discontent amongst the town-based workforce to such an extent that by 1880 the Leicester branch of the union was reporting up to four disputes a day.[92] In some instances the introduction of machinery was increasing costs rather than reducing them, and in 1883 the CWS (Cooperative Wholesale Society) Wheatsheaf works, the most highly mechanized plant in the town, was sending out more work than ever to country villages.[93]

During the late 1880s and early 1890s international competition was fierce. Ominously, for Leicester, the most vigorous participants in the battle for overseas markets were the highly mechanized American factories, whose speciality was high-quality, low-priced ladies' shoes. The initial thrust of the American export drive was directed at Britain's traditional markets in Canada and Australia. In the 1890s, however, the Americans turned their attention to England, Germany, Austria and France. High-powered marketing techniques became the hallmark of the Massachusetts entrepreneurs and soon virtually all the major towns in England possessed an American-owned shop selling American-produced shoes.[94] During 1894 American imports into Britain increased twelvefold and the British industry realized that its very existence was at stake. To survive, however, required a drastic change in working methods and above all the implementation of the team system. The major stumbling-block to the introduction of this system was the restrictive practices carried out by the workers. By 1894 NUBSO was the second largest union in Britain outside coal and cotton, and enjoyed an organizational power commensurate with its size. Leicester, as well as being the headquarters of the union, supported more than a quarter of the membership and it is therefore not surprising that the town became the centre of the employers' concerted attack on restrictive practices. Thus by the early 1890s market forces and technological developments were putting a severe strain on industrial relations in the Leicester trade. Tension between manufacturers and labour was to dominate the industry for the next five years. We have seen the factors at work which impelled employers to try to change working practices. It is now time to chart the emergence of trade unionism in the trade up until the years immediately before the period of industrial conflict.

Labour Organization in the Leicester Footwear Industry 1872–1900

The early organization of British shoe workers has yet to find its historian. The Webbs, in their classic survey, note the formation of a national union of hand seam workers some time in the 1840s,[95] but are silent on subsequent developments.[96] Alan Fox has sketched out the broad outlines of the cordwainers' national organization at the time of the secession of the machine trade workers in 1874 but as yet we have no knowledge of the local structure of the parent union.[97] What is certain, however, is that workers in the new machine-made industry were at first organized by the cordwainers' society. This is only to be expected as the infant machine-made industry was highly dependent on an influx of skilled labour from the hand-sewn sector. When the workers in the machine-made trade decided to secede from the Cordwainers' Amalgamated in 1874 they already possessed a structure of local branches and a tradition of organization typical of artisan workers. The old union also bequeathed to the new organization another important feature, an open mode of recruitment. The cordwainers had recognized early on the importance of and the danger from the mushrooming new trade, and subsequently changed their recruitment rules to facilitate the organization of workers in the machine industry.[98]

Jealousies, especially over finance, nevertheless developed between the two classes of workers. Furthermore the cordwainers, ever aware of their craft status, were often antagonistic towards their less skilled brothers. The campaign for secession began when the secretary of the Leicester Rivetters' and Finishers' Section, Martin Leader, canvassed fourteen other riveters' and finishers' sections on the possibility of a breakaway. The new organization, the National Union of Operative Rivetters and Finishers (NUORF), was formed at a meeting at Stafford in December 1873.[99] The new union took over the system of branch organization founded by the cordwainers and continued many of the activities of the old craft union, such as the tramping system, for many years.

The NUORF adopted a mode of organization that was controlled by the General Council. This body comprised the general secretary, the general president, the treasurer and four members of the committee. The union also followed the 'Seat of Government' device in its ruling structure. The 'Seat of Government' was a method adopted by many early trade unions in order to overcome high transport costs incurred by officials attending meetings. All branches in the union voted every two years to nominate the 'Seat of Government'. Winning the seat, however, entailed more than kudos and convenience as, apart from the general secretary, who could be nominated from any branch, the remaining six posts on the General Council had to be filled by nominees of the branch in the town where the 'Seat of Government' was located. The union was nevertheless distinctly federal in its structure and the branches retained the right to rescind the instructions of council by the device of the 'branch General Meeting'.[100] The branches also retained one-third of all financial income and were thus in a position to fund strike action which did not have the authority of the General Council.[101] This form of organization was to be very important to the Leicester shoeworkers.

Leicester, with its 1,397 members, was by far the largest branch in the new union and easily won the nomination to be the 'Seat of Government'. Thomas Smith, the secretary of the Stafford Rivetters and organizer of the 1873 conference, became general secretary, the only paid post on the council, and removed himself to Leicester[102] to join his Leicester colleagues. Throughout the rest of our period Leicester remained the 'Seat of

Government'. The massive expansion in local membership gave the branch an unassailable position in the organization of the union.

The early years of the union, as should be expected, were mainly concerned with problems of consolidation. Recruitment was obviously the union's first concern and the Leicester branch gained a notable reputation in this activity. Throughout our period the local branch was by far the largest in the union and often contained over 25 per cent of the union's national membership. The massive expansion of the trade in Leicester aided union growth, but nevertheless the local branch pursued a vigorous recruitment campaign especially amongst the finishers and smaller workshops. In November 1880 Leicester reported 130 new members during the previous fortnight.

> The system we have now adopted seems likely to bring about results the most sanguine would hardly have expected. We have divided the town into districts and had over twenty real earnest workers, who are if necessary, doing a house to house call; this is to catch those working away from the factories, in small shops and their own homes, more especially finishers.[103]

Collective bargaining was conducted through the local boards of arbitration that sprang up during the 1870s, and the attitude of the union leadership towards the employers was generally conciliatory. The historian of the union has also noted that 'in each of these centres there was a group of employers who considered that regular joint discussions could play a constructive part in the smooth running of the industry'.[104] Leicester was certainly one of the centres referred to by Fox, and T. Smith appears to have enjoyed the friendship and confidence of local manufacturers.[105]

Yet it would be wrong to regard the 1870s in the footwear trade as a period of total harmony. Even in these boom years footwear, like all clothing trades, was subject to high levels of seasonality in demand. The union therefore normally found itself on the defensive for at least part of the year.

> As the season advances the necessity for increased vigilance, calm reasoning, and firmness becomes greater; questions in dispute must be looked at from as broad a point of view, as it is at all compatible with our dignity as an association, conciliation must be our watchword; and if each officer and member will act upon this advice it will very materially assist us in successfully conducting our union through the difficulties by which our path is surrounded, and land us into the new year fresh and vigorous to meet the troubles we usually encounter at that season.[106]

This statement of the union's attitude in a difficult period captures the ambiguity that surrounded the rhetorical expressions frequently voiced by the union officials. Harmony there may have been and Smith did after all resign his post as general secretary in 1878 in order to become the full-time secretary of the Leicester Liberal Association, but nevertheless it was also a strategy that would 'land us into the new year fresh and vigorous to meet the troubles we usually encounter at that season'. In April the

The Anchor Cooperative factory. These substantial premises were erected in the 1890s. The cooperative ceased trading in 1971. (Courtesy of the British Library of Political and Economic Science.)

Left: The Equity's first premises, 1886. Humble beginnings for one of Britain's most successful producers' cooperatives. (Edward O. Greening, *A Pioneer Co-Partnership*, 1923.)

Below: The Equity premises in 1898: a works most capitalists would be proud of. The factory and the cooperative are still trading. (Edward O. Greening, *A Pioneer Co- Partnership*, 1923.)

Above: Mixed doubles in the Cooperative Commonwealth: tennis courts on the Anchor Tenants Estate, showing the generous, well-stocked gardens at Humberstone 'Garden City'. This development was built by the Anchor Shoe Cooperative in the 1890s. (Courtesy of the British Library of Political and Economic Science.)

Right: 'Why should we not be our own landlords?' An Equity worker's house. (H.D. Lloyd, *Labour Co-Partnership*: courtesy University of Warwick Library.)

Below: The Womens Guild, Leicester Hosiery Cooperative Society. Leicester's producers' cooperatives spawned a multitude of social institutions. Having your photograph taken in 1898 was obviously a serious business; nevertheless, these well-dressed women epitomized the 'respectable' aspect of cooperation. (Thomas Blandford and George Newell, *History of the Leicester Cooperative Hosiery Manufacturing Society Limited, 1898*: courtesy Leicestershire Reference Library.)

Above left: The educational room, Leicester Hosiery Cooperative Society. All local producers' societies devoted a share of profits to educational activities. George Newell, the Society's manager, is seated in the centre of the front row. The predominance of women reflects the sexual division of labour in hosiery in the late nineteenth century. (Thomas Blandford and George Newell, *History of the Leicester Cooperative Hosiery Manufacturing Society Limited, 1898*: courtesy Leicestershire Reference Library.)

Left: Linkers and Cottons Patent machines in action at the Leicester Hosiery Cooperative Society. The women were noted for their contentment at work. They enjoyed singing hymns even in the company of strangers. Note the male Cottons Patent operatives in the background. (Thomas Blandford and George Newell, *History of the Leicester Cooperative Hosiery Manufacturing Society Limited, 1898*: courtesy Leicestershire Reference Library.)

Above: Market Place, Leicester, 5 June 1905. This large meeting was held for the start of the Leicester 1905 Unemployment March. The 'vicar for the unemployed', F.L. Donaldson, blessed the men, who left the area singing 'Lead Kindly Light'. (Courtesy of Leicestershire Museums Services.)

Overleaf: The leaders of the march. George 'Sticky' White, an unemployed, disabled laster; F.L. Donaldson, sometimes referred to as 'the marchers' John Ball' and 'Father Gapon'; Amos Sherriff, a leading figure in the Leicester ILP and the local purveyor of the Clarion Cycle. (Courtesy of Leicestershire Museums Services.)

following year the monthly report was conspicuously lacking in harmonious outpourings, when the General Council denounced in angry terms the attempts by the Leicester employers to introduce a statement that proposed major cuts in piece rates.[107]

Another point which probably had some influence on the harmonious stance of the leadership was the fact that in Leicester at least there existed two systems of collective bargaining. Individual shop floor negotiations on the prices paid to the various groups of workers, all paid by the piece, were necessary in an industry that produced goods that were constantly changing in both type of construction and style. This grass-roots mode of negotiation was complemented by the local arbitration board which in Leicester was designed to act as the court of appeal of the plethora of individual disputes that were constantly arising. Hence by 1882 George Sedgewick, the successor to Smith as general secretary, went so far as to define the purpose of the union as 'to act as mediator between employers and workmen in trade disputes'.[108]

During the early 1880s the moderate stance adopted by the union leadership was being seriously challenged by innovations carried out by employers to meet the needs of rapid technological and economic change during a period of a world-wide decline in prices and narrowing profit margins. The response of the employers to this background of general depression and the threat of competition from more technologically advanced foreign manufacturers was to find ways of lowering production costs. They attempted to introduce labour-saving machinery, new systems of work organization, day work instead of piece rates, and the substitution of less skilled labour.

One of the early innovations to cause disruption in Leicester was the introduction of large numbers of 'boy labourers' into enterprises specializing in low-quality footwear. These products, high in cardboard and low in leather and craft content, were generally manufactured by small and medium-sized employers. The growth of this low-quality sector not only threatened the long-term craft interests of the workers, but the expansion of the numbers of small employers in this area was also being felt in the composition of the local Manufacturers' Association, formed in 1871.[109] The anger vented by the union in April 1878 against the implementation of a new statement designed to lower wages was heightened by the fact that for the first time the Manufacturers' Association had failed to consult the union before introducing the statement.[110] These small firms were also the first to reduce wages and to ignore what was left of the apprenticeship system. The rise of the small firms therefore carried serious consequences for the local labour market, and they also threatened the stability of the larger enterprises which now had to cope with both a declining economic environment and local low-priced competition.

The major craft element in the labour process was lasting, and this was not to be mechanized successfully until the early 1890s, but the

43

implications of the early steps towards a team system, carried out by the larger employers in the early 1880s, were quickly spotted by the workers as a threat to their craft status. The monthly report of the union in October 1881 called for more effort in organizing workshops and gave the following appraisal of innovations and their threat to the craft status of workers:

> The aspects of our trade are constantly changing in consequence of the rapid increase of productive power, caused by new systems of division and subdivision of labour, and the introduction of machinery; in fact many of our large shoe manufactures resemble more the appearance of an extensive engineering establishment than a place for the manufacture of shoes, so largely does the use of machinery obtain.
> The knowledge of leather, its attributes and uses, are becoming day by day apparently less a necessity to the workman than the fact of being competent to direct or control some intricate piece of machinery. We say 'apparently' advisedly, because whilst it may be possible to create a race of human beings – flesh and blood as ourselves – but who, for all practical purposes, would be as much machines as the instruments of metal which they would tend, it is not possible to do this without at the same time destroying that individual tact, taste, and skill which has hitherto been a marked characteristic of the disciples of St. Crispin. The combinations of leather produced under such conditions would be void of those symmetrical proportions, the artistic outlines, and the life – so to speak – which is now so admirably blended in the various samples of our craft, which in their special lines, are today the pride of both maker and vendor. To maintain the position we have acquired in the markets of the world during the past, is none the less duty of the workman than the employer. This cannot be done by the unrestricted use of the automatons before mentioned. We have then, as workmen, the strongest incentive to at least endeavour to restrain, not only the unlimited importation of unskilled ill-trained labour into our midst, but also discourage as far as possible, the use of improper and worthless material.[111]

The workers were of course in an ambivalent position on the question of machinery. 'Machinery has played an important part in the past history of our trade, but we are fully assured that it is destined to play a more important part than it has hitherto done' declared the monthly report of November 1888. The industry was after all based upon and clustered around mechanized forms of sole attachment and it is of no great surprise that the newly designed union emblem of 1885 contained an illustration of the 'Blake' machine.[112] Mechanization in the lasting department, however, not only threatened the workers' major area of skill, but the attendant speed-ups in all the other areas of production the lasting machine would bring in its train would challenge the remaining craft pretensions of the rest of the workforce, and open up the industry to a flood of unskilled, young workers.

Immediately before the first wave of lasting machines a new generation of sole-attaching and finishing machines was introduced. These new machines, produced by the highly competitive American shoe machine industry, often carried inflated productivity claims. The union noted with concern that 'the introduction of machinery is responsible for a large proportion of disputes no one will deny, not because the workmen have in any way attempted to oppose its introduction, but because the inventors therefore, with the view of selling their machines more readily, have led employers to take more from the wages of the men than the portions of the work performed would warrant, hence the men's objections and ultimate resistance'.[113] The core of the problem was the adoption by Leicester manufacturers of American production methods, while at the same time they refused to follow the American policy of paying high wages for high productivity. The Webbs, in their work *Industrial Democracy*, chose this specific problem of the Leicester footwear trade as a major example of obstinacy and conservatism amongst employers. They also noted the obduracy of the workers who clung tenaciously to the tenets of Owenite socialism, which claimed that the legitimate reward of labour was the entire commodity produced or its price on the market.[114] The problems that arose over the machinery question during the 1880s were, however, pale foreshadows of the disputes created when a reliable lasting machine was introduced in 1889. These conflicts will be the subject of later chapters.

Until the mid-1880s disputes over machinery were a minor irritant. The strong undercurrent of craft pride, independence and autonomy can, of course, be detected beneath the rhetorical surface of harmony between labour and capital, but these aspects of artisan consciousness remained submerged yet at the same time flowed into the ideology of self-help liberalism shared by both master and men. As long as workers prospered in their workshops or were left relatively unsupervised, being paid by the piece, harmony would prevail in the factories. The dynamics of expansion, which both increased and strengthened the workshop sector, produced a system of industrial relations that assured the continuation of methods and practices that were rooted in the artisan era. Unlike other mass production industries, most notably cotton textiles, paternalism played a minor role in the Leicester footwear industry. This is understandable given the fact that the manufacturer had little contact with the majority of workers, who worked outside the factory until 1891. Moreover, the vicissitudes of seasonality resulted in much of the workforce constantly moving from one employer to another.[115]

The prosperity of the trade also removed some of the more raucous elements from the shoemaking community. As early as 1862 the St Crispin's day celebration had been relocated inside the Temperance Hall and the highlight of the event was the address by the mayor to the assembled shoemakers. Dare commented hopefully that this new venue 'will furnish a rational holiday instead of his old drunken saturnalia'.[116] More importantly, the regular meeting between union officers and manufacturers that took place in the running of the local arbitration machinery facilitated personal friendships and collaboration between the two groups in areas outside industrial relations. As we have already seen, two systems of collective bargaining existed in the early decades of the trade in Leicester, shop floor negotiations and arbitration. As long as the trade boomed the two did not come into conflict. Thus arbitration during this period tended to concentrate on fixing annual statements rather than involve itself in the cut and thrust of individual pricing negotiations.[117] The officer stratum of the union increasingly came to see their role as that of an industrial police force rather than as champions of shop floor demands. Sedgwick's concept of the union's function as being that of a mediator 'between employers and workmen in time of disputes' underlines this point.[118] Such conciliatory attitudes towards the manufacturers brought rewards to union officials other than endowing them with an inflated sense of their own importance and communal responsibility. Political office was to be the most important of these benefits. Smith, Sedgwick and their successor as general secretary, William Inskip, all sat on the Liberal benches of Leicester council along with the ten or more Liberal councillors who were also shoe manufacturers during this period.

It is not surprising therefore that when the industry became bedevilled by disputes in the late 1880s, disputes that arose from shop floor discontent, conflict soon developed a political dimension. Both Leicester liberalism and the Leicester footwear industry were dominated by a group of men who were firmly based in a system of production that was distinguished by its artisan mode of organization and lack of centralization. Hence conflicts that were to arise over efforts to change this form of manufacture questioned political as well as industrial relationships. Furthermore, change in the footwear industry, particularly centralized production, also entailed important shifts in local social structure. It is now time to undertake an analysis of local politics and social factors, for without such a study the troubles in the industry during the 1890s would be incomprehensible.

3 Work and Consciousness: the Leicester Working Class, 1860–85

The question 'What were the origins of the Labour Party?' is a legitimate historical question. The danger which is constantly faced by historians in answering these backward-looking questions is that of anachronism. Our focus is naturally aimed at those institutions and social groups which formed the roots of the tree whose growth we are trying to explain. In pursuing this tracing exercise the danger is that antecedents may be exaggerated. Furthermore, their relevance and social context during early periods may be misunderstood. A major theme of this study, which will be developed further in Chapter 8, is that a major input into early socialism was a concern to defend certain forms of existing social relationships, particularly those based in the workplace. The ideals of the independent artisan and the self-regulating workman were the central issues in the battle between capital and labour that dominated Leicester during the period 1885–95, a struggle which gave birth to early forms of socialism. This chapter will concentrate primarily on the persistence of artisan work patterns in a more general communal context than the one described in Chapters 1 and 2. It will therefore deal mainly with the world of work as experienced by the majority of the working class in Leicester. Other important forms of class activity such as Owenism in its secularist garbs, and popular religion, will be examined in the succeeding chapters.

The period generally was one of social and political stability. The era of mass movements and social unrest, with the notable exception of the reform agitation, appeared to be a thing of the past. Historians have generally explained this period of working-class quiescence by reference to profound changes in the economy which affected the political disposition of the working class. One group of writers has drawn attention to growing divisions within the working class during a period of increasing economic prosperity and in particular to the important effects of the emergence of a labour aristocracy on class politics.[1] More recently the work of Patrick Joyce, on industrial and communal relationships in the Lancashire cotton towns, with its emphasis on paternalism and deference has offered new insights into the history of the period.[2] Leicester, however, was a community particularly ill fitted to these two modes of explanation. There was no detectable stratum sufficient in size and importance which corresponded with Hobsbawm's list of factors that supposedly identifies a labour aristocracy.[3] Furthermore, the few workers who do broadly match Hobsbawm's category, the clickers in footwear and warehousemen in hosiery, tended to stand on the sidelines of working-class politics.[4] Their role in the production process tended to be somewhat marginal in comparison with that played by the spinners, engineers, hewers and checkweighmen in Foster's Oldham study. The politics of paternalism raises another important set of problems which in the context of Leicester cannot be so easily put to one side as those raised by the Labour aristocracy theorists. Paternalistic interventions were regularly attempted by the Leicester manufacturing class, but because local industry was largely dispersed on a system of outwork, these efforts were mostly carried out by agencies whose aim was morally to uplift the working class. How efficient were these paternalistic devices? Such an assessment will expose the tenacity of the artisan, workshop-based, culture. Finally, an attempt will be made to explain Leicester's political and social stability during the period.

The prevalence of outwork manufacture during the period under review provided fertile ground for the growth and maintenance of popular beliefs, attitudes and practices. It is true, as we shall see in Chapter 6, that the Leicester working class accepted the policies and followed the leadership of middle-class politicians throughout the period, but nevertheless the Leicester workers were rarely subjected to the full range of hegemonic devices practised by manufacturers in other parts of England.[5] Traditions and cultural patterns which can roughly be described as 'artisan' flourished unhindered in this period of massive economic and population expansion. These cultural practices were slowly perceived by manufacturers as presenting a formidable obstacle to productive efficiency, especially during the latter part of the period when foreign competition threatened the viability of Leicester's two major industries. But this recognition of the problem was slow. Most manufacturers were reluctant to change a system that worked and generated profit for a minimal investment.

Some local observers, however, were alarmed and sensed a threat in the growing manifestations of working-class cultural independence during a period of dramatic population expansion. Joseph Dare, the Unitarian Domestic Missionary, was particularly well placed to comment on the subject, being a paid employee of a congregation which largely consisted of the town's major hosiers. His task was to distribute both charity and moral uplift to the lower classes.[6] A recurring theme in the annual reports of this nineteenth-century social worker expressed his concern, and extolled his employers to do something about the audacious behaviour of the growing working-class population. In particular Dare singled out the mass of newly arrived immigrant labour for comment. 'Raw from the country, they are intoxicated with town life and intensify its worse manifestations.' The influx of 'godless' shoemakers caused Dare much concern. In 1853, before their arrival, he noted that 'in reference to the reading tastes of the masses, an intelligent publisher informs me that he supplies now scarcely any of the licentious tales issued by "Lloyds" and "Reynolds". These abominations have been, at least in Leicester, nearly supplanted by the "London Journal", which has reached an immense circulation and is comparatively a serial of a much better kind, though it has some objectionable points.'[7] By 1857, however, Dare was concerned by 'these Sunday strollers who take the Reasoner, or Reynolds, with them, and are settling, with absolute decision, questions that the greatest minds never dare approach'. He went on to complain that 'one cause of neglect of worship is the lamentable prevalence of infidelity, which prevails to an extent few can perceive, who have not mixed with all classes on common ground'.[8]

Dare's solution to the apparent problem of social control over the rapidly expanding working population was paternalism. In the comparatively calm days of 1853 Dare commented with satisfaction that 'a softening influence has been produced by many of the employers and their friends mingling with "the hands" in their summer festivities'.[9] By 1864 the outdoor summer activities of the workers, according to Dare, had degenerated into 'what they call their recreations ... Often the fete ends in a mere riotous debauch, or is continued in the town for many days, to the neglect of employment, self-degradation and the privation of helpless dependents.'[10] Dare's ideal type of summer outing was those provided by some of the larger employers, who would most probably be among his benefactors and thus singled out for special mention. For example:

> I had the pleasure during the summer of spending a day with the hands of a very large establishment. The locality chosen for the holiday was Kenilworth. The heads of the firm accompanied their hands, numbering about five hundred, together with several friends who were specially invited to join them. They sat at tea, mingled in the country dance, or rambled over the magnificent ruins together, or as 'fancy will determine' the employers or visitors referring to the various interesting legends or historical associations connected with them for the information and amusement of the merry group. All enjoyed themselves without restraint, neither quarrel nor drunkenness disgraced the scene, and the whole of the hands were at work the next morning at the usual time.[11]

Dare's reports do, of course, require cautious treatment as he was undoubtedly prone to exaggerate the effects of the paternalistic interventions of his larger benefactors. We must in particular bear in mind that only a tiny proportion of the Leicester working class would, in this period, have been directly employed by the manufacturers on a regular basis and thus benefit from their paternalistic largesse. Patrick Joyce in his study of paternalism during this period has noted that 'Season, fashion, foreign tariffs, variations in raw material costs and a lack of alternative workers all compounded to depress the condition of the operatives and sever the link between master and man which continuous, dependable work created.'[12]

Joyce here is referring to the failure of paternalism to establish itself in the West Riding. Many of his factors were found in both footwear and hosiery and if we add the vital feature of outwork to Joyce's list, relationships between master and men must have been extremely fluctuating in Leicester.

Nevertheless, the collective conscience of the Unitarian manufacturers as expressed through the mission did not eschew innovation and intervention in the affairs of working-class everyday life. Education was a central objective of the mission. In the decades before the Education Act, the mission school provided lessons for 742 boys in 1862, by far the largest establishment of its kind in Leicester.[13] Many of these scholars were part-time employees of Unitarian manufacturers.[14] The mission school continued up until 1872 by which time it was rendered obsolete by the new board schools.[15] The Unitarians were also eager to provide adult recreational facilities including Instructional Classes, Sewing Classes, a Provident Club, Discussion Classes, Window-plant Shows and Sunday Schools. But how effective were all these activities in achieving their organizers' aim of producing working men and women of sober dispositions whose value system closely accorded with that of their benefactors? We have no means of gauging the effects of many of these activities and pastimes, but the evidence that is available, particularly on the working men's discussion groups, is revealing.

In the next chapter we shall see how the Domestic Mission provided a temporary home for early secularists who availed themselves of the Unitarians' warmth and shelter during the 1850s when the fortunes of Owenism were at a low ebb.[16] In this chapter, however, the focus will be upon the activities of the Discussion Group during the 1860s. The adult male reading and discussion classes informed Dare in 1865 that they wished to form a working men's club. Dare's initial reaction was favourable. He himself became a committee member, and was chiefly responsible for raising funds from local manufacturers.[17] The club eventually opened on Easter Monday at premises in St Martin's. The Domestic Mission provided newspapers and a library. Middle-class men including Dare were prominent on the committee and the club's future and direction appeared to be in their hands. Within weeks of opening, however, the working-class membership announced their wish to offer 'the means of recreation and enjoyment with no temptations to excess, to enable them to get a glass of ale without the inducement of taking two for the good of the house, and to enable them to see in the club examples of moderation.'[18] The wishes of the members prevailed, setting a precedent for the club movement nationally. Dare, naturally, resented this development. By the end of the year the Reading and Discussion classes were moribund, the members having joined the working men's club *en masse*.[19] The club in contrast survived and prospered, and it appears to have been particularly attractive to footwear workers.[20]

There is, however, a danger in oversimplifying rejection from below of middle-class-inspired rational recreational initiatives. The local coffee and cocoa house movement, whose directors included such notable manufacturers as Angrave, Ellis, Simon, Stanyon and W. H. Walker, was established in 1877 and by 1882 the company was running eight separate houses. The question of popular attitudes to drink is a fascinating one but for reasons of space cannot be explored fully here. Nevertheless, the temperance movement did have an effect upon working-class life, especially in the area of politics. For example, in November 1905 the Leicester ILP were anxious to publicize the fact that eight of the nine ILP town councillors were total abstainers, which suggests that abstinence was perceived as a major personal quality amongst working-class political leaders.[21] Yet the reformers were faced with an uphill battle during the period. Footloose workers, probably new to the town, increasingly sought entertainment in drinking establishments, many of which, according to Dare, were expanding their premises to provide singing and dancing rooms.[22] The Unitarians were in the forefront of the campaign to provide counter attractions such as penny readings and factory brass bands. In 1864 Dare warned the mission's benefactors that 'counter attractions alone will do away with the casino and dancing saloon', but added ominously:

> No doubt these moral agencies have produced and are producing very beneficial results as far as their influence extends, but they only reach down to a certain grade of the population, and are chiefly calculated to interest and improve those who already possess some little taste and information. I attended some of these social gatherings to see what kind of audiences came together, and I must say very few were present of those whom it is most desirable to call out. There are whole masses who are incapable of enjoying or profiting ... lower deeps still open wide to devour them.

Given Dare's frequent strictures on the licentious behaviour of young workers in the unskilled sections of the footwear industry it is quite clear whom he was describing. Indeed later in the report he drew attention to the frequent instances of 'the embezzlement of materials entrusted to them'.[23]

Dare's was not a lone voice in advocating the paternal approach as a solution to the problem, or potential problem, of social stability. Both the Tory *Journal* and the Liberal *Chronicle* contained columns entitled 'Treats for Workers' which eagerly charted instances of employers' munificence. Yet by the end of the period up to 1885 only one firm appears to have successfully established a paternalistic regime of a permanent nature. This, not surprisingly, was Corah's, who with their large new St Margaret's works were the biggest hosiery firm in the town and thanks to their innovations in machinery and marketing were the first and perhaps the only company able to provide continuous factory-based employment.[24]

Other middle-class-inspired forms of working-class improvement produced more tangible results. In particular the Freehold Land Society is worth attention. Founded in 1849 by such staunch Liberals as the Biggs brothers, Joseph Whetstone and the two local MPs Harris and Ellis, together with James Thompson, the editor of the *Liberal Chronicle*, the society's initial objectives were 'to overthrow the Tory domination of the County' by gaining the freehold county vote for subscribing artisans. Although at first bedevilled by speculators and jerry builders, the society eventually provided 2,550 housing sites, one-fifth of the total new stock erected in the period 1851–81. The society eventually became the Leicester Permanent Building Society and appears never to have played the political role intended by its founders.[25]

Joyce has also noted that, in general, old cities and towns were difficult locations for the practice of thoroughgoing paternalism and the politics of influence.[26] Alternative employment opportunities to those offered by the potential paternalist obviously made the price of a fully-fledged system of influence too high. Furthermore, the process of mechanization and centralized production, an essential feature in Joyce's typology, was accompanied in Leicester by intense class struggle in both footwear and hosiery. Industrial relations were thus well soured by the time that the process of factory building had been completed. Indeed, worker-employer conflict was deeply rooted in both industries decades before factory production. The issue of frame rent in hosiery was a constant source of acrimony amongst stockingers in the apparently stable years of the 1860s and 1870s, especially when no other employer followed John Biggs's example of abolishing rent in 1859.[27] The evidence of the stockingers' leaders to the commissioner examining the truck system in 1871 highlights the stockingers' long-held anger on the frame rent question.[28] In footwear during the same period, the continued adjustment to statement prices necessitated by the trade's seasonality and sensitivity to fashion militated against long-term harmony.[29] The net result of these sources of conflict in Leicester's two major industries was to produce an undercurrent of discontent amongst the workers that ran through the period under survey.

These widespread antagonisms ever present in work-based relationships, together with the spirit of artisan independence nurtured by the outwork system, negated the effects of paternalistic devices. Judging by Dare's comments, and, despite his obvious bias, he was a well-situated observer, the effects of the mission's activities were minimal. The main recipients of the rational recreation movement were usually the better-off artisans who already possessed a modicum of 'knowledge and taste'. These men were also unlikely to be over-impressed by the sanctimonious preaching of Dare and his ilk, preferring instead to avail themselves of those facilities that they found personally useful. Below this stratum we find the mass of semi- and unskilled labour, many of whom were new to Leicester. This sector of the population caused Dare the most anguish. Not only

52

were they usually found outside the factories in the small workshops well away from the potential sobering effect of the entrepreneur; they were also developing the artisan's spirit of independence, albeit in a less sober form.

If paternalism and the labour aristocracy are to be rejected as explanations of social stability in the period 1860–85, what were the factors that underpinned this era of harmony? The answer is rather simple and unsurprising. Leicester experienced in these decades an unprecedented economic expansion. Work, if always prone to seasonal fluctuations, was freely available, but more importantly the type of work undertaken represented no great break with past practices. The shoe workers and stockingers, never at the top of the wages table, enjoyed a lengthy period of relative prosperity. The pioneer factory operatives who worked the Cotton's frames still enjoyed craft status inside the factory. Furthermore, this economic expansion, being essentially an expansion of the outwork system, widened employment opportunities for the whole family. The sons of these workers may have endured the hardships of the shoe finishing workshops, their daughters and wives probably laboured over sewing machines, or stitched hosiery by hand at home, but the effect on the family economy must have been considerable. Seasonality only confirmed the continuation of traditional work patterns. Fluctuations were often predictable, and reinforced work rhythms that were the antithesis of factory discipline. If Leicester's stability was based as much upon an expansion of handicraft as of factory production, how does this accord with the national picture? One critic of Joyce has drawn attention to the narrow geographical area upon which he bases his generalization, an area distinguished by early large-scale factory production, highly untypical of the period.[30] Similar criticism has been levied against Foster's labour aristocracy thesis.[31] One writer has recently argued that the British industrial revolution was founded on a broad handicraft sector, a situation which continued late into the Victorian period.[32] This argument suggests that Leicester was probably closer to the norm than, say, Lancashire.

The workers in Leicester's two main industries in the period 1860 to 1885 continued to enjoy artisan life styles and work patterns. The process of proletarianization outlined by Marx entails both the removal of the instruments of production from the worker and the imposition of strict capitalist control over the work process.[33] Up until the mid-1880s in Leicester only the first part of the Marxist formulation had been completed. The inefficiency of the outwork mode of organization resulted in a low degree of capitalist control inside the workplace. Thus the forms of social control, albeit historically contentious ones, which have often been ascribed to the world of work during this period, had little effect in Leicester. Pollard's findings that 'the worker who left the background of his domestic workshop or peasant holding for the factory entered a new culture as well as a new sense of direction' and that 'continuous employment was one of the most hated aspects of factory life' were, generally speaking, still to be experienced by the majority of Leicester workers.[34] The pinnacle of artisan culture was the persistence and growth of free-thought activities organized around the local secular society. It is this particular area of working-class cultural life that will be examined in the next chapter.

4   Radical Free-thought in mid-Victorian Leicester

With the persistence of the workshop economy and the influx of large numbers of shoemakers, widely acknowledged as the most radical section of the English working class,[1] it is not surprising that Leicester was a major centre of secularism. Since the time of Tom Paine this particular strain of artisan culture had produced some of the most radical working-class leaders of the nineteenth century. The role of notable members of the free-thought and secularist movement such as Robert Owen, Richard Carlile, G. J. Holyoake, Charles Bradlaugh, Annie Besant, Edward Aveling and John Burns in working-class political movements is, of course, well known and has already been the subject of two major works by one historian.[2] In this chapter the survival and rising fortunes of secularism in Leicester will be surveyed in the period between the demise of organized Owenism and the arrival of socialism. Such a survey, while providing interesting material on the persistence of artisan political culture, is also necessary if we are to answer the questions posed later on about the intellectual traditions and beliefs of early socialists and to what extent they helped shape the nascent socialist movement in Leicester.

Working-class secularism in Leicester had deep roots. Radical artisans in the town corresponded with Paine in 1789[3] and during the first decades of the nineteenth century Leicester was an active centre of the Hampden Clubs movement.[4] Secularism, however, began its formal existence with the foundation in 1838 of Branch 26 of Robert Owen's socialist organization at the Commercial Rooms in the market place.[5] Attempts to chronicle in detail the workings and social composition of marginal provincial Victorian institutions is a notoriously difficult task for the historian. The Leicester Secular Society does possess archive material, but all that is extant is post-1880. The financing and building of the Secular Hall in 1881 was apparently the occasion which instituted an orderly process of bookkeeping.[6] Before the 1880s we have no detailed knowledge of membership. What follows is largely based on autobiographical material produced by members,[7] contemporary sources and recent secondary material.[8]

By 1846 Robert Owen's Branch 26, under the guidance of two of its leading members, Josiah Gimson and W. H. Holyoak, formed itself into a branch of the national society. Gimson (1818–83), an Owenite artisan engineer, who later became the owner of a large engineering concern, became the branch president, while Holyoak (1818–1907), a local tailor, played a leading role in the branch's affairs as well as performing the function of bookseller to the society.[9] Under the guidance of Gimson and Holyoak the Leicester rationalists became close adherents to the brand of secularism advocated by G. J. Holyoake, with a strong emphasis on respectability, a concern for philosophical and intellectual issues and a belief that secularism was more concerned with constructive measures, such as cooperation and social improvement, than with the 'infidel's' traditional activity of 'bible-bashing'.[10]

Before the formal foundation of the Leicester Secular Society in 1866 the Leicester Owenites appear to have experienced difficulties in establishing a permanent organization. The remnants of the National Secular Society (NSS), headed by Gimson and Holyoak, found a temporary home in the evening discussion groups of The Unitarian Domestic Mission Hall. At first glance this may appear an incongruous location for 'infidels' to gather but the Unitarians themselves were experiencing a major theological crisis. Owen Chadwick has identified this crisis as being essentially rooted in a growing division between those Unitarians whose main beliefs were evangelical biblicism and those who were heirs to the sect's tradition of rational deism.[11] The first group were in essence ordinary bible protestants distinguished only by their disbelief in the Trinity, while the second were 'the heirs of old deism, preaching rational religion, unpoetic common sense, anti-evangelical, suspicious of fervours and enthusiasms, calm in religious life, and in religious thought, believing that more good was done by books than sermons'.[12] In Leicester the first group appear to have formed the post-1832 political oligarchy, while the second, including Coltman, Bilson, Wright and Sladen, all wealthy manufacturers, but imbued with the intellectual traditions of a congregation that was once closely related to Joseph Priestly, became attracted to the secularist doctrine formulated by Holyoake and locally advocated by Gimson.[13]

The influx of lapsed Unitarians into Leicester's old artisan organization, while it may offer little direct evidence about working-class culture and consciousness, does testify to the existence of a group of mostly working-men whose intellectual activity was of such a high order that it attracted local middle-class radical intellectuals. Yet what evidence can we furnish on the social composition of Leicester secularism below the level of the society's middle-class patrons? As we have seen the society's records are silent on this subject. We are therefore obliged to rely on evidence of a more impressionistic nature which generally describes Leicester secularism as largely a working-class phenomenon. Gould in his history of the society noted the early involvement of working-class political leaders, especially the former Chartists J. Seal and J. Sketchley.[14] The early period of the society's formal existence consisted mainly of discussion classes on 'the Peoples Charter, frame rents, Popular Education and Secularism, for the benefit of a group of working men'.[15] During the 1860s, apart from Dare's regular warnings to his congregation on the growth of popular free-thought, our sources are silent. By 1873, however, the society had established itself in permanent rooms of a humble nature, in Humberstone Gate. Young Malcolm Quin, the future positivist socialist who spent part of his youth in Leicester, attended the society's weekly meetings in that year and found the membership to be 'largely proletarian with a few shopkeepers and manufacturers'.[16] Gould, in a similar vein, asserted that 'Our membership – a motley of some two hundred – included nobody with a University degree and nobody who possessed a carriage.'[17]

The membership of the society expanded during the 1870s to the extent that Gimson was able to embark confidently on plans for a new purpose-built hall. A Secular Hall Company was established in order to raise the capital. Two thousand square yards of land was purchased in Humberstone Gate and in 1878 the secularist architect from Leek, Larner Sugden, was instructed to design the building which was to include an auditorium capable of holding an audience of 600.[18] The finance was raised by the sale of £5 shares, the majority of which, over 80 per cent, was owned by the Gimson, Wright, Sladen and Coltman families, the rest being held by a medley of small traders, with a few shares bought by hosiery and footwear workers.[19]

The public face of Leicester secularism tended to portray the solid, rational respectability of the society's larger patrons. These were a group who eschewed the tub thumping style and political techniques of Bradlaugh in favour of Holyoake's quieter, more constructive form of free-thought. In many ways the society represented the embodiment of Holyoake's ideals. The spare land owned by the society was either rented for income, or parcelled out to members for use as allotments, organized on cooperative lines.[20] Both the finances and image of Leicester secularism received a further boost when T. H. Huxley sent a large undisclosed sum of money to Gimson towards the upkeep the hall and Holyoake also assisted by purchasing £500 worth of shares.[21] Gimson was thus able to organize the society's activities upon a solid financial foundation. By 1885 the society was employing Thomas Slater, the Bury cooperator, as full-time manager and librarian, and a swimming club, gymnasium, Sunday school, evening classes and a women's group became regular features along with the weekly debating sessions.[22]

Yet the society included other groups whose ideas and beliefs were somewhat different from those embraced by the now prosperous ex-Owenite Gimson and his lapsed Unitarian manufacturing colleagues. One important strand of Leicester Owenism had marched up the path towards Comteian religion alongside Holyoake in the 1850s and continued long after Holyoake halted.[23] The Leicester society therefore contained from its earliest days a group of avowed positivists. The leader of the Leicester Comteians was George Findley, an old Chartist, who kept a second-hand bookshop in the High Street.[24] Findley was a remarkable personality who corresponded with Congreve, Crompton and Carson, who were also occasional visitors to his home. His son, also George, shared his father's beliefs and together with Malcolm Quin began to inject an element of religiosity into the society's proceedings. This first took the form of giving a short reading before the commencement of the Sunday lecture, a practice which began in 1878 and was later followed by glee-singing with piano and harmonium accompaniment.[25] In 1882 the positivists introduced a secularist hymn-book, which openly referred to secularism as a new religion,[26] formed a choir and appointed a choirmaster. The positivists soon found their niche in the new hall when Findley and his followers took over the Sunday school.[27]

Despite the positivists' influence on the nature of Leicester secularism, a form of free-thought that caused one officer of the NSS to comment that the secularists in Leicester behave as 'if they had signed a peace treaty with the Christians',[28] tension always existed between the Findley group and the society's patrons. The latter, like Holyoake himself, admired the constructive nature of Comte's system but were deeply suspicious of the priestly rituals associated with the Church of Humanity. This suspicion was perhaps reinforced by the habit of Leicester positivists of attending high church services in order to partake in the study and benefits of ritualism.[29] The compromise between the Holyoakeians and the positivists, however, lasted for many years. It was not until the early years of the present century when the positivists became attracted to the ILP, whose political philosophy, in the words of Quin, promised the fulfilment of the Comteian ideal of 'a risen proletariat and a world at peace', that the tensions between them and the liberal Gimson group became unmanageable.[30]

The society was also subject to pressures from another quarter during the same period. Politically it represented in microscosm the various elements that formed radical liberalism. For example, in 1876 the shoemaker secularist Charles Eagle was jailed for ten days for disobeying the vaccination law, while the secularist manufacturer Michael Wright became one of the leaders of the local anti-vaccination movement.[31] During the 1880s there is much evidence that working-class membership of the society was increasing rapidly, a development that was at first welcomed but was ultimately to divide the political loyalties of Leicester secularism. The factors which produced the growth of working-class secularism during the 1870s and 1880s appear fairly obvious, yet they are frustratingly difficult to document. As we have seen, free-thought in Leicester always contained a large working-class element, but the expansion of working-class membership during the 1870s and 1880s was supplementary to those older strands of popular unbelief. The influx of 'godless shoemakers' may have played a part in the society's growth and a few boot lasters and riveters do appear on the Secular Hall Company's list of shareholders.

Disenchantment with the orthodox religions during a period of economic upheaval may have been another element, but apart from the few memoirs which have survived, there is not enough evidence to warrant theorizing about collective mentalities. Probably the most important factor in the Leicester secularist expansion was the same which produced the major growth in secularism nationally: the personality and charismatic leadership of Bradlaugh.[32] This may appear paradoxical for a provincial society that led the revolt against the NSS and played a formative role in the British Secular Union (BSU), but by 1884 the BSU was a spent force, having realized that there was not enough room for two national organizations.[33] Thus for the sake of unity the Leicester society had to tolerate the existence of a Bradlaughite faction amongst its membership. Bradlaugh himself was a frequent lecturer at the society and was one of the guest celebrities at the hall's opening ceremony.[34]

Prominent amongst the Leicester supporters of Bradlaugh were a group of hosiery factory workers led by Tom Barclay and George Robson from Corah's St Margaret plant. Barclay, the Leicester-born son of Irish parents who eked out a living as rag and bone collectors, was converted to secularism during the 1870s.[35] His conversion occurred during a period when he was deeply troubled by his declining faith in catholicism. This religious crisis coincided with his new employment at Corah's where he was befriended by Robson and other working-class secularists. His parents, poor yet devout, were appalled by their son's free-thought and young Tom was forced to seek lodgings with Bill Lee, a secularist colleague at Corah's. In his autobiography Barclay paints a vivid picture of the working-class auto-didact culture with which Corah's and secularism brought him into contact. He described Robson as 'that *rara aris in terra*, the working man scientist; he didn't speak grammatically, and rather depended on me for a little polish in that direction, but he was an enthusiastic naturalist and gave all his leisure time to the practical study of Geology, Botany and Entomology'. Barclay himself undertook an intensive course of self-education, studying geology, physiology, biology, hygienics and economics, as well as attending the Rev. D. J. Vaughan's Working Men's College. This was followed by a course in Political Philosophy organized by the Cambridge University Extension Scheme which triggered off a lifelong interest in the subject. Barclay became an avid reader of George Carruthers and Ruskin which, along with the secularist classics by Draper and Ingersoll, were to form the bulk of his intellectual capital. Bradlaugh, however, was his main hero in this formative period of his development. Although he gave him little attention in his autobiography, his editor has noted that Barclay was found by a friend 'crying like a child' in St Saviour's Road overcome with grief on the news of Bradlaugh's death.[36]

Increased working-class involvement in the working life of the Secular Hall brought distinct changes in the society's programme of events. In particular the weekly diet of rational recreation was injected with an element of worldly indulgence when the society succumbed to working-class demands and opened a bar serving alcohol to members and visitors in the early 1880s, an event described rather tersely by F. J. Gould as 'a measure to enhance their relationship with the non-teetotal working class'.[37] Other significant signs of greater working-class involvement in the society can also be detected. The new hall became the venue of the footwear workers' annual St Crispin's day celebrations[38] and in the turbulent period of the mid-1880s the hosiery workers' union used the building for large general meetings.[39]

The major effect of an increased working-class presence in the society was a distinct change in the subject matter of the weekly lectures and debates. As we have seen in Chapter 1, the 1880s were a period of crisis for hosiery factory workers, a crisis that coincided with an event that shook the foundations of secularism nationally. The debate between Charles Bradlaugh and H. M. Hyndman, which took place at St James's Hall in April 1884, opened up a period of intense discussion throughout the secularist movement. Dr Royle has pointed to the importance of the debate and its effect upon a crucial stratum of working-class secularists. Furthermore, 'the debate about radicalism and socialism, however, took place not between Secularist and Socialist societies but within secularism itself, before there were many socialist organizations in existence'.[40] Royle has assiduously chronicled the connections between local secularist groups and early socialist societies in the period immediately after the debate, and Leicester conforms closely to this pattern.

Sydney Gimson, in his memoirs, has commented on the intensity of the debate on socialism within Leicester secularism that was initiated by the Bradlaugh–Hyndman confrontation. 'Among our members and in our audiences the discussion of Individualism and Socialism went on furiously and, though I was on the other side, I must admit that socialism was rapidly gaining converts.'[41] There is also some evidence that an interest in socialism amongst Leicester secularism preceded the St James's Hall debate. On 16 January 1884 Hyndman had lectured at the hall on 'Constructive Socialism', followed a week later by William Morris on 'Art and Socialism'.[42] The debate, however, increased this early interest both by bringing socialism to the forefront of the secularist agenda and by attracting major figures on to the provincial lecturing circuit. The Leicester secularists certainly had a full exposition of the various competing socialist theories with the Fabian essayists, Belfort Bax, John Burns and even Prince Kropotkin among the many lecturers at Leicester during the period immediately after the debate.[43] The Leicester secularist converts to socialism, led by Barclay and Robson, opted for Morris's brand of the new ideology. On 1 November 1885 they constituted themselves into the Leicester branch of the Socialist League, holding their weekly meetings inside the Secular Hall.[44]

60

Any assessment of free-thought and organized secularism in Leicester between the era of Owenism and Chartism and the socialist period must acknowledge the tenacity of the English working-class radical tradition. To a certain extent the ideas, beliefs and practices of protest of the 1830s and 1840s went underground and survived in the mission rooms and haylofts that were the meeting places of the early secularist groups. Traditions, however, must be treated with caution: we must remember that working-class participation in free-thought activity before even the flimsy documentation that survives from the 1880s was undoubtedly confined to a tiny minority. Furthermore, if we put to one side the political activities of Bradlaugh which did win some working-class support, what remained of secularism's public face was a collection of beliefs that at best could elicit amusement and at worst ridicule. On the other hand we cannot ignore the positive contribution that secularism made to the early socialist movement. The most obvious connection is undoubtedly one of personnel. Aveling, Burns and Besant were national figures who point to the importance of the relationship between the two movements, a relationship which had a local equivalent in the activities of, to cite a few examples, Maguire in Leeds, Snell in Nottingham and, of course, the Barclay–Robson group in Leicester.

The question of the ideological relationship between the two movements is more complex. The Victorian secularist was, after all, the radical individualist *par excellence*, his individuality underlined by his denial of God. Economic circumstances and events were certainly the main causal factors behind the influx of secularists into the ranks of the socialist collectivists. A Leicester-born secularist, Percy Redfern, succinctly summarized his own perception of the relationship between the two movements, after his conversion to socialism in Nottingham during a coal strike. 'The militancy of my freethinking died. What remained was the positive secularist faith in mutual help. Man must aid man.'[45] It is not too difficult to pick out the influence of Holyoake in Redfern's musing. Significantly both he and Snell became major figures in the cooperative world as well as adopting socialism. If the Holyoake strain of secularism found expression in cooperation and 'constructive socialism' where do we find the erstwhile followers of Bradlaugh?

Bradlaugh was undoubtedly the living embodiment of the raucous iconoclastic working-class radicalism the roots of which stretch back to the world of Carlile and Paine.[46] Like their mentor, Bradlaugh's supporters were distinguished by their audacity and willingness to adopt controversial positions. Barclay and Robson personified this tradition and were to bring much of its spirit to early Leicester socialism. Their demand for socialist speakers at the Secular Hall was itself an audacious gesture given the clear radical liberalism of the society's patrons. Moreover, their use of street-corner propaganda meetings links back to the days of the Chartists as well as copying the techniques used by Bradlaugh and his followers, most notably in London's Victoria Park, techniques that were usually frowned upon by the more prim and respectable advocates of Holyoake.[47]

The connections between secularism and socialism will be developed more fully in the chapter on early socialism in Leicester. At this stage, however, it is important to note that radical artisan culture was still lively, and probably as strong as it ever had been in the early 1880s. Although middle-class members largely controlled the purse-strings of the Leicester Secular Society, their rule had never been total.[48] Indeed, even their Holyoakeian orthodoxy provided a platform for discussion of what were to be such formative ideas as cooperative production. Furthermore, middle-class money had provided a home for the dissemination and discussion of radical ideas amongst working-class members. As long as the society existed orthodox political economy could never assume an uncriticized hegemony. Indeed secularism flourished because it was iconoclastic. While much of the movement's audacity was often levelled against orthodox religion, a disposition to challenge and criticize established ideas was nurtured amongst the membership. It is therefore not surprising that when that most established of beliefs, classical political economy, was eventually attacked by the new doctrine of socialism it was the audacious secularist working man who was at the forefront of the challenge.

Yet as has already been noted, secularism, while important, appealed to only a tiny minority of Leicester's working class. Leicester's most notable social manifestation during the mid-Victorian period was not freethought but rather radical nonconformity. It is to that subject and its relationship with the working class that we now turn.

5 Religion and the Working Class in Late Nineteenth-Century Leicester

Religion is a subject that demands great attention in any local survey of the transition from working-class Liberal to socialist politics. Nonconformity in particular has been singled out by many historians as formative in the development of working-class consciousness during the late nineteenth century. Working-class nonconformity has been cited as a major factor in working-class support for the nineteenth-century Liberal Party,[1] while in provincial England Hobsbawm detects an 'intellectual descent' from the dissenting chapel to the ILP.[2] Pelling, in contrast, has cautioned against oversimplification, directing attention to the increasingly middle-class character of nonconformity during the period.[3] Existing local studies have reinforced the pattern of complexity. Clark's work on Colne Valley demonstrated a strong bond between chapel and early Labour Party life, while Thompson's study of nearby Bradford claimed that the local ILP was founded by a mixed group of secularists, catholics, followers of Edward Carpenter and a 'happy pagan', together with a few nonconformists.[4] Clearly religion and the popular beliefs of any given community reflect variables in local traditions, class structure and power relationships, and can only be understood by observing the interaction of these factors.

This chapter will explore what changes, if any, took place in the nature of working-class religiosity and denominational allegiances during the second half of the nineteenth century. The findings of this examination will then allow an assessment of the relative importance of religion to working-class cultural and political activities. It will also help to evaluate the extent of nonconformist hegemony and patterns of worship that expressed both independence of, and resistance to, the dominant orthodox denominations.

Leicester's nonconformist character and its claim to the title 'the capital of dissent' was widely acknowledged by the mid-nineteenth century, but how true was this generalization during the 50 years after 1850? Did the unifying role played by nonconformity during the church vestry disputes of the 1840s, which led to the formation of the Liberation Society by a local dissenting minister, E.T. Miall,[5] continue during the subsequent decades? What changes occurred in the pattern of working-class religion during the period of massive population and industrial expansion?

Table 5. Religious attendances in Leicester, 1851.

Denomination	Churches	Morning		Afternoon		Evening		Best Attended service
		Churches open	Attendance	Churches open	Attendance	Churches open	attendance	
Church of England	9	7	3,344	6	1,058	7	3,763	5,119
Wesleyan Methodists	2	1	600	1	31	1	800	831
Primitive Methodists	3	1	250	2	100	3	880	880
Other Methodists	3	2	570	2	230	3	1,140	1,140
General Baptists	5	5	1,419	—	—	5	2,197	2,197
Particular Baptists	2	2	1,156	—	—	2	1,326	1,326
Congregationalists	2	2	970	—	—	2	977	977
Calvinists	3	3	930	1	200	2	550	1,050
Roman Catholics	1	1	546	1	56	1	497	546
Others	5	4	953	2	161	4	1,076	1,324
Total	35	28	10,738	15	1,836	30	13,206	15,390

Source: D. M. Thompson, 'The churches and society in Leicestershire 1851–1881' (Ph.D. thesis, University of Cambridge, 1969), Table 15, p. 66. This table was compiled by Thompson from the census schedules and omits the 'Sunday School Scholar' category included in the published returns. Thompson's table also tidies up the idiosyncrasies of denominational titles published in the returns. For Thompson's methodology utilized in the compilation of this table see his 'The 1851 religious census: problems and possibilities', Victorian Studies, 11, 1 (1967).

Perhaps the best starting-point in answering these questions is to look at the two statistical tables that are available on church attendance in Leicester.

Table 6.   Church attendance in Leicester, 1882.

Denomination	Buildings	Accommodation	Morning	Attendance Afternoon	Evening
Church of England	24	16,408	5,904	2,180	9,783
Baptists	20	12,475	5,087	1,001	7,346
Congregationalists	8	5,132	1,765	—	2,607
Wesleyan Methodists	6	4,015	1,359	—	1,898
Primitive and other Methodists	9	4,450	1,381	147	2,587
Presbyterians	1	700	89	—	107
Roman Catholics	2	900	547	—	863
Salvation Army	1	1,500	337	870	1,420
Others	14	4,220	1,069	1,497	3,339
Total	85	49,800	17,538	5,695	29,950

Source: A. Mearns, *Statistics of Attendance at Public Worship, 1882* (citing the *Leicester Daily Post*)

Table 5 is taken from the 1851 Census on Religion and Table 6 was compiled by a local newspaper which carried out its own survey in 1882. The 1851 survey has of course received much scholarly attention and criticism, and most agree that despite its obvious imperfections the census does provide a useful yardstick on the subject.[6] The same must also hold true for the 1882 exercise which was undertaken using methods similar to those applied in 1851. The most striking feature of Table 5 is that the total number of sittings could accommodate only 41 per cent of the population, a proportion smaller than most comparable towns.[7] Furthermore, the established church appeared to be filling more of its available seats than the main dissenting chapels. A comparison with the 1882 table reinforces this finding. Accommodation did increase over the 20-year period broadly in line with a population rise of 120 per cent, but in terms of numbers by 1882, 72,576 people in Leicester did not have a church seat, in comparison with 35,576 in 1851. The trend in actual attendance is also revealing: in 1851, 48,387 people did not, or could not, visit the largest attended service in the evening, a figure which rose to 92,426 in 1882.

The failure to fill even existing seats was a serious concern for local religious workers. In 1846 Dare noted the religious sentiments of some of the recipients of the Unitarian Domestic Mission's charity: 'We do not go ourselves to a place of worship because our clothes are not fit; the rich tuck up their fine things and sit away from us, as if we were filled with vermin.'[8] This sense of class divisions within congregations was probably amplified by the high number of appropriated sittings, especially in the dissenting chapels.[9] Dare also pointed out that many of the poor whom he attended were never visited by a minister of religion, while others claimed that they needed Sunday for rest, many staying in bed all day 'while their body-linen is being washed, and to rest their limbs, as the work is too much for the food they got'.[10]

Perhaps the major factor, however, in the low rate of working-class attendance was the ever-growing proportion of immigrants attracted to Leicester's expanding industries. Religious habits established in the source areas could be quickly discarded by the immigrant, a phenomenon that Dare well understood and frequently commented upon. The following statement by an immigrant worker quoted by Dare in 1857 was probably typical of many in a similar situation: 'Now change of place has brought change of habit, and although my predilections in favour of religion are as strong as ever, yet the habit of non-attendance seems confirmed.'[11]

Recognition of the problems facing local religious bodies in the area of working-class attendance gave rise to a spate of church and chapel building. Table 6 shows a rise in the number of places of worship between 1851 and 1882 from 35 to 85. The established church was clearly leading with an increase of 15 churches, while the main dissenting groups grew by 23 chapels. Nonconformity, however, found much difficulty in keeping together the new congregations. For example, seven Primitive Methodist chapels were closed between 1873 and 1900, some after only six years.[12] Furthermore, other dissenting sects had similar experiences and more than one chapel proudly built during the 1860s ended its life as an early cinema.[13]

Perhaps a major factor that militated against the success of dissent's attempted expansion was the often close association between middle-class manufacturing patrons and individual chapels.[14] The Hilton shoe manufacturing family dominated the Leicester Primitive Methodist congregations during the second half of the nineteenth century and many members of the family served as local class leaders.[15] Similarly the Harrises were the mainstays of the Harvey Street Chapel and the Evanses of the fashionable 'Pork Pie Chapel' in Belvoir Street,[16] while the family of Thomas Walker and Sons were the main benefactors of the Melbourne Road Baptist Church and Sunday School.[17]

Nevertheless, it would be a distortion to claim that orthodox nonconformity was becoming totally class-based. Some working-class Congregational and Baptist chapels with deep communal roots continued to prosper. The building of the Free Christian Church at the corner of Harrow Road continued the working-class, orthodox nonconformist tradition, albeit independent of the mainstream denominations.[18] The process by which working-class support for nonconformity declined was, it must be remembered, gradual. Working-class allegiance to the political aims of dissent remained considerable, a point reinforced by working-class support for nonconformist Liberals in the school board election struggles of the 1870s.[19]

The failure of dissent to meet the challenge of the 1851 census report is underlined by comparing the attendance figures for nonconformity in 1882 with the number of seats available listed in Table 6. The Primitive Methodists could not fill one-third of their available places. The Congregationalist chapels managed to half fill their benches during the evening service, while the Baptists did slightly better than the congregationalists. The Wesleyan Methodists equalled the dismal performance of the Primitives, while the Unitarians, never ones for proselytizing and not included under a separate heading in Table 6, ended their expansion programme by closing down their newly opened second chapel in Wellington Street.[20]

The established church, generally, out-performed dissent, in the field of expansion. They built proportionally more places of worship, which became established features of the Leicester skyline, and enjoyed more success than dissent in filling seats. The average best-attended Anglican congregation in 1882 was 408 in comparison to the Baptists' 367 and the Primitive Methodists' 287. Further evidence suggests that some Anglican churches, particularly the new ones built in predominantly new working-class areas, were achieving remarkably large congregations. Several of these churches, most notably St Mark's, St Andrew's and St Paul's, had Tractarian ministers who proved highly successful in attracting large working-class congregations. The first ritualist minister in Leicester, however, was Anderdon, the vicar of the ancient parish church St Margaret's. Anderdon, a follower of Newman, was appointed to St Margaret's in 1846, and later left Anglicanism with his mentor to become a Jesuit after building up a large, successful congregation.[21] The new churches of the 1870s were staffed by Tractarian incumbents appointed by Bishop Magee of Peterborough. James Mason of St Paul's, distinguished by his flowing robes and luxuriant beard, attracted a working-class congregation which in size soon rivalled St Margaret's.[22] We know less of the early Tractarian vicars of the other new churches, but by 1903 St Mark's under the direction of F. L. Donaldson was reported as having one of the most impressive working-class congregations in Britain.[23] The successor to Magee at Peterborough was Mandell Creighton, Beatrice Webb's close friend, who, if he did not openly advocate Tractarian practices, continued to support incumbent ritualists.[24] His daughter described one of her father's visits to a ritualist church in Leicester in 1891. '[They drove to] a great ritualistic church where father was to preach. I got there about a quarter of an hour before service, but it was crammed and I got about the last seat. There were chairs all up the aisles and people stood all through the service and some hundreds were turned away.'[25]

Did ritualism attract the working class?[26] At the level of appearances and imagery we may agree with the old adage that what unites the English aristocrat and working man is a love of pomp and pageantry, especially as the ritualists so skilfully introduced the qualities of colour, music and ceremony into the often bleak working-class urban environment of the late nineteenth century. The ideology of the ritualists, which gave prominence to the concept of immanence, offered the vision of a return to a fantastic golden age where all men were both equal in the eyes of God and united in a classless society, rather like the medieval organic parish or the early community of the Christian church. In reality the leading ritualists, especially those close to Maurice and the Christian Socialism of Headlam, were advocates of class collaboration via the medium of cooperation and self-governing workshops.[27] But, nevertheless, the arrival of the ritualists in Leicester brought tangible benefits to the working class. Not only was life slightly more colourful, but the emphasis placed by the new vicars on parish work with its plethora of clubs and parish organizations and the ritualists' willingness to enter even the poorest homes went some way towards relieving urban alienation.[28]

In contrast, evangelical Anglicanism appears to have been more middle class in complexion in late nineteenth-century Leicester. One writer on the subject has detected a drift by some wealthy manufacturing families away from the dissenting chapels, especially the Great Meeting, into fashionable Anglican evangelical congregations.[29] This was particularly the case amongst the second and third generations of such formerly illustrious nonconformist families as the Corahs, Pagets, Gees, Faires, Russells and Viccars. The attraction of evangelical Anglicanism to certain nonconformist manufacturing families fits the pattern of socialization experienced nationally. Prominent Leicester manufacturers began to favour public schools and Oxbridge for their sons, while the 'republican austerity' which prevented Joseph Whetstone, the hosier and wool spinner of the Great Meeting, from accepting a title at the time of Queen Victoria's coronation seems to have disappeared from among Leicester manufacturers by the latter part of the nineteenth century.[30]

Despite the nonconformist manufacturer's ingrained suspicion of the established church, many found little difficulty in changing their allegiance. After all, Leicester Anglicanism had traditionally been evangelical, sharing the nonconformist's hatred of Rome. Thus the prosperous entrepreneur, with his desire for status and perhaps a small country estate, could find common ground, perceiving moderate nonconformity and evangelical Anglicanism as being the mainstream of English protestantism. It would be a mistake, however, to depict Leicester evangelical Anglicanism as an exclusively middle-class congregation. While there were undoubtedly fashionable middle-class congregations such as that at St James's facing Victoria Park, some evangelical ministers did extend their ministry to the working class.

The vicar of St Martin's, the Reverend, later Canon, Vaughan, was undoubtedly the most active evangelical in attending to the needs of the working class. Vaughan distinguished himself in the field of adult working-class education with the opening of the Vaughan Working Men's

College in 1862.[31] The aims and objectives of the college were given a clear exposition in 1869 when Vaughan changed the name of the school from 'working men's institute' to 'working men's college', saying that it was 'important to mark in this way the characteristic features of the institute, an institute for self-improvement, for mutual improvement, and for cooperation in a humble yet earnest, endeavour to improve and elevate the working classes of the town intellectually and morally'. Fired by such evangelical inspiration, Vaughan was able to fill a gap in the town's education system, particularly amongst those who suffered from the inadequacies of the pre-1870 period. By 1869 the college was enrolling over 500 students, a figure which rose to 1,200 in 1880.[32] Vaughan was held in high esteem by many of his former pupils which included men prominent in the Labour movement, such as Merrick, Chaplin, Barclay and Robson, but there is no evidence that large numbers of his students themselves became active evangelicals.

Perhaps the most interesting feature of Tables 5 and 6 is the growth and relative strength of those congregations gathered under the heading of 'Others'. This group in 1851 included both the Quakers, who could attract 78 members to their morning service, and the Unitarians, whose morning congregation totalled 350.[33] There were also 400 members of a church or chapel of whom we have no information, the census listing this group as an 'isolated congregation'. The final group in this census category is the Mormons, who could boast 296 members attending their evening service inside a hall with 250 seats.[34] If we now examine Table 7, printed in the *Nonconformist* in November 1872, we can detect a rapid growth in the places of worship of the fringe sects.

If we exclude the traditional, small, congregations from this table's

Table 7. Places of worship and accommodation, 1872.

Denomination	Places of worship 1872	Sittings 1872	Changes since 1851	
			Places of worship	Sittings
Church of England	15	13,178	+7	+4,350
Baptists	12	8,793	+2	+2,150
Congregationalists	4	4,400	+2	+2,650
Wesleyan Methodists	2	2,070	+1 −1	+ 498
Primitive Methodists	5	2,221	+2	+1,100
Other Methodists	2	1,550	+1 −2	− 510
Presbyterians	1	650	+1	+ 650
Roman Catholics	2	555	—	—
Others[35]	10	4,670	+5	+2,191
Total	53	38,087	+21 −3	13,079

Source: Nonconformist, 6 November 1872: Supplement

category of 'Others', we are left with a host of new groups, including the Union Church, the Gospel Hall, Brethren, Christians,[36] Hallelujah Band and the Catholic Apostolic Church. It is interesting to note that the *Nonconformist* appears to have overlooked, perhaps deliberately, the Mormons. Given the strength of this church in 1851 it seems unlikely that even in a period of emigration it should have totally disappeared.[37] By 1882, as Table 6 shows, the 'Others' had expanded to 14. If we discount the Quakers, Unitarians and Calvinists we are left with possibly 11 places of worship which most probably belonged to the new marginal sects. Interestingly the Hallelujah Band by 1882 was now the Salvation Army whose hall during the evening service was virtually filled to capacity. Taken collectively these new congregations, together with the Salvation Army, represented the third largest denominational category in 1882, overtaking both the Methodists and Congregationalists.[38]

Is it possible to detect a trend or pattern in the changing religious complexion of Leicester in the period under study? By 1882 the three main nonconformist churches, Baptists, Congregationalists and Methodists, still represented, collectively, the largest portion of church attendance with 11,851 worshippers. This figure, however, represents 39.5 per cent of total evening worshippers in comparison to the 1851 percentage of over 63 per cent for mainstream dissent. This decline must pose a major question-mark against the use of the appellation 'Nonconformist' Leicester during the last two decades of the nineteenth century. Can we discern any other trend or tendency to this pattern of declining traditional nonconformity?

The most interesting aspect, perhaps, of the rapidly changing religious contours of the late nineteenth-century Leicester is the decline of working-class allegiance to middle-class-dominated evangelicism with its emphasis on remorse, despair and the fear of Hell and its replacement by ritualistic Anglicanism and the rise of new sects, all of which gave liturgical centrality to the sacraments. We have already looked at ritualistic Anglicanism in Leicester; can a similar pattern of support and beliefs be found in the newer sects?

The first factor that we must note when surveying the new religious groups of late nineteenth-century Leicester is that they appear to have played a similar role to that performed by Primitive Methodism in areas of rapid industrial and social change earlier in the century. Their appeal was directed to, and support came from, sections of the working class who were unreached by or shied away from bourgeois nonconformity. Leicester was, after all, experiencing a population growth of 42 per cent in the period 1871–81. In what must have been a period of generalized social 'anomie' many took solace and comfort from sects that offered both salvation and a sense of communal bond via common participation in the breaking of bread. Horton Davies, in his survey of English theology, has categorized these new sects as 'New Forms of Primitivism', representing, often in advance of orthodox christology, a shift in emphasis, in both liturgical form and beliefs, towards the ideas and practices of the early church,[39] a trend which was eventually to permeate most Christian denominations, as can be witnessed by the triumph of the Gothic style of religious architecture during the second half of the nineteenth century. Davies has drawn attention to six common characteristics shared by the new sects: a strong biblicism; the revival of charismatic practices such as 'prophesying' and 'speaking with tongues'; sensational methods of attracting attention such as bands, banners, uniforms and processions; the rebirth of the impetus to revivalism connected with the conviction of the impending second coming of Christ; a marked fervour for the reunification of Christendom; and an appreciation of both the sacramental and ceremonial.[40]

The Church of Christ was founded in the United States of America by Alexander Campbell, a former Baptist with a strong belief in the imminence of the second coming.[41] The English branch of the Church of Christ was started in 1843, although its numbers were to remain relatively small. Leicester appears to have been a provincial stronghold of the sect. The first church was started by two shoemakers, James and Thomas Levesley, in their own home in 1859. The congregation, mainly composed of shoe workers, expanded steadily so that by 1879 the sect had two chapels in Leicester.[42] By the 1890s members of the sect were active in establishing a footwear producers' cooperative, were planning their own garden city, and two prominent members of the Church of Christ became important activists in the Labour movement.[43]

Less is known of the other new sects in late nineteenth-century Leicester. The Salvation Army was probably the largest new group, warranting its own separate heading in Table 6. Yet, as Davies has shown, the early Hallelujah Bands placed the celebration of the sacraments as central liturgical features.[44] It was not until the 1880s that Booth was able to place the Army on a more evangelical keel by rejecting sacramentalism. Interestingly, during the period when Booth was imposing doctrinal uniformity amongst the provincial Hallelujah Bands, one of the Leicester bands declared itself independent, an incident which required the despatch of William Corbridge, one of Booth's close colleagues, to rectify.[45]

Of the remaining new sects even less is known of their Leicester congregations.[46] They rarely received mention in the local press and no archival material survives. On the other hand there existed other fringe groups in the town who received no acknowledgment in the religious surveys yet constituted another fascinating dimension of working-class religiosity in late nineteenth-century Leicester. By 1859 these small sects were beginning to establish themselves in Leicester, a phenomenon which evoked scornful comment from Dare:

> As regards the religion of the working classes though perhaps there are but few who are wholly destitute of religious feeling, as manifested in seasons of

sickness, death, or other calamity, yet vast numbers attend no place of worship. The existing forms of belief and methods of religious teaching do not interest them. Others who have any active religious sentiment are fond of running after strange doctrines. One while it is 'Mormonism' then 'Spiritualism' or some other 'ism' succeeds; and now a favourite doctrine in the Midlands is 'Brownism'; recently started in Nottingham by an old pensioner named Brown, who is both lame and blind. The practice of this fourth consists of groups sitting in circles and gazing into an egg shaped crystal for divine revelations from the Angel Gabriel. Their doctrines are a sad jumble of vaticinations of Zadkiel and Dr. Cummings, mixed up with Owenism, socialism, Swedenborgism, and divination of the crystal. There are already one hundred Brownites in the town, who are very active in disseminating this wretched blasphemy. Now all this is very lamentable and no doubt originates in the neglect of early education and religious training. Through this neglect one portion of the working classes are filling the beer shops, and another propagating all manner of crude theories in religion and politics.[47]

Logie Barrow has recently drawn attention to another form of popular religion, spiritualism, as a parallel continuity, with secularism, of Owenite ideas.[48] Dare spoke of spiritualism in the passage quoted above; perhaps the Brownites constituted a Midland variant of what was, during this period, an extremely diffuse movement.[49] Spiritualism may also have gathered older, peasant forms of popular belief into the movement. Many of Leicester's poorer inhabitants continued to place great trust in the healing powers of Amelia Woodcock, the Wise Woman of Wing in Rutland.[50] The first mention of spiritualism in Leicester came in July 1875 when the Leicester circle published their first quarterly report. In this brief résumé of their activities Mr Bent, the chairman, pointed out that spiritualism had recently been organized on a permanent basis, although the practice had enjoyed a long existence in Leicester.[51] We have no evidence of the size of the Leicester group, but it was obviously large enough to support a permanent hall in Silver Street.[52] Furthermore, the reports of Leicester spiritualism, in the *Spiritualist*, occasionally mentioned names of leading circle members, most of whose occupations are supplied in local directories. The list of Leicester spiritualists given in Table 8 is not of course comprehensive, and as most of these held some form of organizational office, bias is inevitable.

It does, however, confirm Barrow's argument that both spiritualism and secularism constituted important types of what he has called 'plebeian culture', that is, forms of popular culture that embraced both skilled working men and members of the lower middle class. The main thrust of Barrow's thesis is that while plebeian culture supplied many individuals who were to play important roles in the Labour and socialist movements of the 1890s, their intellectual freight produced a 'subtle and changing mix of individualism and collectivism' in plebeian and working-class politics during the nineteenth and early twentieth centuries.[53] The obvious place to address this argument is in Chapter 7, but it is worth noting at this

Table 8. Occupations of known spiritualists in Leicester in the late nineteenth century.

Name	Occupation
Jabez Chaplin	Full-time Hosiery Union officer
Mr and Mrs Bent	Booksellers and laster
Mr Burdett	Shopkeeper
Mr Grimes	Framework knitter
M. Harkins	Apartment housekeeper
J. Holmes	Newsagent and Hosiery Union secretary
Mrs Mansell	General dealer
Mr Larrard	Factory foreman
Mr Wightman	Butcher

Source: White's and Wright's Leicester Directories, 1875–90

stage those members of the Silver Street circle who became activists in the early socialist movement. Bent became prominent in the Leicester Social Democratic Federation (SDF), later switching his allegiance to the anarchist communists.[54] Chaplin and Holmes were the two full-time officers of the LAHU and founding members of the ILP.[55]

It could be argued that spiritualism should be excluded from a local nineteenth-century religious survey as the organization never embraced Christian or for that matter any mainstream religious beliefs. Spiritualists often travelled back and forth between local circles and secularist societies, and shared the latter's penchant for making derogatory statements about organized religion.[56] Yet while all spiritualists were not socialists they were united by a transcendental faith in the existence of the 'other world'. For the Owenite socialist spiritualist this involved accepting much of the panoply of mediums, pseudo-scientific gadgets, table levitations, and so on, while clinging to the central belief that Owen's socialist commonwealth had been temporarily transmuted into the 'other world', or, as they preferred to call it, 'Summerland'.[57] Thus the socialist spiritualist shared much with the millenarian Christian sects of the period, especially with those congregations, such as the Church of Christ, who placed great importance on community building.

Summing up, several features were prominent in the changing contours of the town's religiosity. Participation in religious worship was in decline, despite efforts by all the major denominations to reverse the trend. This was especially the case amongst the orthodox nonconformist denominations whose congregations were becoming increasingly middle-class dominated. The only area of growth, apart from the catholics, was amongst the smaller dissenting sects, many of which shared charismatic, millenarian and sacramental characteristics. Furthermore, these new sects often gave a central position to a liturgy which emphasized 'brotherhood' and 'community', in place of a dependence on the sermon and the pulpit.

This failure of nonconformity to retain the loyalty of the working class can partly be attributed to the tenacity of Leicester's independent artisan culture which undoubtedly made an important contribution to some of the newer sects, together with the major influx of immigrant workers, many of whom quickly lost their former religious habits. Nonconformity also appears to have failed the challenge presented by the massive growth of the urban working-class population, particularly in the field of proselytizing and ministering to the very poor. The few members of the poor who attained any form of religious experience probably received it by joining the street processions and community activities of high church Anglicans, or by partaking in the ritual ceremony of the Hallelujah Band's parades, or by attending the phantasmagoric meetings of such fringe millenarian sects as the Brownites.

How does this pattern accord with the national picture? Historians are generally in agreement that the second half of the nineteenth century witnessed a decline in religious worship and attendance, together with an increasing tendency towards 'secularization'.[58] At the level of class relationships and denominational adherence the situation was, however, far more complex, being highly dependent on pre-existing forms of worship, local social structure and economic relationships. Joyce, for example, has found that during an era of economic prosperity, religion, for the factory population of certain Lancashire towns, could be an 'expression of allegiances formed at the level of the factory and its environment'.[59] Similarly Moore, in his study of Durham miners, has described the importance of chapel building in the paternalistic policies of the coal owners in the Deerness Valley,[60] while Obelkevich has noted that the 'closed parishes [of South Lindsey] particularly those with resident squires were ... the favoured terrain of the Established Church'.[61] The common features of these three examples is the centrality of workplace relationships to the immediate environment and social milieu of the workforce. No Leicester manufacturer operating in industries which were virtually reliant on 'outwork', and suffering a constant round of seasonal fluctuations, would possibly hope to exercise the same power as a Lancashire mill owner or country squire over his workforce. Thus the 'independent' Leicester worker, typically employed in either hosiery or footwear, could opt out of formal religious activity or experiment with new creeds without fear of recrimination.

Not only did the expanding working class shun religion. Nonconfirmity appears to have increasingly distanced itself from those working-class social and political upheavals that distinguished the last two decades of the nineteenth century. Whenever there was a strike to be settled, a dispute arbitrated, the unemployed ministered to, it was invariably an Anglican incumbent who was first on the scene.[62] This situation, when compared to the part played in working-class life by such notable chapel ministers as Hall, Mursall and Miall in the first half of the century, highlights the shifting lines between class and orthodox nonconformity that occurred during the period. Indeed it was not until the first decade of the present century, when the Leicester Congregationalists appointed an exponent of R. J. Campbell's 'New Theology' as one of their ministers, that mainstream nonconformity, or at least a section of it, attempted to reverse the trend of declining working-class support.[63]

The increasingly middle-class nature of orthodox dissent was not peculiar to Leicester. The rise of the fashionable middle-class chapel was a phenomenon in many large towns, 'the chapel had become the church in name and design',[64] while the previous 'separateness' of the Wesleyans from both church and dissent was replaced by an identification with orthodox nonconformity in order to facilitate broad-based evangelical action.[65] Even in the Pennine heartland of working-class nonconformity, by the turn of the century the mill owners were the main patrons of the chapels, whose working-class congregations were beginning to question their own allegiance.[66]

The social geography of the new sects that emerged in the second half of the nineteenth century has yet to find its historian, and those comparisons which can be made must be extremely tentative. Birmingham, the place of publication of the *Millenarian Harbinger*, together with Nottingham and Leicester, were centres of the Church of Christ, all three towns sharing the characteristics of high rates of immigration and tenacious artisan economies.[67] The spatial distribution of spiritualism on the other hand has received some attention. Barrow has concluded that 'plebeian spiritualism remained predominantly northern and Pennine until the 1900s', a geographical pattern that 'does not contradict that of secularism'.[68] Interestingly, Barrow also points out the close relationship between the 'map of spiritualism' and the early map of the ILP, a connection that the evidence presented above shows to be, in Leicester at least, more than coincidental.

By the final decades of the nineteenth century the Leicester working class manifested less religious enthusiasm than they had during the mid-century and that certainly fits the national trend.[69] Furthermore, working-class nonconformity had entered a process of decline. What growth there was in popular religious activity was more likely to be found in the new Anglo-Catholic churches or in the fringe sects. This process was ultimately to contain a serious threat to the old equation of broad-based, popular nonconformity equalling radical liberalism.

6 Leicester Politics and the Working Class, 1860–85

The two-and-a-half decades reviewed in this chapter were the golden years of Leicester liberalism. The party reigned supreme in both local and parliamentary elections and previous tensions between Whigs and radicals had been overcome with the formation of an apparently enduring compromise. Two questions demand our attention. First, what were the attractions of liberalism to the working class and why did they support the party? Second, how extensive were new forms of working-class political activity and did these activities exceed the boundaries of the Liberal–radical alliance?

1862 presents a convenient starting-point for this preliminary survey of Leicester politics. The unopposed return of P. A. Taylor, a Radical Liberal, as MP for Leicester in the by-election of that year, marked both the reconciliation of the previous warring factions of the party and the beginning of stability within local liberalism. Leicester Liberals had been divided over the question of electoral reform and secular education since the passing of the Corn Laws. The Whig section of local liberalism had viewed major changes in the franchise with caution and had frequently sided with the Conservatives during the 1850s to check the growing momentum of radicalism.[1] The radicals on the other hand, led by John Biggs, the hosier and MP for the town since 1855, refused to compromise on the franchise issue.[2] Biggs and his faction pressed for the return of two Radical Liberal members to Parliament, a tactic designed to silence the Whigs and smash the old political equilibrium of Leicester liberalism whereby the town's two seats had been shared by radical and Whig since the first Reform Act. The division within liberalism, however, created by this strategy allowed the Conservative candidate, Heygate, to gain the first parliamentary victory for his party in over 30 years when he was elected to Parliament in 1861.

Heygate's victory undoubtedly served to bring the opposing Liberal factions back together. The Whigs were greatly disturbed by the victory of their traditional adversary, while the radicals were able to capitalize on Biggs's retirement from politics in early 1862, following the collapse of his firm, by seeking a new compromise with their erstwhile political allies. Biggs, like his Whig adversaries, was a major manufacturer and a leading figure at the Great Meeting, yet a constant feature of his political life had been the propagation of extreme forms of radicalism, particularly over the franchise issue, designed to cement working-class support for liberalism. The founder of the Leicester and Leicestershire Political Union in 1830, Biggs transformed this organization into the Reform Society which by the early 1850s was advocating radical forms of electoral change.

Biggs was partly motivated in the early 1850s by his belief in the necessity to canalize working-class dissent, recently expressed in the Chartist turmoils, into the Liberal Party. The radical candidates who stood for election in 1852 as nominees of the Reform Society went to the electorate with a programme which advocated votes by ballot, the re-distribution of seats, triennial parliaments, the removal of taxes on raw material, the substitution of direct for indirect taxation, religious equality, a national system of secular education, and electoral rights made co-extensive with the payments of taxes and settled residence. Evans has noted that apart from the substitution of a householder and lodger franchise for universal suffrage this programme had much in common with the six points of the Charter. Biggs himself was returned to Westminster in 1855 on the same programme, while his abandonment of frame rent, a unique gesture by a major hosier, must have further endeared him to the working class.[3] Biggs's populism certainly paid dividends; Buckby, the former Chartist leader, constantly advised his followers to vote radical.

Paradoxically, the man who replaced Biggs as MP in 1862 shared most of Biggs's views yet was fully backed by the Whigs. P.A. Taylor repre-sented Leicester from 1862 until his retirement in 1884. His background was not dissimilar to Biggs's. A Unitarian by faith and a member of the Courtauld textile family, Taylor also shared much of Biggs's taste for radical politics.[4] He was the chairman of the Society of Friends of Italy, a friend of Mazzini, a leading figure in the South Place Chapel, and the proprietor of the *Examiner*. As well as being a keen advocate of electoral and religious reform, Taylor was widely acknowledged as the most extreme republican in the House of Commons throughout his parliamentary career.[5] Despite many similarities, Taylor was a very differ-ent politician from Biggs. This was especially the case with Taylor's many international contacts and his deep interest in foreign affairs, a subject which was frequently to dominate British politics of the period. Thus Biggs, an archetypal provincial radical, was replaced by a leading exponent of international republicanism.

The re-establishment of the coalition of liberalism in Leicester was confirmed in 1865 with the defeat of Heygate by John Harris, who stood as a moderate Liberal candidate. Harris, another local hosier, had realized since the early 1860s that electoral reform was to be the key issue of the decade and subsequently adopted a more flexible attitude to the franchise question.[6] The rising popularity of Gladstone, the man who 'by the velocity of his evolution towards many sideness, temporarily squared the political circle', was also of importance locally and helped to heal old wounds.[7] Perhaps of most importance in explaining the moderates' desire to forget old scores and develop a different position on the franchise issue was the changing structure of the local electorate. Heygate's defeat, despite Liberal unity, was uncomfortably narrow.[8] In truth the electorate was becoming more conservative. In particular, the largely Liberal stockingers' freeman vote had declined along with the collapse of the apprenticeship system and its attendant freemen's rights. Table 9 based on existing poll books illustrates this point.

Table 9. Framework knitters and the Leicester electorate.

	No. of FWK voters	Liberal FWKs	Tory FWKs	FWKs as proportion of the electorate
1826	814	Party affiliation not given		20%
1832	No occupation given in poll books			
	425	265	163	15%
1837	533	371	162	16%
1852	390	327	63	14%
1857	278	198	51	8.6%
1861	382	263	119	9.4%

Source: Leicester poll books

Thus the Liberal stockinger who had constituted 10 per cent of the electorate in 1835 had declined to 6 per cent by the late 1850s. A small drop perhaps, but with a margin of only 250 votes over the Tory candidate in 1865, a highly significant one. 'The party needed new blood', declared one speaker at a Liberal electoral reform meeting in 1865, and given the long-standing bias of the working-class hosiery worker to favour liberalism it is not surprising that reform was perceived as the surest way of checking rising Tory fortunes.[9]

The 1867 Reform Act increased the size of the local electorate from 5,736 to 15,161.[10] The enlarged electorate certainly fulfilled the Liberal hope of bringing new blood into the party. The general election of 1868 saw the return of the two Liberal candidates, unopposed by the faction-ridden Conservatives. By 1880 Gladstone mania reached its high-water mark in Leicester when Taylor and McArthur, the Liberal sitting members, defeated the two Conservative candidates by margins of over 6,000 votes.[11] Domination at the parliamentary level was also reflected in local elections. This was particularly the case in school board elections which breathed new life into the old controversy on the role of the established church in the early 1870s. The Liberals certainly relished the challenge at school board elections, perceiving them as a means that would 'throw new life into the party' and 'pave the way to victory at the next general election'.[12] The school board elections also reinvigorated the Liberation Society locally as well as presenting the newly formed Democratic Association with its first experience in organizing the working-class vote.[13]

The Democratic, later, Republican Association was formed in 1871 by Daniel Merrick, the leader of the Sock and Top Union and perhaps Leicester's most prominent working man of the period.[14] The political aims and objectives of the Democratic Association were to organize the newly enfranchised working-class voter to support their call for universal suffrage. Given the fact that Taylor had advocated universal suffrage in the 1868 election campaign the Democratic Association was in reality the organized working-class section of Radical Liberalism, a point underlined by the Association's social policy which was 'to educate the people in the principles of political economy, moral virtue and social advancement.'[15]

In many ways the formation of the Democratic Association was part and parcel of a wider process of reform in the organization of local liberalism. For example, the Leicester Liberal Club was established in 1873 to replace the old Registration Society and by 1878 the Leicester Liberals had adopted a constitution based on the Birmingham model. The close relationship between the Democratic Association and the Liberals was illustrated by the active assistance given to the Association's campaign for Liberal school board candidates by such well-known radicals as Page Hopps and Macdonald, both Unitarian ministers.[16]

It may seem surprising that no important working-class organization, independent from the major parties, was established in this period, especially given the town's recent Chartism. Yet this absence of formal working-class independent politics is understandable in the light of the vigour of Leicester's Radical Liberalism. Indeed, two historians have argued, in an important article, that there was much common ground between the Chartists and the Radical Liberals, particularly in the area of franchise extension, religion and the privilege of a seemingly exploitative aristocracy.[17] Pursuing a similar theme, the research of Kate Tiller has shown the importance of local Chartism in shaping the future character of local liberalism. Tiller's comparative study of Kidderminster, Wigan and Halifax concludes that in areas which possessed a strong Chartist legacy, liberalism tended to be of the radical variety, while in localities which figured little in the Chartist turmoils, middle-class orthodox liberalism became the norm.[18] This pattern is further reinforced by Vincent's work which highlights the importance of the Chartists in the composition of Rochdale radicalism and the election to Parliament of Edward Miall.[19] Leicester radicalism certainly conforms to this model. Taylor, one of the foremost republicans of the day, not infrequently stirred recent memories with his call for universal suffrage.[20]

This perspective which views Chartism as anticipating mid-century liberalism rather than as a precursor and primitive form of working-class political organization is useful in understanding the nature of Leicester liberalism. The subsequent career of John Markham underlines the point. Markham, described by the historian of the Leicester movement as 'Self educated, he was a fine example of the shrewd level headed type of working class leader', had by 1852 been elected to the town council as a Liberal and was a strong supporter of John Biggs.[21]

Yet if during the 1860s and 1870s Leicester politics had generally returned to the old opposition of People and Privilege, did anything remain of the Chartist ethos of working-class isolation? The first and most obvious point to note in answering this question is the fact that despite its closeness to and working relationship with the Liberal Party, the Democratic Association nevertheless appears to have retained a distinct, identifiable working-class image. The nomenclature, 'Democratic', 'Republican', is also suggestive. The brief appearance in the winter of 1861–2 of the *Midland Workman and General Advertiser*, which advocated electoral reforms and contained articles by the Chartist leader John Sketchley, indicates, however slightly, that the embers of the old movement were not quite extinguished.[22] Of perhaps a more tangible nature were the activities of those Leicester men associated with the First International. Exactly when the Leicester branch of the First International was formed is unknown. The only member's name that has survived is that of E. W. Randle, the secretary and an elastic web weaver by trade. It could have been that the Leicester branch was an appendage of the local elastic web weavers' trade union; these workers were well represented on the International and they frequently utilized the executive of the International as arbiters in disputes between various factions in the union.[23]

By February 1873 the local Internationalists had persuaded the Republican Club, the local name for the Democratic Association, which claimed 500 members, to affiliate to the International.[24] The Republicans, however, were somewhat reluctant to change their name, a condition of affiliation.[25] Randle appears to have overcome this initial reluctance and reported that a meeting of Republicans which he addressed on the question of affiliation at 'The British Workman,' a local radical club, had to be adjourned so that larger premises could be found to accommodate the numerous participants.[26] Despite this delay Randle was still confident in March that the Republicans would join and looked forward to visiting 'the villages round the summer and spread our prinsiples and our cause i ham very glad to hear that you are going to lay the foundations of our commune it shall have my warmest support'.[27] This attempt to broaden the base of Leicester's branch of the First International foundered when Leicester became caught up in the machinations between Hales and his British Federal Council (BFC) and Marx. Hales, despised by many elastic web weavers for his support of an employer utilizing female labour, could not count on the support of the Leicester branch. Moreover, this branch, expanded by 500 new members, would probably have wrecked his designs to change the BFC into a working-class political party with little connection with the International. Thus Mottershead, a colleague of Hales, was despatched to Leicester in order to persuade the Republicans not to affiliate. He succeeded, being able to capitalize on press reports of the International which characterized it as a 'secret society' led by sinister foreigners.[28]

The documentation of the activities of the Leicester Internationalists is, of course, not substantial. The Leicester branch could be seen as being essentially a dissident section, the elastic web weavers' trade union determined to pull the carpet from under Hales. Yet the letters from Randle to Jung often contained informed views on wider political matters. For example, his letter of 19 February ends with the following note 'i hope spain will hold her guard and rise mightily as a nation in the hands of a real republican government governed by the people and for the people not the Gladstone class Legulation which we have so much of.'[29] It is also interesting to note that during the aftermath of the Paris Commune[30] the local Internationalists almost succeeded in winning over the 500-strong Republican Club to the cause of Britain's most avowed working-class organization. Indeed it took an alliance of the Hales circle and the Radical Liberal leadership of the Republicans to stop the alliance.[31] This brief surfacing of the old insurrectionary tradition does show, no matter how briefly, that at least a small section of the Labour movement still retained a faith in the importance of independent working-class politics, while the willingness of some Republicans to consider affiliation indicates that unease did exist within the class alliance of local radicalism.

In general, however, the 1870s proved to be quiet years for the Leicester Labour movement. The working class continued to support Radical Liberalism and their leaders gave unstinting support to the party of reform. The most notable event of the period was the foundation of the Trades Council in 1872 by eight local trade unions.[32] No archive material for the Trades Council prior to 1892 has survived, so that any analysis of the first two decades of its existence has to be tentative. A factor which helped to create the Trades Council appears to have been concern amongst local trade unionists over the Criminal Law Amendment Act, while the holding of the TUC Congress the previous year in Nottingham may have kindled local interest. Merrick, the hosiery workers' leader, was in the forefront of the local campaign against the legislation and he advised working-class voters in 1874 to vote Liberal in order to have the Act repealed.[33] Merrick was the first president of the Council and delegate to the 1875 TUC where he claimed to represent 3,170 members affiliated to the Trades Council.[34] The first decade of the Council appears to have been unremarkable. The Council was, however, quickly recognized as being part of the local Liberal establishment. Merrick, already a Liberal councillor, was nominated for the office of JP by the Trades Council in 1886, and served for the two years prior to his death in 1888.[35] Indeed, it was during the 1870s and 1880s that local trade union leaders became part of the fixtures of local Liberalism. Merrick was joined on the Liberal benches of the town council by Thomas Smith, the general secretary of NUBSO, who also became the secretary of the Liberal Association when he retired from union office in 1878. Smith also sat on the school board along with Edward Kell, NUBSO's president, and George Sedgewick, Smith's successor as general secretary.[36]

Despite the apparent calmness of Leicester politics during the 1870s and early 1880s the Leicester working class was never a totally passive component of the Liberal alliance. Perhaps the most interesting manifestation of working-class political activity during these years was the anti-vaccination movement which gave Leicester national notoriety.[37] At first the movement was started by mainly working-class parents who formed a local branch of the Anti-Vaccination League. The early meetings of the branch were poorly attended but with the passing of the 1871 Vaccination Act, with its stricter requirements and compulsory provisions, the movement began to grow, if somewhat slowly. A major impetus to the movement came from the ravages of the 1871–2 smallpox epidemic when Leicester reported over 3,000 cases and 358 deaths, some of the victims having previously been vaccinated. It was later in the decade, however, when the benefits of a locally inspired isolation system became apparent, that the branch received widespread local support.

The notification and isolation system was initiated by Dr W. Johnson, the new assistant medical officer of health, and one of a new generation of medical practitioners who espoused recent 'germ theories' and rejected the 'miasmatic' explanation of the disease. Johnson used Leicester's fever hospital, a remnant from a previous epidemic of scarlet fever, to isolate smallpox victims as part of a new rationalized system which still retained vaccination. The Johnson or Leicester system, as the method became known, soon achieved notable results and helped to convince working-class parents, the main recipients of the Act's provisions, that vaccination was unnecessary. Generalized disobedience of the 1871 Act became the order of the day and in 1881, 1,154 prosecutions were brought against Leicester parents who refused to have their infants vaccinated. Not surprisingly, the movement soon developed a political complexion. By 1882 it was virtually impossible for a pro-vaccinationer to get elected to the town council even though the council had no part to play in the administration of the Act, while in 1886 the Guardians, whose function it was to enforce the legislation, were opposed to vaccination and were frequently to run foul of the law over its lack of implementation. In 1885 nearly 3,000 people were awaiting prosecution. The imprisonment of offenders had begun in 1869 when three Leicester parents were jailed. In 1876 feelings locally ran high when nine Leicester people were imprisoned and demonstrations became common. 'In May 1876 Charles Eagle and Frank Palmer after ten days in jail for disobedience to the vaccination law, went in a procession to the Market Place, and received the homage of fifteen thousand cheering townsmen.'[38]

Simmons has argued that this phenomenal instance of civil disobedience owes much to the Leicester radical nonconformist society, part of the dissenter's character being a joy in 'martyrdom'.[39] Fraser, on the other hand, has emphasized the exemplary effect of Johnson's method upon the local population.[40] Nonconfirmity is undoubtedly the weaker explanation. Why for example were other centres of dissent not distinguished by a similar movement? Furthermore, religious objections were rarely cited in the defence of those brought before the magistrates for refusing vaccination. Moreover, if by implication radical nonconformity is meant to include the Liberal abhorrence of an interfering state, why did Leicester accept without complaint other legislation such as the Public Health Act? On the other hand, Fraser's explanation perhaps discounts too greatly the character of the local population. It was after all a working-class secularist, Charles Eagle, who was a dominant figure in the local branch of the League, while his fellow secularist, the elastic web manufacturer Michael Wright, became the leader and main organizer of the local movement.[41]

Politically, the movement became Leicester's *cause célèbre*. Indeed, it was a Conservative councillor who first used the issue to gain electoral support. But the activities of the Leicester branch of the League became closely identified with local liberalism when P. A. Taylor championed anti-vaccinationists nationally.[42] Taylor's successor as the radical member, J. A. Picton, continued Taylor's parliamentary campaign and was able to secure the appointment of a Royal Commission in 1889. The Commission did not go far enough to meet the League's demands but exemption on the grounds of conscience was achieved. Locally the town council put forward a private corporation bill which was passed by Parliament in 1879. This Act placed legislative weight behind the local notification system. Persons who failed to notify the authorities immediately of an occurrence of smallpox were subject to a maximum fine of £10.

Considerable working-class involvement in the Leicester anti-vaccination campaign is acknowledged by all scholars who have previously written on the subject. But it was a movement which tended to affirm rather than question the existing political status quo. Fraser has noted that the anti-vaccinationists in Leicester were composed of two groups: working-class parents who had most to fear from the legislation and produced the majority of members of the movement, and middle-class politicians who used the campaign for political purposes. A continuity can be seen between the class alliances that were gathered within the anti-vaccination campaign and former movements such as the reform agitation of the 1860s and controversy over religious education in the early 1870s. Yet in the midst of the vaccination turmoils, in the mid-1880s, a new issue was beginning to force itself on to the local political agenda. The vicissitudes of factory production in hosiery, and mechanization in footwear, exacerbated by both foreign and countryside competition, were beginning to strain relations between employers and workers. Both these groups in local industry had for many years formed the backbone of Leicester's Liberal coalition and it is to the first serious challenge to the alliance since its formation in the late 1850s and early 1860s that we now turn.

7 Early Socialism in Leicester

Socialism as a distinct and independent ideology emerged in Leicester amongst a small group of young secularists, some of whom were also active hosiery trade unionists. The effect of the new creed upon Leicester politics was miniscule during its first five years of existence. Yet within two decades socialism was to replace liberalism as the main form of working-class political expression, a process which was to culminate in the election of independent working-class candidates to local governing bodies and the victory of Ramsay MacDonald in the 1906 general election. This growth, however, was frequently interrupted and spasmodic. Until 1890, socialism in Leicester consisted of a small branch of the Socialist League whose members were mainly young hosiery workers and secularists. After 1890 young, militant converts of the new movement were able to harness the growing discontent amongst local shoemakers and establish a strong socialist base within the structure of footwear trade unionism. Upon this new foundation a branch of the ILP was formed out of the previous warring factions of local members of the Social Democratic Federation and the anarchist-ridden Socialist League.

During this first phase of local socialism the young men from the Secular Hall were able to establish a footing in the newly formed LAHU. This is not particularly surprising as hosiery had provided recruits to secularism for many years and these men, perhaps because of their disposition to audacity, were often ideally suited to trade union work. Indeed trade unionism itself had often provided a refuge for working-class radicals and, as we have seen above, it was the secularist and trade union celebrants of the Paris Commune who embarked upon the formation of a Socialist Club in 1888. The problems which beset the hosiery factory workforce were to hasten the development of local socialism. Yet during a period when local advocates of socialism were as muddled as their national mentors on what strategy the new movement should follow, this new movement grew but slowly.[1] Other factors were also at work in limiting the growth of socialism. Hosiery was increasingly becoming an industry of female workers. This is not to suggest that women were uninterested in politics; women in hosiery gave tacit support to the socialist-inspired leadership of the LAHU throughout the period, but during an era when

85

politics was, formally at least, a 'man's business', they provided few recruits to the new movement. Shoe workers, on the other hand, offered greater opportunities. Steeped as they were in their tradition of radicalism and well versed in assuming the leadership of past popular movements, it is surprising that we find so few from this trade in early Leicester socialism. Shoemakers were eventually to become the driving force of local socialism during the 1890s but why do they figure so little in the development of the Socialist League? Footwear was still relatively prosperous, and the radical liberalism of the NUBSO leadership, for many, still appeared to work. Moreover, as we shall see in the next chapter, rising discontent amongst shoe workers continued to be channelled into their formidable local union organization. There were also problems of proselytization. The early members of the Socialist League in Leicester were generally earnest and inward looking and rather obsessive about the need to make socialists through study rather than by propaganda. By the end of the period of this chapter a few leading militant shoemakers had joined the ranks of local socialists and they were to play key roles in the future. Their presence, however, was disproportionately small considering the size of their occupation in Leicester.

The meeting in King Street in 1888 to celebrate the Paris Commune, referred to in Chapter 1, was more than a gathering of frustrated trade union activists impelled towards considering the benefits of socialism by the specific circumstances of the Leicester hosiery industry. Many of the celebrants were active secularists and the heirs of an indigenous working-class tradition that stretched back to the days of Robert Owen. Moreover, the purpose of the meeting was to commemorate an important event in the history of the European working class. The presence of LAHU officers who were not secularists shows that participation in the working-class radical tradition extended beyond the ranks of organized free-thought. For at least three of the celebrants, Barclay, Robson and Warner, the decision taken at the meeting to found a Socialist Labour Club was another step forward in a process of political education and activity which had been under way since the early 1880s. All three were active working-class secularists who had followed with intense interest the emergence of socialist ideas at the weekly lectures in the Secular Hall. Barclay and Robson's radicalism had been reinforced and enhanced by a vigorous process of self-education, while Warner, who along with Barclay was an officer of the LAHU, was ever aware of his family's past involvement in the Chartist movement.[2]

Barclay was in many ways the key figure of this group. An avid reader of Ruskin and the literary classics, this young bachelor of Irish extraction was equally involved in both trade union and working-class political culture. He was first to involve himself in the socialist movement when he debated against Bradlaugh's anti-Hyndman position in the Secular Hall early in 1885, supplementing his crude Marxism a few months later with a lecture

on 'John Ruskin's Political Economy'. Barclay's early lectures at the
Secular Hall received a mention in *Justice* which in turn prompted J. L.
Mahon of the newly formed Socialist League to make contact with the
young provincial. Barclay's reply to Mahon clearly demonstrates the role
of the Secular Hall to the early socialist movement:

> Dear Sir,
>   I received a letter from you through some other person unknown to me,
> some two months ago ... You heard that I was interested in the Socialistic
> movement and I may say that I am very much so. At the Secular Society, at
> which I am a member, I lectured in answer to Mr. Bradlaugh's 'Some
> Objections' ... For two or three weeks I purchased a quire of Justice to sell.
> But I got poor encouragement here in Leicester. I may say that in answer to a
> question of yours that The Commonweal is sold at the Secular Bookstores
> and that it is on the Society Club Room tables ... Commonweal is much
> superior to Justice since the new editorship of the latter. I will do my best to
> push it [Commonweal] amongst my class. But it is hard. They are ignorant,
> selfish, apathetic ...
>   With best wishes for and thanks to all connected with The
> Commonweal.
>   believe me yours,
>   Thos Barclay,
>   wage slave.[3]

The decision as to which strain of socialism local groups affiliated was
often an historical accident. Provincial socialists making their first stumbling steps into the new theory could find difficulty in differentiating
between the various versions on offer and tended to make their choice on
personality rather than policy, as Barclay's subsequent letter to the Socialist League clearly shows:

> Gentlemen,
>   You must excuse me not answering before this, your notice of my letter
> and your requests. I have been Secretary pro tem on our Trades Union, and
> now very busy for over a week preparing for half yearly meeting. I am already
> a member of S.D.F.[4] but I send you P.O. and ask you to enrol me one of the
> Socialist League. One is liable to get confused among Fabians, Anarchists,
> Socialists and Socialists. I have looked through your manifesto and compared
> it with that of the S.D.F. and the difference as far as I can see is 'non
> est'.
>   Nevertheless I shall be glad to belong to a Society that has amongst its
> members Wm. Morris and the daughter of Carl Marx.
>   I ask your Council's permission to form a branch of the Socialist League
> in Leicester which I shall try to do.
>   ... My personal thanks to Dr. Aveling for his lucid lessons in Socialism,
> which it is a pity all Socialists will not read.[5]

Yet personality and policy are often not so easily separated. Barclay,
with his love of literature, and especially Ruskin, obviously felt an
empathy with Morris and *Commonweal* rather than the arid pages of
Hyndman's *Justice*. Moreover, Morris exerted an influence over the bohemian culture of young working- and middle-class intellectuals, centred

at the Secular Hall. One of the outstanding members of this informal society, Ernest Gimson, the son of the Secular Society president, was soon to join Morris as a furniture designer.[6] The question of whether Morris's socialism was essentially moralistic rather than based on a material analysis of society has already been explored by historians.[7] The main appeal of the League to Barclay and his circle was Morris's insistence that socialism had to be made by making socialists, an idea that found a ready response amongst these self-taught, bookish, workers. One of Barclay's early branch reports underlines the point:

> As regards the branch I must report that the whole of the organization devolves upon me. After Dr. Aveling's lecture I expected to see more at our meetings, but very few came up. Then two or three of us put our heads together and resolved that we would not force the thing, for we saw that Socialism had to be acquired by gradual study and discussion.[8]

Such a mode of proselytization could not, however, quickly establish a large political movement. The membership of Branch 13, Leicester, of the Socialist League does not appear to have ever been more than 20 subscription payers.[9] Even these often found difficulty in paying their weekly sixpence and there appears to have been much internal dissent and suspicion over the state of the branch's finances.[10] Furthermore, the seasonality of local trade, especially in winter, could affect both subscriptions and sales of *Commonweal*: 'We are only a small branch at best two thirds of our members are out of work or on short time – we find it very difficult to get any money in at all – I have not sold more than 10–15 *Commonweals* per week for several months.'[11] Problems also arose from the section of the membership based in the older artisan trades and thus susceptible to the itinerant work cycles. John Fowkes, the secretary, spent the autumn of 1888 taking samples of his work around potential employers in London and was finally reduced to begging his fare back to Leicester from the staff at the League headquarters.[12] His predecessor as secretary, P. C. Copeland, had left Leicester in similar circumstances the previous summer, taking the branch funds with him.[13] Another obstacle to growth during the League's early period in Leicester was the tendency for the membership to continue the old pattern of meetings typical of the era of self-educating artisans. Thus while the Leaguers could use their membership of the Secular Hall to press for leading socialist speakers at the society's weekly lectures, their own weekly meetings and talks were often more narrow in appeal. For example, Barclay frequently spoke to the branch on Ruskin and Zola.[14] On the other hand we must not dismiss these literary interests as insignificant for what we are witnessing is a vital aspect of the intellectual development of a group of young men[15] who were to play an important role in the development of socialism in subsequent years.

With its roots firmly planted in the milieu of Leicester secularism the League attracted other young men from a social background markedly different from that of radical young hosiery workers. These young middle-class members shared Barclay's and Robson's love of learning and the arts and became interested in Socialism largely because of the elegance of Aveling's 'scientific' lectures at the hall. Typical of this group was Maximillian Bunting, a young, well-to-do cashier of Arthur Street and an early secretary of the branch. Bunting corresponded with Aveling, finding the latter's 'rational, scientific' image commendable and intellectually respectable.[16] His support for the socialist cause was, however, put to the test when he studied the League's manifesto for the first time, finding the word 'revolution' particularly irksome: 'This word is a great stumbling block to us in the provinces. It has been so much applied to pikes and staves that for the progress of our movement it would be well left out.'[17] Bunting soon left the League but his gifts of cash and his ability to procure national speakers through his role as secretary of the Secular Society undoubtedly assisted the League in its formative period.[18] Similar assistance came from James Billson, a son of the substantial manufacturing family and a friend of G. B. Shaw.[19] The most enduring of these middle-class supporters was Archibald Gorrie, a lifelong supporter of Barclay's political campaigns, who gained a certain notoriety in the early 1890s as the only Christian in British anarchism.[20] Gorrie was converted to socialism after hearing Barclay lecture, and subsequently became branch secretary and benefactor and established ties with Edward Carpenter.[21]

This early bohemian phase ended with the departure of the majority of the branch's middle-class supporters and a quickening of the tempo of upheaval in the hosiery industry. The branch's initial reluctance to push propaganda seriously hampered recruitment; so much so that a group of hosiery workers at a Leicester factory, unaware of the existence of the Leicester branch, contacted the *Commonweal* to enquire about membership.[22] The Leaguers' focus of attention did, however, move towards industrial matters. The branch, which had moved from the Secular to the Spiritualist Hall in Silver Street, moved again to the offices of the Hosiery Union in Horsefair Street. The Horsefair Street period was in many ways the League's most creative one. Warner and Barclay were union officials, while the union's up-and-coming officer, Jabez Chaplin, was increasingly being influenced by Barclay.[23] Furthermore, the union's full-time secretary, James Holmes, whose membership of the League is uncertain, was a long-standing friend of Barclay and sympathetic to socialist ideas. These were frequntly expressed in the union's 'Monthly Notes' which were distributed amongst the membership, and socialists joined the union's campaign to recruit country workers.[24]

If the Socialist League in Leicester was changing in social composition from a group of working- and middle-class young intellectuals into a body of politically minded young trade unionists, was this shift reflected in the political ideas of the Leicester Leaguers? In one sense this question has already been answered. During the first 18 months or so of the League's existence the main concern of the group was to build up the membership slowly by encouraging other like-minded young people to join their study and debating circle. The sloughing off of the initial middle-class support and the accompanying crisis in the hosiery industry resulted in the League changing its focus from making socialists to making trade unionists, especially in the country villages. In this respect the League members were following an age-old Leicester pattern of trying to unite town and country against the manufacturer, an idea last voiced a decade-and-a-half earlier by Randle of the International. Despite the political rhetoric of Barclay and his colleagues, this aspect of country propaganda was politically circumscribed by the League's refusal to participate in parliamentary and local government elections. Thus the political campaign in the country was essentially a consciousness-raising exercise which ran in harness with Holmes's efforts to establish country branches of the LAHU.

The methods adopted by the League in their country campaign followed old patterns as well as introducing ingenious new ones. There are numerous references in both the Socialist League press and a recently compiled archive on early socialist handbills to the League's village lecture tours.[25] The main topic was invariably Barclay's set piece 'Socialism, Rent, and Profit', although how these lectures were received and the size of attendance is a question that our sources cannot answer. Even if the League did contribute noticeably to the LAHU recruitment drive, that contribution has to be assessed alongside the shortlived success of the LAHU in the villages.

In many ways, the League's efforts to assist the LAHU, noble as these were, offered little political potential. Holmes was already sympathetic to socialism and the union's regular Trades Council delegate, Warner, was a leading member of the League. In reality the most active sector of the LAHU, the male Cotton's patents operatives, numbered only 600 and all the signs indicated a growing presence of females in the hosiery factories.[26] This is not to argue that women workers were always politically passive. Indeed it was a crowded meeting of women workers in the Secular Hall during the 1886 February strike who noisily shouted down the proposal that Merrick 'the G.O.M. of the Leicester working class' should act as arbiter in the dipute.[27] Yet the problem still remained that it was difficult enough to encourage women to participate in trade unionist activities, let alone political organization.

Barclay's most original contribution to the village campaign was the production of his weekly newspaper the *Countryman*.[28] This newspaper was distributed free to over 50 villages and was remarkably similar in format to present-day weekly giveaways. The idea to launch the *Countryman* came from J. W. Barrs, a well-to-do secularist tea merchant. Barrs was a well-known local radical with idiosyncratic tastes in both arts and politics. 'Twas a habit of him to purchase and read any book that the popular and ordinary critic condemned.'[29] On hearing that Barclay had left Corah's factory, Barrs contacted him with the idea of launching the paper, handing over to him complete editorial rights. The first issue came out in March 1886 and displays Barclay's pen in full flow, with numerous articles tucked between the copious advertisements. There were features on village hosiery strikes, political economy, magisterial appointments and an essay competition for agricultural workers. By the following year Barclay was exhorting the Leicestershire miners to form a strong trade union, informing the country folk of the Chicago anarchists, the London Trades Council and statistics of national income. The *Countryman* claimed a circulation of 5,000, although this figure cannot be corroborated. By 1889 Barclay became increasingly hostile to the Tory squirearchy and began to utter anti-royalist sentiments, calling the queen 'a useless woman'. Not surprisingly advertisers began to fight shy of patronizing such a newspaper and the *Countryman* ceased publication in the early 1890s.[30] This early venture into journalism was, however, to provide crucial experience in the formation of a local Labour newspaper in the early 1890s.

As the 1880s drew to a close the League's political thinking became increasingly muddled. This was probably caused by the fact that apart from their trade union activities the members, having eschewed electoral politics, had no central concern upon which to focus their ideas and formulate policy. Their lectures and speeches more and more began to appear like an assortment of the various bees in the few bonnets that constituted the membership. For example, Barclay, possibly because of his impoverished background, held a long-standing aversion to cooperative production. This proposed solution to the ills of the world was designed, according to Barclay, to enhance the status and economic position of the few well-to-do workers who were able to fund such ventures, and thus left untouched the deeper problem of poverty.[31] Despite the perceptiveness of this critique, Barclay, by constantly attacking cooperators,[32] was isolating himself and the League from a considerable group of potential supporters, particularly among young militant boot and shoe workers. There is also some evidence that Barclay's feelings on cooperation caused friction within his own group; on one occasion the branch went so far as to pass a resolution supporting cooperative production.[33]

Another source of weakness was an increasing ambivalence towards trade unionism. Robson, in particular, specialized in giving open air lectures on the 'iron law of wages'. This position was somewhat contradicted by their own trade union activities and the frequent praise which they lavished on James Holmes for the latter's writings on socialist matters. Warner, on the other hand, fell under the sway of anarchism which was beginning to receive a fair amount of exposure from Socialist League lecturers near the end of the decade.[34]

Judged in terms of membership and tangible connections with the Labour movement, the League's record during the 1880s was not particularly impressive. Branch membership was always miniscule and they never managed to increase their toehold in the trade union movement. Indeed Barclay, who had shared a position of almost equal power with Holmes in 1885, had retired from union activities into full-time journalism. Warner remained a union officer throughout the period, but his influence was slight. Although he was the LAHU delegate to the Trades Council he must have been an isolated figure being the only anarchist on the Council. With a penchant for advocating direct action, he probably suffered much ridicule from the majority of delegates who still espoused a Lib-Lab political outlook.[35] Furthermore, the membership of the LAHU, although relatively small, never demonstrated any overt socialist attitudes. In 1885 as in 1890, there were but a few socialist hosiery workers.

Yet there is a danger of underestimating the effect upon the Leicester Labour movement of Branch 13. Although few in number they had managed to give an airing to virtually every major socialist speaker in the country. Their campaign of outdoor propaganda, begun in 1888, reactivated the tradition of popular oratory on the time-honoured pitches of Russell Square, the Market Place and Humberstone Gate, where many of Leicester's future socialist leaders first came into contact with socialist ideas.[36] Furthermore, their proposal to set up an independent working-class political club, first raised at the 'Commune dinner' of 1888, had by the early 1890s reached fruition with the opening of the Leicester Labour Club and Socialist Institute, pledged to the improvement of the Conditions of the Working Classes, not only by the organization of the workers, but also 'by all constitutional and political means'.[37] Finally Barclay's journalistic ventures were to provide the base for the setting up of Leicester's Independent Labour Press in the early 1890s.

Measured against the national picture, the achievements of the Leicester branch were considerable. They were one of the few provincial groups to send delegates regularly to the League's conferences and in 1890 Leicester was one of the organization's six remaining provincial locations.[38] Leicester socialism undoubtedly had a strong advantage over that of other provincial towns, being able to draw upon and utilize the resources of the town's notable secularist tradition. Conversely, Barclay and his colleagues changed the direction and began to reshape Leicester's most notable radical working-class institution. After Barclay's 1885 lectures and the influx of socialist speakers, the orthodoxy of Holyoakeian free-thought ceased to dominate the thoughts and discussions of the more advanced sections of Leicester's radical working-class culture.

Perhaps the major reason for the lack of organizational success for the Barclay circle was the fact that the largest and best-organized section of Leicester's working class, the footwear workers, enjoyed relative prosperity throughout the 1880s. William Inskip remained in firm command of NUBSO and enjoyed considerable local political success, eventually becoming Leicester's first working-class alderman. When the economic climate in the footwear industry altered dramatically in the early 1890s the remnants of the League were committed anarchists, with a puritanical disregard for organization and therefore ill disposed to capitalize on the growing unrest amongst footwear workers. Unlike the numerically small LAHU, NUBSO was the the dominant working-class organization in Leicester with a virtually all-male membership, organized in two branches whose combined total was over 12,000 workers. Moreover, NUBSO dominated the Trades Council, and enjoyed much local political patronage. Thus problems in the footwear industry had manifold implications for Leicester's political and economic life. It is these problems that must now command our attention.

8 Labour Struggles in the Leicester Footwear Industry and the Decline of the Liberal Old Guard

This chapter will analyse the growing turmoil amongst boot and shoe workers and its effect upon trade union politics. In order to answer the question, why was the leadership of NUBSO in Leicester, a group of men who were a classic example of late Victorian Lib-Labism, replaced by staunch socialists, emphasis will be given to the fundamental industrial changes that took place between the late 1880s and 1895. The complexities of this industrial theme are of crucial importance and in order to deal with them adequately it is necessary to put to one side, until the next chapter, the wider political developments which accompanied these changes. It will be argued that increased mechanization and new work patterns fundamentally threatened both the old system of informal work relationships and status divisions within the workforce. The increasing reality of this threat provided a platform upon which a young generation of socialist shoe workers could stand up and act as the defenders of the autonomy and independence of the 'disciples of St Crispin'. The success of the socialists in these disputes had wider communal importance which will be dealt with fully in the next chapter.

In the years before the industrial turbulence of the early 1890s, NUBSO experienced its golden age of Lib-Labism under the general secretaryship of William Inskip. His career began as a laster in the Leicester trade but his organizing ability and tactical skill soon won him union office as an 'investigator'.[1] This important post involved travelling around the various centres of the trade, investigating and attempting to settle local disputes and in the last resort authorizing strike pay. His talent as a negotiator and the respect which he gained from both employers and workers assured him a base of support that extended well outside Leicester. Fox has summarized Inskip's social and political philosophy. 'In general he accepted the economic framework of the society in which he lived, looking rather to a strong trade unionism for amelioration than to any fundamental change in that economic structure. In general too he accepted its social values. He was contemptuous of egalitarianism, and convinced that progress required the generous rewarding of individual ability, thrift and energy.' Similar to his predecessors, Smith and Sedgewick, he was a staunch Liberal in politics and upon his promotion to the office of general secretary he was also elected town councillor for St Margaret's ward. Such attitudes and political trappings were, of course, highly suitable to a representative of workers in an industry that was enjoying a long period of prosperity and whose main sub-group of workers, the lasters, continued to enjoy craft status. The majority of footwear workers were still employed in small units, outside the factory, a milieu favourable to the ideology of self-help and personal economic independence.

The decade 1885–95 was, however, to see a major shift in both the outlook and politics of Leicester's footwear workers. The Lib-Labism of the mid–1880s gave way to socialism which became the dominant feature of NUBSO's policy by 1895. What caused this change in the politics of Leicester's footworkers and how was a self-confident Lib-Lab union leadership replaced by a new stratum of militant activists? Three developments in the industry under way by the late 1880s served to undermine the union leadership: first, growing discontent with the arbitration system; second, the campaign to bring all workers inside the factory; and third, the introduction of the lasting machine. Such fundamental changes in the structure of the industry were not, however, the product of separate independent developments in various sectors of the production process. They have to be seen as the logical actions of employers to modernize and restructure the Leicester trade in response to the competition of American manufacturers in both the home and export markets. As we saw in Chapter 2, the technologically superior and well-organized Massachusetts industry seriously threatened the British trade during the late 1880s and early 1890s.

The manufacturers' first problem was to retain their place in the market by producing footwear as cheap and as attractive as the American product. The disputes which accompanied such extensive changes of style forced some manufactureres to resort to an older strategy of introducing a day-work wage system.[2] The attractions of such a mode of work organization for employers were considerable. New products could be introduced without price negotiations with the workers and labour could be more flexibly deployed. The workers, however, reared in an artisan tradition rooted in the piece-work system, resented such new methods of payment which entailed not only more work for possibly the same or less money, but also threatened the autonomy of the operative and his control over the pace of production. Yet while Leicester had been an acknowledged centre of the piece-work method the union had never been able to eradicate local pockets of day work. The problem faced by the union was that during every slack winter season some employers would engage unemployed workers on the day system. The problem became serious enough in 1881 for the Leicester branch to propose that the rules of the union should be changed in order that

1. No member in any branch shall work day-work, with the exception of overlookers of apprentices and shop-foremen.

2.   No member under any pretence whatsoever must article himself to an employer for any stated term of service, under the penalty of expulsion from the Union.

3.   In cases where the members are already working day-work no action shall be taken on such shop or shops witout first obtaining the sanction of the council to do so.[3]

These amendments were accepted with little opposition, but they did not solve the problem. By 1883 a delegate meeting had to be convened to debate the issue. In the two years between 1881 and 1883 members, particularly in Leicester and Leeds, had been accepting day work during the winter slack season on such a scale that expulsion would threaten the very existence of the two local branches. The rules were again amended to allow those already working day work to remain in the union. Many delegates were concerned at having to make concessions to day work and the new amendment was frequently debated at subsequent conferences.[4]

In Leicester the campaign was largely waged against attempts to expand day work into shops that traditionally paid by the piece. The first signs of competition impelled many local employers to resort to the day-work system. The most noticeable and bitter dispute occurred in 1886 when the large Leicester firm of Walker and Kempson abandoned piece work. This firm, owned by old Unitarian families, considered itself a leader in good industrial relations and enjoyed a close relationship with leading trade unionists in the early 1880s. It became the scene of a protracted industrial battle. The union report commented on the dispute with more than a touch of irony:

> As will be seen responsibilities of no ordinary nature rest upon any one firm, which, whilst seeking to secure its own advantage pertaining to its self-interest alone, ruthlessly destroys the fabric which holds the welfare of the trade together as a whole, and would make impossible the continuance of those harmonious relations without which no trade or community can hope to be successful, or indeed hold its own.

After a long-drawn-out battle the firm eventually conceded to union pressure and piece work was re-established in its factories, but not without damage to employer–union relations.[5]

The day-work disputes of 1886–7 were, however, only the opening salvoes of what was to be a long campaign. Day work having proved too costly a strategy for the employers, was replaced by an increased reliance upon the existing arbitration system as a means of facilitating greater productivity. By resorting to arbitration manufacturers were not trying to recreate the trade harmony of previous decades. Arbitration, by removing the dispute to the slow-moving arbitration machinery, gave the manufacturer both time and greater flexibility in introducing new styles. Moreover, fashions in shoes changed so quickly that by the time a price dispute was settled by arbitration the product under question was often no longer being manufactured, having been replaced by yet newer models, or poor trade had returned, allowing the manufacturer to dictate his own price. The arbitration system produced resentment amongst the workforce but the alternative, a plethora of strikes, threatened both the finances of the union and the political convictions of the union leadership which clung tenaciously to the belief that arbitration was the best guarantee of trade harmony.[6] Indeed Inskip and his fellow council members were caught in the cleft stick of this particular employer strategy. But if the manufacturer felt secure at having neutralized NUBSO'S primary weapons, could they withstand a lengthy period of guerrilla warfare?

The executive council's refusal to abandon arbitration gave rise to wide-spread grass-roots discontent and brought to the fore a new generation of unofficial workshop leaders. The anti-arbitration campaign that emerged in many shoe centres during the late 1880s[7] was as much an attack on the political attitudes of the union leadership as it was a reaction against management strategies. Since Mundella, arbitration had been a political ideology as well as a device for settling disputes.[8] While in the short term gains could be made by the manufacturers by overloading the system, in the long term they stood to lose the benefits that accrued from the existence of a type of trade union philosophy that closely resembled their own world-view. On the other hand it has to be conceded that manufac-turers had little option but to pursue the course which they followed. With increased market penetration by the Americans, the cosy world of first name relations with union leaders and the common language of radical liberalism was no longer tenable.

The union executive, unable to satisfy demands from the membership to suspend the working of the arbitration machinery, could not prevent the emergence of an unofficial grass-roots leadership. It is difficult to chart accurately the arrival of these unofficial leaders. The union monthly re-ports refused to give the militants any direct publicity, and chose instead to attack the unofficial movement in general terms. There is a similar reticence about the militants by the local press. Gradually, however, names do emerge and the militant leadership can be identified. Their undoubted leader was young T. F. Richards, usually called Freddy Richards, who was born the son of a commercial traveller in Wednesbury, Staffordshire in 1863. Richards was apprenticed as a laster in the Staffordshire trade and appears to have drifted, along with the Staffordshire industry, to Leicester in the early 1880s.[9] By 1885 he was a member of NUBSO. A keen student at Barclay's socialist classes, sharing his teacher's love of Ruskin, Freddy was a committed socialist by 1889. He did not, however, figure in any of the activities of the local Socialist League branch. Perhaps he was uneasy at Barclay's hostility to cooperation, Richards being deeply committed to producer cooperatives, or he may have been hostile to the League's later espousal of anarchism. By the early 1890s he was the leading figure in Leicester's Social Democratic Federation branch, although this group never secured permanent rooms nor meeting places.[10]

Richards was supported by two other young socialists of whom we have less biographical information. E. Clarkmead, another laster, was for a while even more prominent in the unofficial movement than Richards. He was the first Leicester socialist to be elected to union office when he became the town's full-time agent in 1890.[11] The third member of this group was Martin Curley, a young laster who was to remain Richards's staunch lieutenant for many years.[12] The anti-arbitrationists were also joined by the fiery figure of George Cores, an anarchist shoemaker from the London trade who moved to Leicester in 1890. Cores combined his brief stay as a laster in Leicester with his activities as occasional editor of the *Commonweal* and organizer of the Walsall anarchists' defence campaign.[13] A staunch member of the *Freedom* circle, Cores was nevertheless often at odds with his anarchist colleagues over his support and belief in trade union organization.[14] Cores sat alongside his fellow ex-Socialist Leaguer turned anarchist, Warner of the LAHU, on the local Trades Council. His rhetoric and skill at controlling meetings soon won him a seat on the executive of the Leicester branch where his ability at passing socialist resolutions at branch general meetings gained him some notoriety.[15]

These young militants exploited the anti-arbitration feelings of the Leicester workforce to organize unofficial strikes and attack the union leadership's liberalism with socialist rhetoric. A series of major unofficial strikes in 1889, led by Richards, proved successful for the workers and provided Richards with a firm platform to mount his challenge against the union leadership.[16] There is, of course, a major difficulty in attempting to assess the consciousness of working people by reference to the views of their union representatives. The election of Clarkmead as a full-time official in 1890 and Richards's impressive performance in the election for the Leicester delegate to the national conference in 1892, where he secured 850 votes, the previous highest total being 228, suggests that the socialists were gaining ground.[17] Yet it could be argued that this growing support was an expression of the workers' approval for the socialists' trade union style rather than their politics. On the other hand the point that arbitration in the Leicester footwear trade was as much a political philosophy as it was machinery for the settlement of disputes has to be noted. Clearly, in terms of local politics in the early 1890s, when there was no separate working-class political party engaging in electoral politics, firm measurements of shifts in working-class consciousness is extremely difficult. We can, nevertheless, detect cracks in the Lib-Labism of the Leicester footwear workforce.

One appeared in 1887 when Inskip brought his colleague from the TUC parliamentary committee, Henry Broadhurst, to Leicester to inaugurate the founding of the Leicester District Labour Association. This organization aimed to secure more working-class candidates for school board and local government elections.[18] Although firmly in the Liberal camp the very existence of the Association indicated that despite the close connection between NUBSO and the local Liberal Association, there appeared to be a need to place some distance between the leadership of the working class and local liberalism. The Liberal leadership was naturally disturbed and the mayor, Alderman Wood, who was also chairman of Freeman, Hardy and Willis, began holding annual grand luncheons for Capital and Labour, Broadhurst being the main guest at the first such event.[19]

Despite these efforts to bolster local Lib-Labism the call for independent working-class political institutions became more persistent. In March 1891 the Leicester Working Men's Political Council was set up, a body whose purpose was to advocate independent Labour representation in Parliament. Similar tendencies were expressed by the previously politically quiescent clickers, whose Number Two (No. 2) Branch demanded that the local May Day demonstration be held on May Day rather than the previous Sunday as well as passing a resolution in favour of a new political party 'separate from either of the great political parties'.[20] These moves by the clickers are also a significant indicator that disaffection with the politics of the union leadership was spreading to wider sectors of the workforce and was not confined to new 'wild young lasters'.

The anti-arbitration movement finally came to a head locally in October 1891. A mass meeting attended by several thousand members was held at the Temperance Hall to debate the question 'Peace or War in the Leicester Boot Trade'. This stormy meeting finally gave a narrow majority to Inskip's appeal to retain the local board of arbitration. Victory, however, was gained at an apparently heavy price. Inskip had to promise the meeting that he would give up all his public offices, including his seat on the town council, in order to devote more time to ensuring the smooth working of the board. It was this concession that won him the vote. Yet in the following month both Inskip and Woolley were re-elected to the council, a perhaps cynical act which was to have dire long-term consequences for Inskip's reputation in the union.[21]

In the midst of the unofficial campaign many local employers resorted to sending out work to unorganized finishing shops both in the town and in adjacent country villages. For many manufacturers this was a short-term expedient rather than a reversal to an older form of industrial organization. A new generation of finishing machines were becoming common features of the larger establishments and NUBSO was at last making real progress in organizing finishers.[22] Nevertheless, up until 1891 the majority of Leicester's footwear workers were still outside factories.[23] NUBSO had traditionally been successful at organizing lasters, whether inside the factory or in the workshop. Most of them would have served an apprenticeship and they possessed a strong sense of craft solidarity. By contrast the finishers had always proved difficult to organize. The job was easy to learn and was often combined with other forms of employment during the seasonal lay-offs.[24]

With the increasing mechanization of the finishing trades, the lasters, who formed the overwhelming majority of the union, were anxious to organize the finishers, an anxiety which coincided with the general upsurge of organizing the less skilled in the late 1880s. There was, of course, a strong sense of self-interest on the part of the lasters behind the campaign to recruit the finishers. The manufacturer was naturally all too keen to promote increased subdivision in the lasting departments similar to that already existing in the clicking process. Thus the finisher was the likely candidate to operate the stitching machine which had been the traditional preserve of the laster. At the same time, they could become the low-cost operatives of the new lasting machines. The protection of demarcation lines was therefore vital to the employment prospects of the lasters, and in order to defend existing work practices, the finishers had to be organized inside the factories and outwork curtailed. It was the latter which gave the employers the ever-present opportunity to start the de-skilling process outside the factory in the workship sector.

These pressures prompted NUBSO to campaign to force employers to bring all forms of production inside the factory walls. The issue of indoor working, however, provided common ground for the militants and union hierarchy. Richards had been active in the fight to make employers provide factory accommodation for the finishing workers in the late 1880s.[25] The union executive had been conscious for many years of the organizational and administrative benefits of 'indoor working'.[26] The campaign in Leicester began with unusually smooth negotiations. The Leicester branch notified the executive council in December 1890 of its intention to demand 'indoor working' from the local manufacturers at the next meeting of the arbitration board. The branch's request for funds for strike action, if negotiations broke down, was granted with no opposition.[27] A meeting of the arbitration board was held the following month, attended by union officials and 140 Leicester manufacturers. To the undoubted surprise of the trade in general, the employers, with only three dissensions, agreed to the workers' proposals.[28]

The Union was jubilant with the outcome of the negotiations, but Day, the editor of the *Shoe and Leather Record*, attacked the Leicester employers for their apparent capitulation.[29] Day's misgivings were, of course, based on the inevitable growth in union power that the decision entailed,[30] but it must also be remembered that Day was the spokesman for the manufacturers nationally, many of whom were not as advanced in factory production as Leicester, and were still highly dependent on outwork. The Leicester manufacturers, on the other hand, realized the determination of the local workers. Even more importantly they saw that the new generation of machinery, especially the lasting machine, demanded the introduction of the Massachusetts-style team system. Such a development would signal the end of outwork.

The rapid transformation of the Leicester trade from a system of work

100

organization highly dependent upon outworkers to a fully-fledged factory-based industry inside 12 months was not without its difficulties or paradoxes. The fact that more than 12,000 of the town's 24,000 footwear workers were removed from their workshops and home-based production units on the insistence of the minority of the local workforce based in factories is not without significance for theorists of the 'proletarianization' process. On the other hand it has to be conceded that the structural changes produced by technological progress contained an element of inevitability. It is, however, the timing and form of these changes in a particular historical setting that are the major concerns of this chapter.

To argue that the outworkers immediately appreciated the benefits of factory-based employment would be a gross mis-statement. Union spokesmen could ally themselves with and use the rhetoric of anti-sweating campaigns[31] in presenting their case for indoor working, but the subject of their concern, the outworker, resisted the benign process of factory life. The problem was based upon the finishers' strong sense of independence and their sub-contractor status. As we saw in Chapter 2 the finisher usually employed up to six youths in his workshop. Thus the seasonality of work, the sense of independence inherent in the workshop and the ability to exploit young labour gave the finisher a set of work rhythms that were the antithesis of factory discipline. Moreover, finishing had always been an occupation notorious for the raucous ill-mannered life style of its practitioners. They lacked the civilizing effects of a craft apprenticeship and artisan way of life.[32] The finishers' hostility to factory life was expressed in different ways. Many continued to ignore regulation timekeeping, choosing instead to wander off during working hours to pubs and other recreational activities. This particular problem became so acute that employers resorted to 'locking in' the workers at the beginning of each shift. Locks were broken by the men and disorder was not uncommon.[33] The problem was exacerbated by the fact that St Monday had traditionally been celebrated by shoemakers in Leicester both in factories and workshops. For example, at the Cooperative Wholesale Society's newly opened Leicester factory in 1874, 40 per cent of the lasters were absent every Monday from March to June, 17 per cent every Tuesday and 12 per cent every Wednesday.[34]

Another sign of disapproval by the new factory workers was their hostility to supervision over the work process. In particular the role of the foreman on the factory floor was difficult for the finishers to accept. Strikes caused by friction between workers and foremen became more common and shop floor relations entered a difficult period.[35] This problem was exacerbated by manufacturers who, wishing to strengthen the supervisory sector of junior management in order to deal with the influx of outdoor workers, actively recruited trade union officials as foremen. The No.1 Branch lost its president, treasurer and secretary within a month. The purpose of manufacturers in recruiting trade union officials may have been more complex than a simple desire to bolster supervision,[36] but all too often the solution backfired as ex-union officers proved to be tactless and overbearing foremen which fuelled the workers' already strong resentment at their presence.[37] Furthermore, the peeling off of this strata of local union officialdom presented the young socialist militants with the opportunity of becoming branch officers. Richards, for example, began his meteoric rise up the union hierarchy when he was elected vice-president of No.1 Branch in 1892.

A much wider and perhaps more important implication of the successful outcome of the 'indoor work' issue was the contribution made by the 'finishers' to the internal relations of production in the Leicester footwear factories. The existing groups of workers in the factories, mainly lasters and clickers, were steeped in craft tradition. The lasters in particular had successfully resisted the process of subdivision and in the years immediately before the implementation of the lasting machine enjoyed a high degree of autonomy over the labour process. The extract from the monthly report of October 1881 quoted in Chapter 2 demonstrates that the lasters shared the language of craft common to other artisans of the period.[38] The historian, however, has to be wary of such florid language as it did, after all, have a propaganda function. On the other hand such rhetoric was a celebration and affirmation of the lasters' independence. The importance of the finishers' arrival in the factories is that this sense of independence endemic to lasters became intermingled with the finishers' own boisterous form of work autonomy. This injection of workshop culture into the existing atmosphere of craft autonomy provided a unique and important dimension to industrial relations in the Leicester trade in the three stormy years between the arrival of the finishers in the factories in 1892 and the lock-out of 1895.[39]

The anti-arbitration movement and the success of the 'indoor working' campaign were both important in the changing pattern of union politics and local industrial relations, but another factor, the arrival of the lasting machine, was to overshadow even these two major developments. Since the start of the trade's industrial revolution with Crick's riveter in the early 1850s, full-flow mechanized production had long been anticipated by Leicester manufacturers. The major obstacles to this process, poor technology and an abundance of labour willing to partake in subdivided work activities, have already been outlined in Chapter 2. Elsewhere in the industry technological development followed a chequered pattern. In Northampton, for instance, which specialized in good-quality men's boots, a certain amount of hand work was still demanded by customers which resulted in smaller units of production and a smaller reliance upon machinery than in Leicester.[40] By contrast the firm of C. and J. Clark of Street in Somerset was in the vanguard of technological innovation. This company had long been hampered by labour shortages and recruitment problems, having on occasion to resort to hiring female workers at agricultural fairs on three-year indentured contracts.[41] Furthermore, the Clark family had long refused to have any dealings with the American shoe machine companies, choosing instead to embark on their own programme of invention and innovation. The result was that by 1880 the Clark factory, with its own closely guarded patented machines, was the first British shoe plant to employ a fully mechanized team system.[42] Similarly the Massachusetts industry, spurred on by high demand during the civil war, had perfected mechanized team production by the early 1870s with lasting remaining the only area of hand work.[43]

Leicester gradually incorporated Massachusetts technology, albeit in a somewhat uneven manner. In 1853 there were four firms in Britain manufacturing the early crude types of shoe machinery and by 1896 this number had expanded to 24.[44] This growth in the number of shoe machinery firms, however, disguises the increasing domination of the British market by the United Shoe Machinery Company (USMC) of America, and the Leicester company of Pearson and Bennion. These two companies eventually merged in 1899, taking over many of the smaller firms in the process, to form the British United Shoe Machinery Company (BUSMC).[45]

The machine companies that existed in the 1880s had concentrated on two types of machinery. The 'stitchers', which attached the soles to the uppers, were produced by the American company, while an assortment of British firms manufactured finishing machinery to compete with those produced by USMC. The domination by the Americans, and their British licensees, Pearson and Bennion, of the 'stitcher' market, and their insistence on leasing rather than selling their products, allowed them gradually to dictate the mechanization policy of individual firms. For example, a shoe manufacturer who wished to lease the American 'stitcher' had to sign a contract with the machine company committing his firm to use only machinery prduced by USMC throughout the factory.[46] The tendency of this development was for USMC gradually to introduce the mechanized team system into Leicester factories. The more progressive manufacturers welcomed this trend and even Day, whose 1903 essay was written as an attack on the BUSMC and their leasing system, gave encouragement to increased mechanization in the 1880s and 1890s.[47]

The 'team system' as devised in Massachusetts finally overcame the remaining obstacle to complete mechanization with the invention of the Consolidated lasting machine in 1889.[48] When this machine was displayed in a Northampton showroom, NUBSO expressed much concern. The machine, which utilized self-adjusting power nippers to form the leather on the last, was considered superior to hand work, and even more worrying was the fact that the laster was demonstrated 'alongside other machines which were all manned by strong youths and linked in a team system'.[49]

It is difficult to gauge accurately the extent to which Leicester manufacturers adopted the new technology. Our sources are silent on the number of firms which introduced the new machines in the early 1890s. We do know, however, that those factories which placed the USMC's Consolidated lasters on the shop floor in this period had great difficulty in persuading the workforce to operate them. Day ruefully compared the performance of a Leicester laster in 1892 with his Massachusetts counterpart:

> In Leicester if they run a machine for five minutes at full speed, they seem to think it necessary to stop it and see that no breakage has occurred. Then they walk about the shop and borrow an oil can or spanners wherewith to do some totally unnecessary thing. This occupies anything from five minutes to an hour, and then the machine is run again for a few minutes, and if the operator is questioned he says 'machines are no good; I could do the work quicker and better by hand'. And so he could, for he takes care not to let a machine beat a shop mate working by hand on the same job and in short does all he can to induce manufacturers to abandon mechanised devices and go back to hand labour and not to earn as much money as possible per week, but as much as possible per job. In other words to keep the cost of production as high as possible.[50]

The manufacturers did not take much persuading to introduce the lasting machines in the early 1890s. As yet American competition was only affecting markets outside Europe and good profits could still be attained from the home market.[51] In January 1890 the Leicester trade was said to be 'the best in living memory', while as late as May 1893 full employment was recorded in local footwear factories.[52] Indeed early 1893 was to prove a watershed in the Leicester trade. Business was so good that the union report for May noted a shortage of lasters in Leicester, an unusual comment as NUBSO was traditionally reluctant to mention the existence of vacancies for fear of a major influx of applicants from other areas which would have the effect of lowering local wages. The report, however, went on to note that Leicester manufacturers were rapidly introducing lasting machines in an attempt to overcome the shortage of workers.[53]

Immediately following this Indian summer the fortunes of the Leicester trade rapidly diminished. By August 1893 the industry was depressed. In September the Board of Trade's correspondent reported that 'The relations between employers and employed are much strained in consequence of continuous disagreements respecting the new system of employment brought about by the rapid substitution of machine for hand labour.' The seasonal cycle of demand asserted itself the following May when lasters were again in short supply, but this revival was not of the same scale as previous years.[54] The demand for lasters does, however, signify the success of NUBSO's rearguard action against the implementation of machine lasting, but as Head's study has shown the British footwear industry in the mid-1890s was on the brink of collapse. Overseas markets were rapidly falling into American hands and the once secure home market was feeling the first effects of the Massachusetts invasion. Most worrying for Leicester

104

was the popularity and high quality of American ladies' footwear and the vanguard role that these products played in their manufacturers' export drives.[55] Leicester may have been in the forefront of British factory production but the town's speciality of ladies' footwear and the dire state of local industrial relations made the local trade an easy target for American competitors.

Under these circumstances the Leicester manufacturers were forced to act quickly. To meet like with like, mechanized lasting had to be introduced. The employers, no longer able to rely upon the moderating role of the old union leadership, began to lay plans for an eventual showdown with the workforce. In December 1890 the union reported in an ominous tone a meeting at the Bell Hotel in Leicester between manufacturers from the town and other footwear centres in order to form a national employers' organization.[56] The first tactic of the new association was to set up an elaborate bargaining machine known as the 'National Conference' and consisting of equal numbers of employers and union representatives. The new device was in reality a grandiose arbitration scheme that relied on the decision of an independent umpire. The first conference was held in Leicester in August 1892 at the Town Hall with the mayor in the chair and each side providing nine delegates. The employers were anxious to settle the question of discipline amongst the workforce and in particular the behaviour of the finishers recently brought 'indoors' from the workshops.[57] The union, however, deftly side-stepped this issue and brought the question of boy labour to the fore. The conference failed to solve this problem and the matter was therefore referred to the umpire, Sir Henry James. The umpire's eventual verdict was that boy labour should be restricted to one youth, under 18 years of age, to every three men.[58] This was undoubtedly a major success for the union and a setback for the employers.

As yet the machines in the factories were still largely operated by men and the union's fear that an influx of 'strong youths' would both displace adult males and facilitate the full implementation of the 'team system' had been averted. Furthermore, the existing status quo had received the highest seal of approval.

Before the conference the employers' association had altered their rules to facilitate a national lock-out. The authority of Sir Henry James's decision had made a lock-out politically difficult but the threat of such action had been made against the Northampton boy labour campaign earlier in the year.[59] The vexation of the Leicester manufacturers was further increased when Richards and the socialist militants began to attack the tendency towards day-work wages that had been creeping into the more mechanized local factories. The socialists embarked on a two-pronged strategy: Richards and his colleagues, who now controlled the No. 1 Branch, ordered union members in those factories who were working day work to restrict output to the number of shoes produced under the old piece-work system that equalled the value of the flat daily wage. Richards shocked the local arbitration board when they sat to consider the union's action, by illustrating the case of one man receiving 34 shillings per week for producing 65 dozen pairs using modern methods, 'thus earning ten pounds eight shillings', the sum the worker would have been paid under the old statement price. 'He [Richards] always told the men to earn their money and no more.' Members who broke the union output quota were summoned before branch officials and fines were imposed varying between 2s.6d. and one pound.[60]

The socialists' second strategy was, ironically, recourse in 1894 to the local arbitration system in order to negotiate a statement for mechanized lasting. Richards, however, insisted that the rate per piece should be exactly the same as the old hand work statement, thus depriving the manufacturer of any benefit from mechanized production. The Webbs point out that this strategy appealed to 'the operative bootmaker [who] has inherited a rooted belief that the legitimate reward of labour is the entire commodity produced, or its price on the market. This idea was the economic backbone of Owenite Socialism, with its projects of Associations of Producers and Labour Exchanges.'[61] The Webbs are typically perceptive in their explanation of the tactic's popularity. They underestimated perhaps the role of the new generation of socialists in propagating the idea, and their leadership. Fox has also qualified the Webbs' argument by drawing attention to the strategy's job protection function; by restricting output the workers were attempting to retain the maximum number of jobs.[62] Fox, however, by being predominantly guided by macro-industrial relations notions, such as orthodox collective bargaining procedures, and employee protection schemes, fails to draw out the important dimensions of craft autonomy and the workers' control of the speed and rhythm of the labour process. Both were at the core of the output restriction and piece-work campaigns of 1893–4.[63]

Given such a combination of motives on the part of the workforce an equally obdurate stance by the manufacturers was inevitable. Inskip and the union executive had become a powerless rump, out of touch with the membership and only retaining office because of the union's system of tenure. Real and effective power was now in the hands of the Leicester socialists whose large branch membership gave them the power to dominate union policy. The confrontation between the manufacturers and the union which took place at the lock-out of April 1895 is a well-documented major episode in British Labour history and it would be pointless to reproduce the full details here.[64] Instead a theme that has largely been ignored but which has been emphasized in this chapter, that of the laster and the lasting machine, will be explored.

This dimension has been hidden from history largely because both the protagonists in the 1895 dispute had interests in keeping it hidden. Furthermore, the events of 1895 were seized upon as an ideal example for their model by the Oxford school of industrial relations. Brunner, for example, notes that 'No lock-out or strike has taken place since 1895.' 'The conciliation machinery then established has been taken as a model for other trades.'[65] Thus 1895 becomes the centre of an industrial storm, which when passed leaves a new system of organizational 'solidarity' based upon strong employers' associations, a strong union leadership and a national system of collective bargaining. This new 'modern' system is contrasted strongly with the defunct pattern of local arbitration, local union autonomy and a weak leadership unable to impose its will. The Oxford school does acknowledge the role played by mechanization in the 1895 lock-out but fails to distinguish between types of machines and the composition of the workforce.[66]

There is a tendency in the historical sources available, particularly union documents, to obscure the lasters' domination of NUBSO. The union after all was seriously concerned with the business of recruiting other sections of the labour force and was thus reluctant to publicize the fact that it was essentially a sectional organization. Great emphasis instead was given to the recruitment of clickers, finishers and women closers. Yet before 1895 these groups were a minority of the union membership.[67]

The union in Leicester was, nevertheless, anxious to present itself as a genuine industrial union. During a period of rapid technological change survival depended upon extending union membership as widely as possible in order to retain the existing demarcation system. Indeed, the lock-out of 1895 was brought about by NUBSO's spirited campaign to gain an advance for clickers. Alongside this claim the union inserted the demand 'that all work cut in Leicester shall be made in Leicester', a long-standing source of trouble no doubt, but one which was gaining a new urgency when NUBSO realized that some manufacturers were threatening to remove the lasting machines to the country villages or had already done so.[68] The manufacturers, in the meantime, had imposed seven principles upon the union to govern the trade's industrial relations. These principles, known as the 'seven commandments' by the workforce, gave the employers arbitrary rights over the working of the new technology, severely curtailed the activities of the local arbitration board and ruled out any wage increase for two years. With the loyalty of the clickers assured the scene was set for a bitter battle, which was to last for five weeks and seriously depleted the NUBSO treasury.[69]

Central to the dispute was the need the manufacturers saw to break down and eradicate the craft autonomy and system of self-regulation amongst the lasters, in order to turn the industry's workforce into semi-skilled machine operatives. As we have seen, the union could not publicize the centrality of the lasters' craft to the dispute for fear of creating sectionalism. The employers likewise realized that if the lasting issue became prominent they could be accused of vindictiveness against the officer stratum of the union. This point was recognized by the Bishop of Peterborough, Mandell Creighton, during his attempt to act as conciliator between the two parties. Writing to Sir Courtney Boyle, the permanent secretary of the Board of Trade, who was also attempting to mediate, the bishop noted:

> At present the position of the masters is very strong. The men are out of their calculations, this is the busiest time of the year, and they thought the Federation would break up through the inability of the smaller employers to hold out; but (1) the Federation has shown unexpected strength; (2) Public opinion has not been enlisted on the men's side. The men cannot expect to win the country work. I think they must withdraw; the question is how?
> ... Clickers and finishers need complicated machinery; but the work of the lasters, though done by this machinery to some degree, is not absolutely dependent upon it. Simpler machinery that could be used even at home would suffice. At present the lasting is done in the factories: but the men know this is not absolutely necessary. Further the lasters are the representatives of the oldest part of the transformed industry. They have the old traditions and are strongest in the Union. If the pressure of the Union was unreasonable, the masters could at a pinch withdraw some of the lasting to the country. Then the clickers and finishers would be dependent on the country workers and the strength of the Union would be broken. Both sides see this and they are fighting with reference to this occult possibility in the future. The present is not of much moment: not much work goes into the country, and not much gain is made of it.
> ... The men's cry "Work begun in Leicester to be finished in Leicester" is like an attempt to build a great wall of China and so be secure.[70]

The lasters failed to build their 'wall' and the manufacturers' victory was sealed by the men agreeing to nearly all of the seven proposals. The settlement which the workers were forced to accept ensured fundamental changes in working practices and industrial relations.[71] The 'Richards principle' of linking payment for mechanically produced goods to the old hand work rates was killed off by making piece-work payments discretionary to the manufacturer. The latter also fixed piece rates based on 'the actual capacity of an average workman'. The employers' ability to impose the day-work payment system, together with the modified method of piece work, no doubt improved productivity and flexibility and, what is often overlooked, tightened factory discipline. For example, the worker paid by the day was always 'in the boss's time', while absenteeism, especially St Monday, became an expensive luxury with workers being unable to make up the loss of wages by extra effort during the rest of the week. Local arbitration was retained but in a diminished form. The right of employers to refuse to employ any particular worker was not now negotiable at the local boards and thus the door was open to victimization. Similarly boards of arbitration could no longer discuss the question of country work.

Manufacturers were also allowed under the settlement to 'make reasonable regulations for time keeping and the preservation of order', a point which was to be seized upon later by employers during disputes arising from pace-driving foremen. The introduction of machinery was now entirely at the discretion of employers. The terms of settlement effectively destroyed the old system of industrial relations. The disciples of St Crispin were now thoroughgoing semi-skilled factory operatives. The previous informal and self-regulating work rhythms had been replaced by the relentless pacing of the foreman and machine.

It will be shown in Chapter 11 that the industry was rapidly restructured during the remaining years of the decade, the factories by 1900 being largely manned by semi-skilled operatives, paid by the day and working to speeds dictated by the machine companies. Such profound changes in the relations of production were quickly to be reflected in local politics. Local class relations became extremely antagonistic. The mood of the shoe workers during the dispute was foreshadowed 14 months earlier when Cores the anarchist, seconded by Richards, proposed to a crowded meeting of No. 1 Branch the resolution that 'Hundreds of unemployed who are able and willing to work are in such a state of starvation that they will be compelled and entitled to take the means of subsistence by illegal methods unless help is speedily forthcoming.'[72] The other side could be equally audacious and there is some evidence that local manufacturers, perhaps with the hosiery strike riots of 1886 in mind, bought firearms during the lock-out.[73] The NUBSO old guard who played such an important role in the local Liberal alliance were already experiencing a decline in their local influence amongst the working-class electorate. By 1899 when Inskip died, the 12,000 NUBSO members in Leicester contributed £2 0s. 3d. to his testimonial fund.[74] Major changes in Leicester politics were under way in the early to mid–1890s and the structural developments in the footwear industry described in this chapter provided the motive power for these political shifts. The next chapter will chart and analyse the changing contours of working-class politics in Leicester during this period and highlight the role of shoemakers in the development of socialism in the town.

9 Leicester Socialism, 1890–95

Socialism in Leicester up to 1890 was largely the product of structural change within the hosiery industry combining with the intellectual ferment that occurred within the local Secular Society during the mid-1880s. Continuities with previous working-class movements are clear. The Leicester Socialist Leaguers were the intellectual heirs of a local tradition that stretched back to Chartism and Owenism. When the veteran socialist John Sketchley lectured at the Secular Hall to a meeting on socialism, chaired by Warner, we can see an extraordinary juxtaposition of historical themes and personalities: Sketchley, the old Chartist leader and founder of Britain's first Social Democratic Club in Birmingham; Warner, the son of another local Chartist; and the Secular Hall itself, the physical expression of the tenacity of local Owenism.[1] The subject of Sketchley's talk was new but the activist circle in which he mixed and whom he addressed at the meeting were remarkably similar to those whom he led 45 years earlier. In particular the presence of the hosiery workers' leaders suggests continuity.

Yet by 1890 hosiery was far less significant to the Leicester economy than it had been in the 1840s. The trade now accounted for only 21.5 per cent of the industrial workforce, a figure which was roughly half the 1840s proportion. Moreover, the industry was increasingly becoming a female occupation. Women made up over 66 per cent of the trade's workforce of 12,667 in 1891. Even the male activists from the LAHU present at the meeting were the representatives of a minority in the trade. The LAHU membership was 1,500 early in 1886 of whom 600 were men, mostly Cotton's patents operatives.[2] Given such a small social base it is not surprising that socialism was still a phenomenon that existed on the fringe of the local Labour movement in 1890.

Furthermore, socialism shared with trade unionism the problem of recruiting women to the ranks. Only two females, Barclay's sister Kate and Warner's daughter Clara, were active in the local Socialist League. Apart from material and sociological obstacles to female participation in Labour movements, which have been explored elsewhere,[3] employment opportunities for women were bright in hosiery, where their numbers rose from 5,308 to 8,381 in the decade 1881–91. Thus women were not subject to the same threats and problems that faced the adult males in the trade.

110

Besides the problem of a small membership, socialism was also beset by other major difficulties at the end of the 1880s and during the early 1890s. In particular the crisis in the Socialist League nationally and the ascendancy of anarchist ideas had important implications for Leicester. The hard core of the socialists including Barclay, Gorrie and Warner attached themselves and the branch organization to the growing anarchist tendency. Leicester also became an important venue for anarchist speakers. In August 1890 Barclay reported that

> Two members of Freedom Group paid visit to Leicester S.L. in July ... The workers of Leicester seem to regard Anarchism with favour ... Municipally Leicester seems to realise Sidney Webb's idea of Socialism ...
>
> Our Leicester comrades although nominally a branch of the S.L. are in reality Anarchist-Communists. They are constantly preaching Anarchism, and they have neither council, committees, rules nor regulations.[4]

Both Creaghe and MacQueen, two leading figures in the Freedom group, became temporary residents in the town, while as we have seen Cores, a future editor of *Freedom*, spent several years in Leicester employed in the shoe trade.[5]

Yet Barclay exaggerated the strength of the anarchist movement locally. The emphasis of the Leicester group's activities was still centred upon propaganda and the need to make socialists. The anarchists refused to organize and their tendency to frown upon committees and rules was perhaps their greatest attraction to the Leicester activists. Having 'neither council, committees, rules nor regulations' allowed them to continue what they enjoyed most: holding public meetings preferably outside in fine weather. Indeed in many respects the Leicester group's espousal of the principles of *Freedom*-style anarchism was paper thin.[6] The Sheffield anarchists, particularly their chief spokesman, Creaghe, opened up a rift between Leicester and the movement nationally when they attacked the Leicester men for religious toleration. Barclay, the long-standing secularist, thus found himself in the paradoxical position of defending Christianity. Creaghe's attack was in fact aimed at Gorrie, Barclay's close friend, who was active in both anarchist and Christian Socialist circles.[7]

If Barclay and his followers preferred to concentrate on *ad hoc* propaganda campaigns, others were showing interest in laying down organizational foundations. J. Billson, the secularist manufacturer who had been a member of the League in the mid-1880s, had by 1890 joined the Fabians.[8] The ascerbic remark about Webbian socialism quoted above from *Freedom*, August 1890, was a veiled reference to the growing interest in Fabianism that Billson was generating locally.[9] More significantly the group were failing to attract new recruits amongst shoe workers in the turbulent years of the early 1890s. In the spring of 1892 the Leicester group reported that 'agricultural workers show more interest in anarchism than shoe hands',[10] while both the last issues of *Commonweal* and the subsequent volumes of *Freedom* refer to local defections to the SDF.[11] If

Barclay and his followers refused to dilute the purity of their beliefs with organizational compromises, others were not so inflexible. The question, of course, had to be asked, what were the alternatives to 'making socialists' and were they as undesirable as the 'Socialist Leaguers' feared?

Stephen Yeo, in an important essay, has argued that the fervour and enthusiasm of socialist activists in the 1880s and early 1890s were dissipated when socialists began to compromise their religious-like faith in their dealings with other sections of the Labour movement.[12] David Clark in his recent book on Colne Valley has enlarged Yeo's ideas by firmly pointing the finger of guilt at trade unionism as the major obstacle to the growth of ethical socialism during the period.[13] The very concepts of a 'religion of socialism' and 'ethical socialism' are of course highly problematic,[14] but a more important aspect of the debate has perhaps been left untouched. What were the alternatives on offer in the early 1890s to, on the one hand, the nihilistic activities of the anarchists, and the apparently teutonic statist obsessions of the social democrats on the other? Furthermore, the debate on socialist strategy in Leicester was carried out against a backcloth of large, popular trade union organizations. The major weakness in the Yeo essay is that he is discussing in general terms what was essentially a local problem. For example, Clark's survey on the fellowship of socialism in Colne Valley and the community spirit engendered in the Labour Clubs of the constituency is a description of political activity undertaken in unique circumstances. The valley had an unusually low level of trade unionism for an area noted for its lack of religious participation, and, more important, was physically made up of small towns and villages with no focal centre. In such an area socialism was able to fill the many gaps available in both working-class political and communal life. In contrast, Leicester already possessed strong working-class institutions, most notably trade union branches,[15] working men's clubs and cooperative societies as well as informal areas of working-class community activity such as pubs, football grounds, cricket pitches, parks and a racecourse. Ultimately the growth of socialism in Leicester was to depend upon winning over existing working-class institutions to the socialist cause.

Such a strategy was largely precluded by Barclay's firm espousal of Morris's nostrum that socialists had to be made, his growing impatience at working-class apathy as shown above by his derisory contrast between agricultural and industrial workers, and the growing local presence of anarchism. Nevertheless, it was during this period of apparently personal political impasse that Barclay undertook what were perhaps his greatest contributions to the local Labour movement.

The most enduring of Barclay's achievements during this period was his establishment of a local Labour press. Mention has already been made of his journalistic activities with the *Countryman* but this venture was to be overshadowed by his initiative in setting up a socialist weekly exclusively for the Leicester Labour movement. Exactly when the *Pioneer* first saw the light of day remains a mystery. The earliest surviving copy is in the IISH periodical collection in Amsterdam, numbered 'new series No. 6, old series No. 157' and is dated 3 January 1895. The journal appeared weekly which suggests that it was at least three years old in 1895. This issue was edited by Barclay and published by the *Countryman*. The *Pioneer's* style and sophisticated layout are testimony to Barclay's quickly acquired journalistic expertise. Despite its humble size, eight pages, the *Pioneer* was a lively read. For one halfpenny the claimed 5,000 readers were given football reports, league tables, train timetables and, theatre and book reviews, as well as information on the local Labour movement. Barclay may have been borrowing techniques from Blatchford's *Clarion*, but this should not detract from his own strong ideas on what a good socialist newspaper should contain, ideas that we have already seen expressed in his comparison between *Commonweal* and *Justice*. Approximately 15 per cent of the paper's contents were advertisements, although we have no way of assessing what this meant in income terms. It does, however, question his claim that advertisers fought shy of the *Countryman* because of its strong political opinions.

The *Pioneer* represents another continuity with Barclay's roots in the Socialist League, this being yet another tool employed to make socialists. The political position of the *Pioneer* also reflects Barclay's own tolerant attitude to various socialist groups and personalities. In a particularly fierce debate in 1891 between anarchist revolutionaries and the followers of Morris, Barclay gave full expression to this toleration. 'I am a friend of Creaghe and a friend of Morris and Carpenter, but a greater friend of Socialism.'[16] The consequences of such a political position were that Barclay failed to give leadership to the local socialist movement in the early 1890s, while his easygoing attitude to anarchism precluded him from playing a more formative role in the establishment of links between socialism and the larger Labour movement that were to take place in the mid-1890s. The earliest surviving issue of the *Pioneer* displays Barclay's political predicament clearly. Barclay had opened up the pages of the *Pioneer* to the recently established local Independent Labour Party activists. A fierce debate was waged between the groups. Salt, of the ILP, charged that the 'Anarchists were unwise in not trying their strength by getting on Councils of different kinds. Why not improve the people immediately if possible? The people did not understand anarchism but they could understand the ILP.' Warner replied for the anarchists saying that they were 'more numerous than the ILP but kept no books and levied no subscriptions'.[17] This reluctance to organize was to prove the Achilles heel of Leicester anarchism. Two issues later Barclay had been removed as editor, the newspaper was firmly controlled by the Trades Council and the ILP, and to rub salt into the wounds of the anarchists the new editor gleefully reported that the anarchists had been expelled from the Labour Club.[18]

113

LEICESTER LABOUR CLUB,

The Home of Socialists.

JUBILEE BUILDINGS, Bedford Street.

All sympathisers should join the above at once whose objects are to elect, morally and financially, persons to all public bodies, pledged to the Programmes of the I.L.P. and S.D.F., and to encourage healthful enjoyment, recreation, and mental improvement. All kinds of games provided.

Spacious Library	**Skittles**	**Drafts**	**Cricket**
Billiards	**Cards**	**Chess**	**etc., etc.**

HEADQUARTERS OF THE **I. L. P.**

LECTURES.—Sunday Morning, 11 a.m., and 6-30 p.m.
CONCERT.—Saturday, 8 to 11. Sunday Evening, 8 to 10.

ENTRANCE FEE, 1/- CONTRIBUTION, 6d. per month.

Present Membership, 540.

ALL KINDS OF NEWSPAPERS AND PERIODICALS PROVIDED.

Fig.2 Advertisement for the Leicester Labour Club, 1894 (Leicester Trades Council Annual Report, 1894: courtesy London School of Economics and Political Science Library)

The Labour Club was another of Barclay's bequests to the Leicester Labour movement. Again, as with the *Pioneer*, it is difficult to establish its exact date of origin. The initiative for the club's formation, as we have seen, was taken by Barclay and other radical hosiery workers at a dinner to celebrate the Paris Commune in 1888. The club is mentioned in the Trades Council report for 1893 and was to figure in the formation of the local ILP in 1894. The club appears to have acted as an umbrella organization for various socialist groups, providing the platform for the open debate between anarchists and ILP members in January 1895. By this time, however, the socialist activists of NUBSO began to apply their organizational experience to the affairs of the club. Martin Curley, the staunch lieutenant of T. F. Richards, in his capacity of club secretary, carried out the expulsion of the anarchists.[19]

Barclay appears to have been disillusioned by the events that surrounded the *Pioneer* and the Labour Club and soon left Leicester for London and a short career in the Gaelic League.[20] Surprisingly little reference is made to the Labour Club in his autobiography, while no reference at all is made to the *Pioneer*. Perhaps the events of the period left deep scars in his memory; after all his closest friend Archibald Gorrie, who continued his anarchist activities up until the late 1890s, must have been somewhat annoyed at Barclay for having provided their rivals with two major local institutions that were eventually used against the remnants of Branch 13.[21] The *Pioneer* continued for a few more issues after the anarchist expulsion but then disappeared for several years. The precedent of a local Labour press had, however, been set and the newspaper was to re-emerge and perform a useful service after a five-year lapse.

Despite Barclay's efforts in laying down socialist institutions, as the 1890s progressed he and his followers found themselves forced to the margin of the political arena by a second generation of young socialists, based in the footwear industry, whose conception of socialist strategy was markedly different from that of the Socialist League.

Barclay's problem was that his long commitment to the philosophy of Ruskin and Morris had endowed his group with a deep suspicion of 'statism' both nationally and locally. Such a stance held little attraction for shoemakers in Leicester who had long enjoyed the benefits of organization. The young socialist shoemakers from the No. 1 Branch, in particular Richards and Curley, were becoming increasingly aware that they could follow the example of the union's Liberal old guard, and harness the power of NUBSO in Leicester for local electoral purposes.[22] The SDF were never to be popular in Leicester, but in the early 1890s they filled the vacuum created by the Barclay group's refusal to participate in organizational work. Like the League, the Federation found difficulty in both establishing permanent accommodation and presenting regular activities throughout the year. They did, however, manage to recruit Richards and the other young NUBSO militants.[23]

The failure of the SDF to establish itself in Leicester poses many important questions. Why, for example, did they fail to attract more disaffected shoemakers in a period when the industry was experiencing painful structural change? This failure is even more curious when we consider that both the shoe town of Northampton and the shoe districts of London were to become SDF strongholds.[24] Yet we must remember that Leicester was different from other shoe towns in several key respects. First, trade unionism was more important in Leicester than other shoe towns. For example, NUBSO in Northampton could only muster 600 members in 1888 compared with Leicester's 6,323.[25] This represented one trade unionist to every 20 shoemakers in Northampton, in contrast to the Leicester figure of one trade unionist to every 2.4 workers in the Leicester trade in 1891.[26] Trade unionism amongst London workers was as weak as it was in Northampton. Secondly, the structure of the industry in Leicester was far in advance of the Northampton trade, being increasingly dominated by mechanized factory production. Thirdly, the difference between local popular traditions was most marked, especially the role of secularism. In Northampton the organization of free-thought had never been as strong as in Leicester, a fact which is perhaps obscured by the close identity

115

between Bradlaugh and Northampton.[27] Secularism in Northampton thus took on the colour and tub-thumping style of the town's MP, a movement dominated by a demagogue which displayed more affinities with Chartism than with the studious Owenism that characterized the Leicester movement.[28] It was from the working-class followers of Bradlaugh that the SDF emerged in Northampton. In particular, James Gribble, a member of an old 'infidel' family who became leader of the local movement, displayed many Bradlaughite characteristics.[29]

These factors do not, of course, give a total explanation for the success of the SDF in Northampton and its failure in Leicester. But they do question the model put forward by Hobsbawm, which equates social democracy with a strong Anglican tradition, while the Independent Labour Party emerged in areas of nonconformity.[30] Both Leicester and Northampton considered themselves centres of dissent. What moulded the nature of early socialism in both towns was the interplay of distinct local forces: in Leicester a rapid process of mechanization, strong trade unionism and a rather studious cadre of young socialists; in Northampton a slower pace of mechanization, the persistence of small units of production and a stratum of activists drawn from the town's rumbustious political tradition.

Thus social democracy in Leicester faced an array of obstacles in the early 1890s. First they had to compete with anarchists to gain popular attention.[31] This split in the working-class political movement further deprived the SDF of the services of a significant sector of the local activist stratum. Furthermore, in a period when the SDF was trying to overcome its recent identification with riots and demonstrations the party locally often found itself being drawn along similar lines in their efforts not to be outdone by the anarchists. Richards's seconding of Cores's demand for looting illustrates the point. The social democrats were also hampered by their politics of 'statism'. Such a belief in abstract notions of nationalization, and the state ownership of manufacturing industry, held little appeal to a generation of workers who were only just beginning to experience the rigours of factory life. The response of these workers to the factory regime was to be, as we shall see in the following chapter, a demand for self-regulating producers' cooperatives. The most important check, however, on the growth of local social democracy was the strength of the existing Labour movement, especially trade unionism.

The attitude of the Federation's leadership to trade unionism and their espousal of the concept of the 'iron law of wages' is well known.[32] This ideology was largely propagated by Londoners in London, where there was a very narrow trade union base and where the problem of cooperation between social democrats and trade unionists was virtually non-existent. Harry Quelch, the editor of *Justice*, summarized the relationship between the Federation and trade unionism in 1891 in the following terms:

> The business of the social democrats as trade unionists is to permeate their
> trade unions with social democracy and on no account whatever to sacrifice
> to mere trade organisations that energy and enthusiasm which ought to be
> devoted to the spread of social democracy and social democracy alone. Look
> at it how we will trade unionism, old or new, can never reorganise society.[33]

The problem was, of course, that Richards and his colleagues owed their
position, and its continuation, to their vigorous pursuit of trade union
matters. The Federation has undoubtedly received a bad press on its
attitude to trade unions, and recent work on Burnley suggests that the
SDF could, on occasions, find a niche in local trade union organization.
But the role of the Burnley social democrats was always on the fringe of
local trade unionism and they were never tested by the reality of assuming
power. Indeed, the buoyancy of the Burnley economy, prior to 1914,
sustained the Lib-Lab leadership of the local trade union movement and
contained the socialists to a marginal role, while the strength of local Lib-
Labism served to confirm the SDF belief in the inherent limitations of
trade unionism.[34] In contrast the problem faced by the Leicester social
democrats was highly specific and touched a nerve in British social democratic philosophy. They were attaining union office and local prominence
by their fierce campaign to protect the autonomy of the laster and by
attempting to stop the encroachment of mechanization. Such forms of
trade unionism were anathema to the SDF leadership who held rather
crude evolutionary ideas on the whole process of industrialization. Their
position was spelled out with the utmost clarity by H. W. Hobart of the
London Society of Compositors, and SDF spokesman on trade union
affairs, at two lectures he delivered to Leicester social democrats in 1892.
Hobart informed his Leicester audience that 'Trade Unionists unfortunately do not appreciate the economic forces at work in society, and the
consequence is that instead of giving way voluntarily on certain points,
which evolution in production and distribution render inevitable, they
turn obstinate, and false issues are raised which bring defeat.'[35] What
Freddy Richards, who chaired the second lecture, thought of such ideas
we can only imagine.

The nostrums of the SDF leadership did not, however, curtail the
energy and enthusiasm of Richards and his colleagues in their trade union
activities. The emergence of the socialist leaders of the No. 1 Branch and
the issues which accompanied their progress have already been surveyed.
The questions which now have to be asked are, what were to be their
political objectives and how were they to use their recently acquired
power? The answer to the first question is that the young socialists,
prompted by both the Championite ideas on a working-class political
party, allied to the trade union movement, and the sheer weight of local
circumstances, were to set off hesitantly down the path, first mapped out
by Engels, towards the formation of an independent party of labour.[36]
The SDF's critique of such a strategy was to be abandoned, in the firm

belief that the first and most important task facing socialists was to form a truly class-based organization. Vast layers of the working class had to be peeled away from liberalism and moulded into a new party, a party which they believed because of its composition could not be anything but socialist. With the benefit of hindsight such a strategy can be considered naïve in the extreme, but when we consider both the local context and the political alternatives available, what other direction could socialism in Leicester have taken?

The tactics for achieving this goal were largely determined by the answer to the second of the above questions. The power available to the Richards circle was largely contained in the No. 1 Branch. To achieve their political objectives the socialists had to harness this power to change the union's political policy, which in turn would facilitate the intervention of socialism into local electoral politics. This strategy, however, was not as clear-cut nor as easy as the above formulation would suggest. Two obstacles had to be overcome. First, Inskip's political control of NUBSO had to be broken, and secondly, the local Trades Council, the major local working-class political institution, had to be won over to the cause of socialism.

The political position of NUBSO, which under Inskip's control had been firmly Liberal, had to be changed in order to gain union support for socialist candidates. The demands of both No. 1 and No. 2 branches for independent political representation, voiced in 1891,[37] were again expressed at the 1892 biennial conference. Support for this change in policy came from the London Metro branch whose representative, Votier, pointed out that only independent working-class Members of Parliament would be able to secure the legislation necessary to ensure the full implementation of the London indoor work agreement.[38] The resolution put to the floor by Votier calling for union support for independent Labour representation in Parliament was carried by 42 votes to 4. This decision came too late to facilitate any intervention in the July general election, but it did have the important effect of stemming the growth of Lib-Labism in local elections as the resolution was generally interpreted as applying to both local and national polls.[39]

Inskip's control was further eroded by Richards and Curley's resolution calling for union support for cooperative production schemes. The general secretary was particularly hostile to the socialists' demand that union funds should be used as venture capital for cooperatives. The idea of cooperative production was deeply held by the socialists, who saw it as no mere palliative but rather as the building blocks of the socialist commonwealth.[40] More importantly, in terms of union politics, cooperation could provide a common cause for both socialists and the less doctrinal Liberal delegates. Thus by pushing the issue of cooperative production the socialists were able to increase Inskip's isolation from the main body of delegates. The resolution proposed by Richards committing union funds to cooperatives received widespread support, but an amendment left the initiative to individual branches rather than to the use of central funds.[41]

During the two years between the conferences of 1892 and 1894, Leicester No. 1 Branch had been extremely active in supporting cooperative schemes. A committee had been elected to implement cooperatives, members were levied, £1,000 of branch funds had been placed at the disposal of cooperative pioneers, and shares in the new factories had been sold to NUBSO members. By July of the following year the main recipient of this support, the St Crispin's Cooperative, began production.[42] Set against the background of the union leadership's growing unpopularity throughout the membership during the last phase of the anti-arbitration campaign, cooperative production appealed to both moderates and militants as an escape route from the industrial anarchy of the period. Thus when Inskip protested at the space given to a display of St Crispin products on the conference floor in 1894 he found himself under bitter attack from all sections of the union.[43]

The majority of delegates who supported cooperative production did not, of course, see such schemes in the wider political context of a socialist strategy. But the debate increased their growing suspicions that Inskip was firmly rooted in the past and was failing to alter his beliefs with the rapidly changing economic and political circumstances. His isolation and loss of control over the union machine was completed when the conference turned its attention to political matters and in particular the troubled question of his proposed candidature for one of the Northampton parliamentary seats. Inskip, who was also the union's parliamentary agent and therefore the union's potential MP, had put himself forward to stand alongside Labouchere as a Liberal for Northampton. Richards, with a touch of sarcasm, suggested that Inskip was getting a bit too big for his boots, pointing out that as well as being the union's general secretary and parliamentary agent, he was also an alderman, a magistrate and the treasurer of the TUC parliamentary committee. The resolution by Votier and Richards to make the post of parliamentary agent a distinct one and 'that in no case shall it be held in conjunction with the General Secretaryship or the General President' was passed unanimously.[44]

Inskip clung to the belief that this rules amendment did not affect his forthcoming electoral position. This hope was reinforced by the growing dissatisfaction with the resolution passed at the previous conference which committed union candidates to stand independently of the two major parties. Many delegates pointed out that the possibility of local Lib-Lab pacts was being thwarted by this rule. Richards, however, strongly protested against any revision: 'he could not ... support the candidates of Liberal Associations ... That very class of people were their enemies ... They must go step by step to educate the constituencies.' Conference was not persuaded. Many delegates came from areas where Lib-Labism still had much appeal, particularly Leeds and Northampton, and, of course,

Woolley and several Leicester men were in favour of revision, while those London delegates grouped around Charlie Freak of the Metro branch were anxious to join hands with London progressivism. Richards did not lose entirely. His rider that committed the candidates to the political programme of the union was accepted without argument.

This last point was to be the undoing of Inskip's parliamentary hopes. No sooner had the issue of independence been settled in the general secretary's favour than an amendment to bring the political programme of the union in line with the socialist one adopted by the TUC the previous year was put to the floor. It was decided that a hastily convened special committee composed of Freak, Poulton, Richards, Woolley and Bradley should present a new programme to the conference the following day. Their document presented to conference for approval was virtually the same as that adopted by the TUC and called for the 'Nationalisation of the Land and the implements of production'. The mood of the conference was that the union, then the third largest in the country, should fall in line with the TUC, while the more flexible Lib-Labers such as Woolley and Poulton envisaged little difficulty in continuing their political careers under the new programme. Indeed when Inskip, objecting to the clauses on nationalization, tried to pass an amendment for their exclusion from the programme, no delegate was prepared to second it. Inskip, outmanoeuvred, steadfastly refused to forsake his *laissez-faire* credo and announced to the departing delegates his intention not to stand as the Liberal candidate for Northampton.[45]

The socialists had not been totally successful in their attempt to harness union power to their political carriage. Lib-Labism remained as a form of political organization which had the approval of the union. Yet the spread of Lib-Labism had been checked in the important years between 1892 and 1894 by the socialist resolution at the Stafford conference. Moreover, when Lib-Labism was re-established as an approved form of political activity in 1894 its potential for future growth was checked by the new political programme. The socialists were, however, victorious in breaking Inskip's political control of the union. The close relationship between the NUBSO executive and the Leicester Liberal Association was now a thing of the past. Furthermore, as Richards and Curley increased their control over the No. 1 Branch, they were secure in the knowledge that any future shoemaker councillor would have to tie himself to the union's political programme in order to gain both the support and resources that were at the disposal of the branch.

Parallel to these developments in union politics, initiated by the socialists, was the local campaign to gain Trades Council support for the growing new movement. The Leicester Trades Council, like so many others, was formed in 1872 in the midst of the 'Criminal Law Amendment' controversy. Initially representing eight societies, by 1900 it provided a forum for 34 organizations representing over 20,000 members.[46]

During the 1870s and 1880s the Council had been in the mainstream of working-class politics, endorsing candidates to the town council and school board. Daniel Merrick, the Council's president, was their first nominee, winning a seat on the school board in 1877. Ties with the Liberal Association were further cemented in 1886 when Merrick and Sedgewick nominated the Liberal parliamentary candidate, McArthur.[47] The bonds between the Council and the Liberals were finally sealed in 1890 when several Labour Association candidates were elected. Such ties were, however, to prove shortlived. The Council's report for 1891 decorously noted the elevation of Inskip to the aldermanic bench, an act which was to prove the last of Liberal patronage towards the Council.

The socialists' presence on the Trades Council and their growing influence in the organization's affairs was made relatively easy by the large presence of hosiery and footwear delegates. By 1891 these two unions accounted for 13,500 of the Council's 17,000 membership.[48] It was not long before Holmes and Warner of the LAHU were joined by socialists from NUBSO. The first issue which expressed the changing political complexion of the Council was over the call for a May Day demonstration in support of the Eight Hour Day in 1893. After some hesitation, which included changing the Council's rules on representation to reduce NUBSO's presence,[49] the demonstration was held on 7 May.

Five meetings were held in various parts of the town and the events of 7 May reached their climax when a reported 10,000 people crowded the market square in the evening.[50] The anarchists who had long lobbied for the demonstration were active at each gathering, much to the Trade Council's chagrin.[51] The major controversy, however, was created by Joseph Potter, a local shoemaker and future leader of the Equity Boot Cooperative, when he spoke to the crowd in the market square. Potter, a well-respected local trades unionist, sat on the Trades Council as the delegate for the local branch of the Labour League. This organization has been described by the Webbs as being essentially a friendly society, while Clegg, Fox and Thompson have noted its close association with the Land Nationalisation Society.[52] Whatever its genealogy the Leicester branch is shrouded in obscurity, only ever receiving mention in Trades Council reports. The fact that the League locally claimed 800 members suggests that it may well have been a friendly society. Potter's speech was highly rhetorical, claiming that Picton, the local MP, who had recently voted against the Miners' Eight Hour Bill, 'was, or had been a parson and a capitalist'. He went on to note that 'They might as well send a leopard in sheep's clothing amongst a flock of sheep as send a capitalist to represent the workers in Parliament.'[53]

Potter may well have been the local 'championite' sarcastically referred to in the anarchist account of the meeting.[54] The fact that the Labour League ceased to be represented on the Trades Council after 1894, when the local branch of the Independent Labour Party was formed, may be

121

more than coincidental. There is much evidence to suggest that H. A. Champion did have a provincial network of activists in the early 1890s pursuing his plan for the organization of an independent labour party closely linked to trade unions.[55] Further evidence to support the claim of a 'Championite' presence in Leicester is furnished by the arrival of Arthur Field in the town. Field, an itinerant photographer, was at the ILP inaugural conference at Bradford where he sat as the Leicester delegate and won election to the executive, a curious fact as no branch of the ILP existed in Leicester at that time.[56] Field, despite being a firm follower of Champion, nevertheless was on good terms with Champion's political opponent, Joseph Burgess.[57]

Despite the obscurity that surrounded local Championite activity it is clear that the idea of an independent working-class political party, closely linked to trade unionism, was gaining a local hearing. Moreover, other sections of the local Labour movement were becoming sympathetic to socialist ideas. Carter, the secretary of the engineers' branch, and the local typographers, helped to swell the socialist presence on the Trades Council. This trend even began to thin the ranks of local Lib-Labism. J. H. Woolley, Inskip's main lieutenant on the NUBSO executive, Trades Council delegate, and a successful Labour Association candidate at the 1890 local elections, quickly trimmed his political position to take account of the growing call for independent Labour politics. Perhaps Woolley realized that Inskip's orthodox liberalism was becoming untenable during a period when industrial turbulence in the shoe trade was being increasingly identified with local liberalism, especially when shoe manufacturers formed the largest single group of Liberal councillors. Woolley cleverly began to distance himself from Inskip. At the May 1894 NUBSO conference he opposed Inskip and supported the socialists' resolutions in favour of cooperative ventures and banning overtime. More importantly he gave guarded approval to the resolution calling for independent working-class political candidates.[58]

Woolley was not the only important Lib-Laber to alter his political beliefs in the light of changing political circumstances. George Banton, the carpenters' delegate, president of the Trades Council and Liberal general committee member for the Westcotes ward,[59] became increasingly disenchanted with liberalism. Jabez Chaplin, a full-time official of the LAHU, Trades Council delegate and Liberal general committee member for Latimer ward,[60] had long toyed with socialist ideas, and he also began to climb off the Lib-Lab fence. There is even some evidence which suggests that Potter was an active Liberal in the Westcotes ward.[61] With such a growing defection of important local working-class figures from liberalism the Lib-Labism of the Trades Council was weakening. This is not to suggest that there was a stampede to socialism. Many Trades Council delegates, particularly from the smaller trades and occupation groups, continued to support liberalism locally. The initial vote on whether or not to hold a May Day rally in 1893 went against the socialists.[62] It was the narrowness of the decision and the uproar which followed that made the council reverse its original order. Moreover, the Trades Council tactic to limit subsequent demonstrations to bona fide trade unionists has to be seen as both an attempt to preclude anarchist lecturers and a strategy to reduce the socialist aura of the event by including non-socialist speakers.[63]

This lukewarm response to the growth of socialism in the ranks of the Trades Council finally foundered on the unique electoral events of 1894. In March Picton, the senior member, announced his retirement from the House owing to ill health. The Trades Council held a meeting to consider their likely nominations or endorsements of potential candidates. The name of Henry Broadhurst was mentioned as a possible choice which provoked the anger of the socialists.[64] Despite Broadhurst's previous reputation as the premier working man in Parliament, the scandal which surrounded his involvement with the Brunner Chemical works and his attacks on socialists at the TUC had both tarnished his reputation amongst trade unionists and made him a prime target for a socialist attack. Furthermore, his long-standing partnership with William Inskip gave his nomination a certain piquancy amongst some sections of the local Labour movement. The outcome of the Trades Council's deliberations on the subject was a compromise. They decided to back Broadhurst only if he stood as a Trades Council candidate, independent of the local Liberal organization. Such a position was, of course, unacceptable to the Liberal Association, which went ahead and nominated Broadhurst as a Liberal-Labour candidate.

The decision of the Liberal Association gave the socialists on the Trades Council the opportunity they had been waiting for. The Richards group still retained tenuous membership of the SDF and under the auspices of this organization and the local Labour Club they invited Keir Hardie to speak at the local ice rink on 2 June.[65] The meeting was organized by 'Mr. Chatterbox'[66] of the SDF and chaired by Richards. The meeting was ostensibly designed to satisfy a growing local interest in the ILP. The new party's leader did not have an easy time. He was grilled by the Leicester men for over an hour on the integrity of his commitment to socialism. Hardie concluded with a statement that stressed the ILP's strong espousal of the collective ownership of land and capital 'without which political reforms were the merest shadow'. He then visited the Labour Club where he warned the members against 'turning the Club into a lounge for loafers', pointing out 'that liquor and labour don't mix'. The article in the *Labour Leader* which reported these events also went to great lengths to praise NUBSO's 'splendid organisation in Leicester'.[67] Hardie's visit was in many ways a softening-up operation designed to bring the Richards group into the ILP. His warning against alcohol had often been given locally by Richards, himself a staunch teetotaller, while Hardie's interest and support of NUBSO's 'militants'' organization was in stark contrast to the utterances of the SDF on militant trade unionism.

Richards appears to have quickly embraced the ILP brand of socialism, particularly its emphasis upon socialism being allied to the broader Labour movement. The following month he wrote to Hardie requesting the party's National Administrative Council to forward a candidate for the coming by-election.[68] Richards asked for a 'strong candidate to oppose Broadhurst' saying that 'only a very strong man could bring about Broadhurst's defeat'. What Hardie wrote in reply to Richards is unknown but an unusual twist to local politics was to accelerate the growing relationship between the NUBSO militants and the ILP.

Before the by-election could be held the junior member for Leicester, Whitehead, also tendered his resignation in early August. Rather than hold two separate polls it was decided to hold a double by-election on the date originally set to find Picton's successor, 18 August. The Liberal Association had to find another candidate to join Broadhurst. They chose W. Hazell, the owner of several printing works, including a profit-sharing plant in Aylesbury, and a man who considered himself 'a friend of Labour'. Richards wrote to Hardie pointing out the new circumstances and demanding a firm reply to his request for a candidate.[69] Hardie responded by sending no less a person than Tom Mann, the secretary of the party, to investigate the possibility of fielding a candidate in Leicester. The arrival of Mann was to prove a turning-point in Labour politics in Leicester. David Clark has already shown the effect that Mann had upon Colne Valley, especially his ability to attract wide sections of the Labour movement to the ILP.[70] Mann's reputation as both a leading trade unionist and a socialist was the ideal combination for winning over the Trades Council in support of Joseph Burgess, the hastily nominated ILP candidate. So effective was Mann's speech to the Trades Council that George Banton, of the carpenters' union, president of the Council and erstwhile Liberal committee member, joined the ILP, becoming the first president of the Leicester branch. Mann's role as campaign organizer was assisted by the Liberals' choice of Hazell as Broadhurst's partner. The local branch of the Typographical Association, a union which was also threatened by structural change from the new linotype machine and consequently adopting a socialist position in politics, was notified by its executive of poor labour conditions in Hazell's factories.[71] In particular Hazell's non-union Aylesbury plant was singled out for comment by the typographers who described it as 'one of the worst rat-houses in the country'.[72] This intervention by the typographers was to be vital in winning the support of the Trades Council for the ILP candidate. At first Banton had pointed out to the Trades Council meeting that Hazell and Broadhurst were satisfactory candidates. The Trades Council had had a good record in nominating Lib-Lab candidates for local elections and most importantly the Council was short of funds.[73] Mann countered with his impressive speech which appealed to the Council's sense of class by pointing out that Hazell was an employer. Burgess had a deep knowledge of the hosiery trade.[74] But the decisive point was that the NAC would make money available for Burgess's campaign.[75]

The Liberals were not disturbed by Burgess's intervention. After all, the ILP man had no local organization and his financial resources were meagre in comparison with those available to Broadhurst and Picton. The Conservatives saw the by-election as their chance to score their first victory since 1861. The Conservative candidate, J. L. F. Rolleston, a local surveyor and land agent, enjoyed the advantage of being a local man, while his strong imperialist beliefs, which emphasized the need to acquire new markets, could appeal to both workers and manufacturers in the footwear industry who were beginning to feel the harder effects of international competition. Rolleston was also prepared to trim his policy to suit working men: for example, on the issue of the 'Miners' Eight Hour Day' he was at one with the Liberal candidates.[76] Burgess, by emphasizing the need to nationalize land and the means of production, set himself well apart from the other candidates. His statement that 'Socialism would have to be carried out either by the vote or the bomb' may have been designed to silence local anarchist opposition but it must have also left the electorate in no doubt as to his own political position.[77]

The rush to hold the double by-election left the ILP little time for preparation. Burgess did not arrive in Leicester until four days before the poll. Burgess and Mann, his campaign manager, were, however, joined by Hardie and Clynes in what turned out to be a spirited campaign by all parties.[78] Although Burgess came bottom in the poll the voting figures were highly encouraging for the ILP and shocked the local political establishment. Broadhurst was returned as senior member with 9,464 votes while Hazell, who was also returned, could only muster 7,184 votes. The Tory hope that the Burgess candidature would take votes from the Liberals and let their man in was nearly realized. The 6,967 votes cast for Rolleston were only 217 short of the total gained by Hazell. The ILP were even more heartened than the Conservatives by the result. Burgess, in only four days of campaigning, received 4,402 votes, nearly 16 per cent of all votes cast, and as each voter had two votes, a considerable larger percentage of the voters must have marked their ballot papers in favour of the socialist. Hardie was jubilant, calling the Leicester by-election 'the thousand votes a day campaign' and claiming that the newly established Leicester branch of the ILP had over 700 members.[79]

Hardie may have been exaggerating the size of the membership of the new branch. The earliest precise figure that is available is contained in the ILP conference report for 1897 which credits Leicester with 120 members, making the branch the thirteenth largest in the country. It was, however, to be unusually well grounded in the local Labour movement. Banton, the Trades Council president, became branch president. Richards, the main initiating force in the emergence of the Leicester ILP, was also undoubtedly the most powerful local trade unionist of the period. Holmes and Chaplin, the two leading officers of the LAHU, became founder members. The branch also enrolled trade union leaders from smaller occupational groups. Lowe and Hill of the Clickers No. 2 NUBSO branch were both prominent party members as was Carter of the Amalgamated Society of Engineers (ASE) and Kenny of the trimmers, while print workers were always present in the early period of the party. Tomblin of the Shop Assistants' union was soon to join the new branch and became an early delegate to national conferences.[80]

Such a solid base in the local Labour movement augured well for the new branch. Membership continued to grow throughout the 1890s, against the national trend, while the financial condition of the branch was constantly being praised in the ILP press.[81] During the early years the branch was to remain a solid working-class organization with no prominent middle-class members. With the exception of Tomblin of the Shop Assistants' union, most of the men mentioned in the above paragraph were representatives of skilled manual workers, the majority of whom considered themselves craftsmen. Furthermore, all these trades were experiencing major structural change, which uniformly carried the threat of craft dilution. What attracted this section of the Labour movement to the ILP?

We have already surveyed the growing relationship between the NUBSO militants and the young ILP in detail but some general comments are required to make sense of the party's wider appeal. First the ILP, as seen through the eyes of the leaders of those sectors of the Leicester Labour movement facing a crisis of craft, was essentially a party led by men not unlike themselves. Clynes, Hardie and Mann, who shared Burgess's electoral meetings, were all men with a strong trade union background and like the Leicester activists they too had sound knowledge of the limits of trade union activity. But unlike the leaders of the SDF, the ILP officers realized the importance of harnessing trade unionism to political activity. Socialism, whatever its merits might be in offering a solution to the ills of the world, could not win votes if it was seen to be in isolation from the major institutions of the working class. With the backing of a local Trades Council and the presence of local trade unionists, the socialist candidate could appeal to the class instincts of the working-class voter. Richards understood all too clearly that his power-base in trade unionism existed not because of his socialist beliefs but because of his activities as an ardent advocate of his members' interests. His socialist faith obviously played a major part in determining the overall trajectory of his trade union actions but his members' growing exposure to socialism came from a different perspective. For them socialism was inextricably identified with a new style of trade union action. Socialism above all was about work, its organization and the social relations of production inside the Leicester factories. Burgess and the coterie of ILP speakers recognized this fact clearly from the start. The campaign conducted by Burgess made little reference to poverty or wider social issues, choosing instead to concentrate attention on Hazell in his capacity as a dubious employer and on Broad-hurst's association with the Brunner chemical firm. Thus socialism in its first outing into local parliamentary politics was presented as a further extension of the battle against the employer class.

The ILP could also appeal to the sense of status within the local working class. By presenting an array of youngish successful trade unionists as their main representatives in the town, the party was perceived in both class and status terms. On the one hand none of the party's major representatives in Leicester could be seen as class collaborationists during this period. They were, after all, in Leicester trying to dish the most notable Lib-Laber in the country. On the other hand they were not riff-raff. Burgess was the editor of the *Workman's Times*, a newspaper whose appeal was largely directed to the organized and hence by definition better-off worker. Hardie, with his background in the proud collier tradition of Scotland, positively oozed working-class respectability.[82] Mann, a skilled engineer, was in this period returning to the problems of the skilled worker, a point emphasized by his advocacy of cooperative production schemes.[83] Perhaps all these figures had learned vicariously from the SDF the small returns that were to be gained in political terms from fighting for the unemployed and disorganized. Even if this was not the case they all knew that what political power the working class possessed lay largely in the hands of the organized worker.

The composition of the Leicester branch endowed the party locally with an ethos not dissimilar to that of a trade union branch. The assumption of officer roles came easy to a group of men well experienced in organizing trade union branches and Trades Council meetings. Despite these advantages the domination of the Leicester ILP by trade union officials did have some shortcomings. Women, for example, found difficulty in both par-taking in and identifying with a political group that closely resembled the intensely masculine milieu of local trade unionism. This problem was compounded by the ILP holding its meetings in the Labour Club, an establishment from which women were excluded.[84] This male exclusive-ness on the part of the ILP is of course a manifestation of the origins of the local party in the trade union movement, but it also reflects a distinct cultural shift in local socialism. Gone were the days when Kate Barclay and Clare Warner shared stints with their male colleagues on Socialist League platforms. Similarly, Mrs Saunderson's article in the *Pioneer* of 3 January 1895 was laden with references to Carpenter and Bebel, references that can be interpreted as both an appeal for feminism and a lament that the new socialist organization was cutting itself off from all forms of influence that did not have a direct bearing on 'the Labour Question'.

It would, however, be unfair to characterize the early Leicester ILP as only a slate of trade union branch officials. The composition of the party was tempered by a small yet significant group of members whose background was in local marginal religious organizations. The ILP was to draw support from three such bodies, the Church of Christ, the Salvation Army and the spiritualists. It has been pointed out in a previous chapter that these three bodies were part of a wide expansion in fringe religious organizations during the period, but what exactly the connections were between the ILP and this form of religious affiliation is difficult to establish. Millenarianism was a strong theme amongst these groups and perhaps the ILP was seen as part of some wider benign convulsion. All three groups had strong traditions of sacramentalism which may have disposed some of their members to the egalitarianism of the socialist doctrine. Yet what scant evidence is available does not support such generalizations. ILP members from this type of background rarely spoke on the links between their religious and political beliefs. Furthermore, this type of ILP member was often acting in isolation from other members of his congregation. The Church of Christ, for example, was extremely active during the 1890s establishing a boot manufacturing cooperative and a garden city at West Humberstone, developments which coincided with many socialist ideas of the period. Yet only one member from the sect, J. T. Taylor, as far as can be established, joined the ILP. It must, however, be noted that Taylor, the ILP branch treasurer, future town councillor and conference delegate, was the manager and first president of the sect's cooperative which suggests that a major section of the congregation saw no contradiction between Taylor's political and church activities.[85]

On the connections between spiritualism and socialism, Barrow has drawn attention to continuities between Owenite socialism, spiritualism and the socialism of the late nineteenth century and it is not surprising that Leicester, with its strong Owenite tradition, gave expression to this development. Both the Socialist League and the SDF used the Spiritualist Hall in Silver Street for meetings at various times. The Silver Street circle contributed three founding members to the ILP branch, Chaplin, who was also an LAHU official, Bibbings, their full-time lecturer, and Bent, an unemployed laster.[86]

Amos Sherriff, a notable Salvationist, left the Army when he joined the ILP. Sherriff had no trade union background, having raised himself from being an illiterate brickyard labourer to owning his own cycle shop. Like so many other young socialists, Sherriff's first exposure to the new doctrine was at a Barclay lecture.[87] Sherriff was elected as a reserve executive committee member at the branch's formation meeting. He was also the central figure in the small local *Clarion* readers' group, his shop being the outlet for the official Clarion cycle.[88]

This group of activists in the early Leicester ILP tended to be overshadowed by the trade union officials. This is not surprising given the local context of industrial upheaval which dominated the 1890s. Yet their presence widened the appeal of the party, particularly amongst those sections of the working class who were not fully employed skilled workers, a factor that was to prove crucial to the widening local electoral success of the ILP in the early years of the following century.

The branch's first activity in local elections followed rapidly on the heels of Burgess's late August campaign. Flushed with the success of the 'thousand votes a day' by-election the newly formed branch announced that it would contest the forthcoming November 1 local polls if resources could be found.[89] Banton, never one to exaggerate, told a crowded meeting, convened in the Cooperative Hall to discuss election policy, that although the branch had 800 paying members on the books, the party had not enough funds to mount a campaign. The question thus shifted to the Trades Council who decided that individual societies would have to decide their own electoral policy.[90] This decision was obviously sensible. Many unions were still firm believers in Lib-Labism and some of their delegates sat on the Council on the Liberal side.[91] To commit Council funds to wage battle against leading delegates would create deep wounds. Moreover, there may have been a feeling that NUBSO, having solved the question of election finances at its recent conference, was in the best position to carry the major burden. The LAHU, which was expected to join NUBSO in providing electoral money, was, however, faced by strong opposition from its members in the country villages who objected to 'being mulcted by Leicester'.[92]

The issue was resolved at a meeting in the Cooperative Hall when NUBSO claimed their right to 'call the tune' and nominated Curley as candidate for Latimer Ward and Richards for the Wyggeston Ward. Despite the obvious domination of NUBSO this choice received the universal approval of the meeting. The significance of working people acting independently in elections without outside aid was not lost on the local press who gave the meeting wide coverage, while Barclay found the event so stirring that he forgot his long-held objections to electoral politics and gave a strong speech in support of Richards.[93]

The problem of contesting local elections raised other issues apart from organizations and finance. What were the significant issues for the Labour movement in terms of local politics? The experience of the recent by-election and the campaign of the ILP was not instantly translatable into local affairs. Attacks against Hazell as both an unscrupulous employer and a carpet-bagger could feed into the rising discontent against the employer class in general but the local Liberals, lionized by the local press and with their many local connections and Lib-Lab allies, were not so easily vilified. It is true that many local manufacturers were also members of the town council, but the local Liberal Association had astutely nurtured a policy of placing Lib-Labers or 'friends of labour' in working-class wards. Furthermore, local government politics in this period could be intensely parochial in character and the determining electoral issues could often be particular to a ward rather than to the town in general. The traditional way of coping with this problem would have been to embark upon a muckraking campaign, keeping 'personality' constantly to the fore. Yet both Curley and Richards were themselves controversial figures and thus open to retaliation.

The problem was solved by the Leicester ILP's programme of municipal reform. The central focus drew attention to the council's role as an employer both currently and potentially. This position undoubtedly harmonized with the growing resentment against employers expressed during the recent by-election. The major plank in the ILP municipal programme was the demand for better pay for council manual workers. Banton demanded that all municipal workers should be paid the same rate as police constables.[94] This was more than an attempt to court the council workers' vote; it is doubtful if they were a large enough group with the ability crucially to influence the poll. Rather the wages strategy has to be seen in a wider perspective, alongside the campaign being waged throughout the country, particularly by the followers of Champion, to force local councils to establish a 'Fair Wages' policy.[95] This tactic, moreover, was designed not only to improve the material circumstances of municipal workers, but also to establish a system of model employment which could eventually be emulated throughout the community.

The working out of this policy can be clearly seen in the rest of the ILP municipal programme, especially the way the various components slotted together to form a cohesive whole. For example, the socialists demanded that the local bakery, milk and coal industry be municipalized which would not only ensure greater quality control but also expand the 'Fair Wages' sector and perhaps enable work to be found for the unemployed.[96] A further call was made for slum clearance and the erection of municipal artisan dwellings, controlled not by the private landlord but by the corporation.

Both Curley and Richards were defeated in the November poll, but Richards was given a second chance when the councillor for Wyggeston was elevated to the aldermanic bench. This ward by-election was to prove the first victory for the new party. Richards reversed his defeat of three weeks previously with a majority of 81 votes.[97] So with a slightly higher turn-out, and presumably a more prepared organization, Richards showed that an independent Labour candidate could win. It must, however, be remembered that Richards was a minority of one in the council chamber and it was not until 1896 that his lonely presence was supplemented by the arrival of George Banton, the representative for the Latimer ward. Despite these two successes the party faced an uphill climb in local elections. The ILP's first attempt to gain a foothold on the Board of Guardians was a total failure, all six candidates coming bottom of the poll.[98] The branch had gained a toehold but nothing more. This is perhaps surprising considering the fact that the party was fielding local working men as candidates in working-class wards, most of whom were already established figures in the Labour movement, during a period of serious industrial disruption. How do we explain the ILP's poor electoral performance at municipal elections?

130

The answer to this problem is complex and like most electoral analysis involves an element of speculation. The first and clearest factor working against the ILP candidates was their youth. Richards was undoubtedly hurt by charges from the opposition that the ILP candidates were 'beardless youths'.[99] He attempted to ignore the taunt but the charge was loaded with an important electoral significance. For example in March of the previous year Richards, while addressing a union recruitment meeting for women workers, told his audience in jest that half of his branch's 11,000 members were single men and that he would 'forbid any of them to court a non-unionist (laughter)'.[100] In this joke Richards exposed his political vulnerability. He was after all only 30 years of age himself, while his political base in the union was founded upon his popularity amongst the young, and probably single, shoe workers. The battles within NUBSO were fought along generational as much as political lines. Translated into votes at municipal elections his industrial strength counted for little. How many ardent supporters of Richards possessed the municipal franchise? It is impossible to answer this question, but intuitively one suspects that the support for the older Lib-Labers was more concretely expressed at the ballot.

Despite the emergence of class as a political phenomenon in Leicester politics it is important that sight is not lost of the shifts being made by the supporters of class collaboration. Woolley as we have seen had been careful to distance himself from Inskip in NUBSO policy, while Amos Mann of the Church of Christ and the Anchor cooperative factory made a point of sitting next to Richards on the council bench.[101] Indeed most of the local Lib-Labers, with the notable exception of Inskip, trimmed their political beliefs in the face of the rising socialist tide. Woolley in particular made a point of speaking in support of Richards in the November campaign, while in the following October the ILP municipal programme was accepted by the Trades Council with no opposition. The Lib-Labers were also actively drawing attention to the traditional radical Liberal alliance with progressive working-class movements. The *Midland Free Press*, the most radical of the local Liberal newspapers, ran a series of weekly articles in 1893, entitled 'Former Struggles of Labour', which emphasized the old relationship between working-class movements and radical liberalism. This initiative by the Lib-Labers culminated in the setting up of the 'Cooper Memorial Fund' headed by Cort, the NUBSO branch president and a Lib-Lab Guardian, to raise money for a statue to commemorate the Chartist leader.[102] The ILP no doubt felt affronted by Lib-Lab attempts to claim the heritage of past Labour struggles. Even Burgess had referred to it, telling his audience at a crowded public meeting that the Liberals 'expected the I.L.P.ers back in the fold just like the Chartists'.[103]

This Liberal hope was not to be realized. Eight years were to pass before the ILP were able to expand their electoral base, but what they achieved in 1894 remained solid and withstood Liberal attempts to undermine it both at local and parliamentary elections. The general election of 1895 was largely a repeat performance of 1894. Broadhurst and Hazell were again returned, while the Conservative, Rolleston, narrowed his margin with Hazell to 99 votes.[104] Burgess polled nearly 400 votes less than at the by-election, a drop which can be explained by the ILP's holding Sunday election meetings which offended some sections of the local community. The demand by Burgess to outlaw the employment of children under 15 may also have upset some shoe finishers, many of whom still retained the privilege, granted in the 1891 indoor working agreement, to employ two boys on a sub-contract basis inside the factories.[105] Thus 1895 was not to be a repeat of the 1894 'thousand votes a day' campaign but the ILP had proved their durability, while the narrowness of Hazell's victory over Rolleston gave the Liberal Association much cause for concern.

By 1895 the Leicester socialists had achieved as much as circumstances would allow. Major sections of the local Labour movement were now allied to the ILP, while the grip of the Liberal Association over working-class politics had been broken. Moreover, the new generation of working-class leaders, men like Banton, Chaplin and Potter, who under different conditions would have taken over the reins of the working-class Liberal alliance from Inskip and Smith, were firmly based in the socialist camp. Deprived of this new blood the future of the old alliance was bleak. Yet while the future offered little hope for liberalism, socialism had reached an apparent impasse. Four thousand votes for the ILP candidate may have seemed a respectable turn-out for a new party, but the ILP had neverthe-less failed to expand its appeal to wider sections of the working-class community. The truth was that the party was still essentially rooted in the skilled section of the two local major trades. During the mid to late 1890s Richards, Curley, Chaplin and Holmes were to expend as much energy pursuing cooperative production as that spent on purely political work. The problem faced by the socialists was in a curious way similar to their failure as trade unionists to recruit greater numbers of female and less skilled male workers. Perhaps the socialists, despite their youth, were in many ways stuck on the tracks of craft sectionalism. Despite the arrival of class, both as a form of language and analysis, politics were still perceived as being primarily about the world of work. Indeed it would be difficult to refute the cynic's charge that Leicester socialism circa 1895 was little more than an expression of the enlightened self-interest of certain previously privileged sections of the workforce responding to new economic circum-stances. Yet we can detect an emerging consideration for less fortunate members of the community, especially in the formulation of the ILP municipal programme. On the other hand this new dimension was largely overshadowed by the class struggles in the footwear industry. The poor showing of ILP candidates in the 1894 Guardian elections reflect more than the electors' political weariness at having to cast votes for the third, and in some cases fourth, time in five months. The truth was that the ILP found little time or energy to spend in this area of local politics and six years were to pass before they took the election of Guardians with the seriousness that it deserved. Yet if they were to turn their backs upon the important social questions that were expressed in Guardian politics how could they hope to expand their electoral base? Before this theme is developed and the ILP's growing emphasis upon palliatives and the arrival of James Ramsay MacDonald as their parliamentary candidate are explored, it is necessary to probe more fully the concept of cooperation and its importance in Leicester politics during the 1890s. Without a fuller understanding of the changing role of the cooperative ideology the important political changes that were to take place in subsequent years cannot be understood.

10 Towards the Socialist Commonwealth? Cooperation in Leicester in the Late Nineteenth Century

An important component of local socialism in the 1890s was the idea of cooperative production. Such forms of industrial organization could appeal to both socialists and those workers whose sense of exploitation was heightened by the encroachment of mechanization. For the socialists, cooperative production had many attractions. Factories organized on co-operative principles were to provide the foundation of the cooperative commonwealth, while the emphasis upon internal self-management appeared to provide a clear-cut answer to the socialist dilemma about the relationship between workers and the state. The state was to nationalize the factories and hand them over to the workforce who would then organize production along cooperative lines. The socialists were also provided with a further bonus in that cooperative production in a town such as Leicester, with its radical traditions and particular economic structure, had an appeal far wider than socialism. In short, cooperation had theoretical, material and ideological functions of such potency that the idea became central to the socialist platform during the 1890s. Moreover, many workers were all too willing to follow the socialist crusade for the setting up of such schemes. To the embattled workers in both hosiery, footwear and other local trades, cooperation offered the possibility of controlling the influx of new technology, removing the sharp edges of exploitation then being felt by the arrival of new machines, and freezing the existing status divisions and relationships of production within the workforce. Thus for many workers, unlike the socialists, cooperation was to serve essentially conservative aims.

Yet cooperation in Leicester during the late 1880s and early 1890s was not a virgin field upon which Messrs Richards, Curley, Clarkmead, Leedham and Holmes could establish the foundations of an edifice that, given favourable political conditions, could eventually constitute a new commonwealth. Indeed the field was cluttered with the debris of the valiant attempts of more than three generations of Leicester men to build similar structures. Moreover, well-intentioned outsiders, in particular Christian Socialists, were already on the scene, superintending the erection of what were, to the socialist puritan, shaky, jerry-built walls. The vista was further complicated by the growing presence of the cooperative retail society whose new premises dominated the town's High Street. How were relations to be established between the two forms of cooperation? The men who had founded and built the retail society were local men, sharing similar ideals and impelled by similar forces to those pioneers involved in production ventures. But were the interests of the two forms of cooperation not fundamentally different and thus antagonistic? The distinction between the interests of the consumer and those of the producer may be too clear-cut to offer a meaningful explanation of the activities of men who often perceived themselves to be engaged in the single cause of cooperation. More importantly, was it possible for the socialist cooperators to find a space at all on this very crowded field? And if space was available, how were they to assume the ideological leadership of this deep-rooted movement?

The purpose of this chapter is not to present a detailed account of cooperation in Leicester. Such a task would demand a separate study. Rather its function is to illuminate the role of cooperation in the formative period of Leicester socialism in order to promote a more thorough understanding of the nature of the socialists who were shaping the new philosophy and those supporters whose aims were more conservative. The ambiguities between these two conflicting interests represent the key to understanding the social relations within the working class during the period when Leicester socialism established its first firm foundations. The first part of this chapter will examine cooperation, in both its productive and retail forms, up until the socialist intervention around 1890. This will be followed by a survey of cooperation during the period 1890–5, when a vast amount of socialist energy was expended in pursuit of cooperative goals. Finally the decline of the cooperative ideal amongst socalists will be discussed and an attempt made to explain it.

To explain the presence of cooperative concepts amongst the Leicester working class during the closing decades of the nineteenth century by reference to local radical traditions would be both a tautology and a neglect of the short-term structural factors endemic to Leicester's industry during the period. The role of tradition is, of course, crucial to the development of cooperation in the town, but the material world essential for such traditions to endure persisted in Leicester up until the years under review. The small workshops and domestic workrooms, populated by self-regulating workers, were the natural habitat of the producer's ideology of cooperative production. Since the days of Owen and beyond the device had been perceived by workers as a means of closing the production process against the exploitative activities of middlemen and capitalists.

As early as 1817 some striking stockingers had attempted cooperative production as a means of alleviating the hardships caused by the dispute.[1] Similar ventures were launched in the comparatively peaceful and prosperous years of the early 1820s, which suggests that the stockingers viewed cooperative production as more than a mere device to assist strike action. The Leicester hosiery workers were also participants in Owen's Labour Exchange scheme during the 1830s.[2] In addition there is some evidence that the young Josiah Gimson and his fellow members of the local Owenite branch practised communal living in the 1840s.[3]

During the 1850s and 1860s cooperative production appears to have lost its appeal for Leicester workers. The cooperative doctrine was, however, kept alive by Daniel Merrick, the stockingers' union leader, who together with Thomas Cook, the erstwhile Chartist sympathizer and pioneer travel agent, opened a stall in Humberstone Gate in the late 1850s for the retailing of 'essentials of home consumption' on cooperative principles.[4]

This early initiative proved to be short-lived but was reputed to have had an educative effect upon future pioneers. By 1861 a group of five elastic web weavers who lived in Wharf Street, together with J. Woodford, a glove worker, had started the Leicester Cooperative Retail Society based upon the 'Rochdale' system. Both glove workers and web weavers were amongst the highest-paid section of the workforce,[5] a point which accords with the general conclusion that early retail societies tended to be organized by and catered for the better-off sections of the working class. Elastic web weavers also tended to work in factories rather than workshops which underlines Webb's point that workers based in workshops suffering from the vagaries of seasonal employment found it difficult to start retail societies.[6]

During the late 1860s elastic web weaving in Leicester was suffering from the effects of competition from new areas of production. By 1870 men from the Leicester trade were reported to be in London offering their labour at lower rates than those paid to London weavers.[7] In the midst of this trade crisis a group of Leicester web weavers formed the Cooperative Manufacturing Society of Leicester, a producers' association that manufactured webs for the local shoe trade.[8] The web workers, however, were not the first society to revive cooperative production in Leicester. A small association of stockingers had begun a cooperative venture in 1867 with £176 of share capital and £14 of fixed stock. Profits never exceeded £28 per annum, but the venture survived until 1875 when it was bought out by the Hosiery Operatives' Union.[9] A common feature of both societies was their closeness to and ultimate reliance on the local retail society. Web weavers were dominant in the early years of the retail society and appear to have used this influence in the sale of their products to the newly established Cooperative Wholesale Society's boot and shoe factory. This plant was one of the first manufacturing initiatives undertaken by CWS. Production at the CWS works began in 1873 under the management of John Butcher, the secretary of the Midland section of the Cooperative Union.[10]

Butcher was undoubtedly the pivotal figure in the revival of cooperation in Leicester during the 1870s. Born into a Northamptonshire shoemaking family in 1833, in his early life Butcher was a follower of Ernest Jones and took part in the Birmingham demonstrations of 1867.[11] A staunch radical, he eventually settled in Banbury where he combined the managership of a small boot factory with local cooperative activities. He became the driving force behind the Banbury cooperative movement and soon rose to a position of prominence in both the Cooperative Union and the CWS. It was upon his advice that the CWS embarked upon their second productive enterprise, the first being the manufacture of biscuits, with the opening of the CWS boot factory in Leicester. His experience both as a manager of a footwear establishment and as a notable cooperator made him the prime candidate for the top post at the new factory. Yet in the early years of the CWS Butcher appears to have had no fixed opinions upon the growing debate within the society on the question of workers' self-management and profit-sharing schemes. Indeed, before the opening of the new CWS West End works, Butcher was actively engaged assisting the web weavers to establish their society. As well as being an adviser to the web weavers he also became a shareholder and used his influence on the board of management of the Leicester Retail Society to gain 'store' capital for the new enterprise.[12]

The hosiery society enjoyed similar assistance. Soon after it had been taken over by the trade union the enterprise was threatened with closure when many local trade unionists objected to funds being expended to allow the society to produce for stock.[13] This was a pertinent reminder that while workers may have given their blessing to the concept of co-operative production they were reluctant to finance such schemes themselves. This point may not be as damning as it seems. If the society was producing for stock then there was a strong possibility that the trade generally was suffering a cyclical downturn and trade union members may have objected to a group of workers enjoying the privilege of full employment based on the very money that was going to the society for unemployment relief. The simple fact was that such a small local trade union did not have the resources to back fully such a scheme. The situation was saved when G. Bastard, a member of the retail society management committee, persuaded the 'store' to assist the hosiery society.[14] Funds were provided in the form of share capital and part of the 'store's' new premises, recently built under Butcher's initiative in the High Street, were handed over to the society for manufacturing purposes.[15]

In the period when the CWS was limited to the manufacture of biscuits and boots the field was wide open for producers' societies to use the market provided by retail societies. Even in local terms the Leicester store, the ninth largest in the country with over 6,000 members in 1880, provided a major outlet for the hosiery society's products.[16] Other retail societies, who had often found difficulty in dealing with capitalist manufacturers, became both customers and shareholders.[17] This widening of the ownership base soon resulted in the society becoming embroiled in the debate amongst cooperators, during the 1870s and 1880s, over the role of labour in manufacturing enterprises. Blandford and Newell, in their history of the society, are not very informative on the early constitution. It does, however, appear to have been a self-managing workshop in the years prior to the union taking over control in 1876. After this date control first passed exclusively to the union, with Jimmy Holmes playing a prominent part, but following the influx of outside capital from retail societies, managerial power was shared by 'store' representatives and trade unionists.[18] Growing dissent, particularly by northern stores, over both the management of production enterprises and the thorny question of the 'bonus to labour' led to a crisis in 1883. The problem was solved by the society adopting a constitution drawn up by E. V. Neale similar to the one which he had recently introduced at Hebden Bridge.[19] Neale's constitution was in many ways a compromise. Managerial power was handed over to the 'stores' with the workers' committee men being reduced to a token presence of two representatives, while a bonus of 10 per cent of profits was paid to the workers.[20]

The elastic web society appears to have followed a course similar to that taken by the hosiery cooperative. A share of profits was retained by the workers but management became the prerogative of the shareholders. It could be argued that the workers in both enterprises were more interested in the financial benefits of profit-sharing than with self-management. The debate at the Hebden Bridge Fustian Mill in 1872 over the role of labour was to set a precedent for other producers' societies.[21] The sale of shares to retail societies had been under way for a number of years with the result that the management board had become diluted with outsiders. The problem came to a head when the directors from the 'stores' attempted to remove the 'bonus' from the workers. The confusing debate which followed was settled by Neale's constitution which preserved the bonus but ratified the presence of 'store' directors. Yet this was not a direct trade-off of power for money. The mill was largely capitalized by the 'stores' who had exercised *de facto* control for a number of years. The issue of the bonus, although couched in the language of cooperation, has to be seen as a last-ditch attempt by the workers to limit the rate of profit extracted from their labour. By all accounts the closely related problems of control of the production process never figured in the Hebden Mill debate. The workers were probably more than satisfied with regular wages and half-yearly bonuses; most importantly, one of the worker pioneers at the mill, Joseph Greenwood, remained as manager throughout the period. Thus it is likely that the experience of work altered little despite the change in ownership.

The experience of the hosiery society was similar to that of Hebden Bridge. Newell, the manager, positively welcomed the influx of the stores:

> The committee of the Trade Union, who were of course all framework knitters, had the management. They had plenty of knowledge how to make the goods, but they lacked commercial knowledge, what to make, and how to sell ... The chief causes of our success have been the help which the

cooperative societies have given us in capital and trade, and the fact that we have learned to put the welfare of the society before our own opinions ... [22]

Again the transition was eased by the continuous presence of Newell, one of the pioneer framework knitters, as manager. Moreover, with only 91 workers inside the factory, regular work and relatively high wages, things appear to have been generally cosy for the workers. A journalist from the *Workman's Times* described to his readers a visit he had made to the factory in 1890 in the following terms:

> I saw enough during my tour to convince me that Mr. Holmes had not exaggerated when he described the situation of those employed under the society as being a very comfortable one. There are a large proportion of women and girls employed in the factory, and as I was passing through I heard many a snatch of a hymn, with an occasional chorus; and when I can hear the melody of human voices rising above the noise of mill machinery and blending in harmonious strains of praise, I need no further evidence to convince me that the iron has not entered into the souls of the singers, and that they are as happy as it is possible for people to be in the presence of their manager and strangers, and I will give you the character of the place at which they are employed without any assistance but my own intuition.[23]

With such congenial working conditions it is perhaps surprising that local shoemakers were not active in launching similar ventures during the 1870s and 1880s. Jones, in his major survery of cooperative production during this period, lists a plethora of boot and shoe cooperatives in the East Midlands but all were located outside Leicester.[24] The main reason for the dearth of such enterprises in Leicester was the dominating presence of the rapidly expanding CWS works. It was claimed that the workers employed in the West End works 'had expected that they were producing the new millennium'.[25] Clearly many local workers predisposed to cooperative schemes were delighted with the location of the CWS plant in Leicester, especially as it was being managed by Butcher, a man with an impeccable cooperative pedigree. These aspirations, however, began to dissipate as the factory assumed a growing importance for cooperation nationally.

CWS output in Leicester mushroomed from 90,000 pairs in the first year of production at the West End works to 1,237,701 pairs in 1896 at the new larger Wheatsheaf factory.[26] As Leicester rapidly became the principal supplier of footwear to virtually every retail society in the country it became the major focus of contention on the problem of bonus payments to labour. Indeed at the moment of establishment of the Leicester works an argument developed between E. O. Greening and W. Nuttall on the bonus question. Greening, a former northern wire mill owner with a long-standing interest in cooperation, and along with Neale the major propagandist of the Christian Socialist school, proposed that labour in the West End works 'should be made partners and sharers in the profits which they created'. He added, 'They must also have the right to invest their savings in the concern, and have votes in its management.'[27]

Nuttall countered that 'the better policy was to let every worker be a member of the store and let the store make what is sold. He was then his own producer and would receive everything back in the form of dividends, and would be better off in the long run than if engaged as Mr. Greening proposed.' The debate ended in a compromise with the workers receiving a bonus but with no investing or voting rights.

The compromise proved to be short-lived. In 1876 the CWS abolished the bonus system. Just how the employees reacted to this development is unknown. But as the workforce expanded from 420 in 1876 to 1,295 in 1890, eventually reaching 2,249 in 1892,[28] relationships between the CWS and the local Labour movement began to sour. Difficulties arose when the CWS increasingly resorted to country labour for the finishing processes. The West End works were halted by a series of strikes in 1879 followed by another in 1880, and in April 1883 the CWS was accused of utilizing 'the obnoxious system of the "Middle Man" for work made at considerably lower prices than called for upon the Leicester statement'. Indeed NUBSO became so concerned with this situation that they threatened to report the CWS to the TUC.[29] Butcher, in his evidence to the 1876 Commission, admitted, under pressure from Balfour, that all the finishing work in Leicester was put out to small shops.[30] The CWS obviously did not want to incur the cost disadvantage entailed in factory finishing during these years and Butcher appears increasingly to have relished his role as an efficient manager.[31] Yet such a situation could only antagonize the trade union whose affairs were dominated by the issue of country work during this period.

Butcher was persuaded to return to the helm of the CWS works from his stint as a capitalist manufacturer in 1880. Having sat for the previous two years with his fellow capitalist manufacturers on the Liberal benches of the town council, Butcher by 1885 was a long way removed from the cooperative idealism that inspired him in the early 1870s. Indeed he now saw himself as the improving technocratic manager giving his undivided attention to 'preparing to meet an increased demand by securing the most modern English and American machinery, which is necessary to success-fully meet the evergrowing competition'.[32] Relations with employees had never been good and the factory was bound by the patterns of work that prevailed throughout the trade.[33] The return of Butcher also brought a further deterioration in industrial relations. His plans to build a branch factory at Enderby just outside the town, a village which was already being used extensively by the CWS for finishing, brought an upsurge of hostility against his new regime culminating in a major strike in 1886. The strike lasted for two weeks before the workers returned without obtaining any of their demands, but in the midst of the strike many of the workers began to discuss the demise of cooperative principles within the plant. The workers must undoubtedly have been aware of the laudatory reports like that in the *Workman's Times* on the nearby hosiery society, while their early champion, Greening, had constantly raised the question of their status at cooperative conferences.

Some of the strikers were acquainted with Greening's recent publication in the *Cooperative News* dealing with the Familistere cooperative system at Guise in France, and invited him to Leicester for informal discussions about launching a similar venture in Leicester.[34] Greening was initially apprehensive. He did not wish to raise the hopes of the workers for a venture that would have to compete against the highly capitalized CWS works and he did not want to undermine his own position in the cooperative movement.[35] The feelings of the workers, however, ran higher than he had anticipated. Charges of the misuse of boy labour and disputes over piece rates had added to the workers' anger over the 'country' question. The strikers were given a chance to express their wishes on the formation of a new society in a ballot. Over 200 workers agreed to invest in the venture and Greening was asked to draw up a constitution.[36]

The end result was a cooperative which incorporated both the Christian Socialist ideals of the self-managing workshop and the workers' desire for independence from outside investors. The new enterprise, called the Leicester Manufacturing Boot and Shoe Society and known locally as the 'Equity', began production in 1887 and by 1890 was employing 170 workers. What made Equity unique in Leicester was the fact that it came close to realizing the ideal of a 'brotherhood of workers', a point which brought grudging admiration even from Beatrice Webb.[37] All the workers were shareholding members and outside investors were only allowed one-third of the 15 seats on the management committee.[38] The start-up capital consisted of £380, £100 coming from the local NUBSO branch, the remainder from the workers. Further capital was soon provided by southern retail societies, including the Arundel and Hackney stores, while the local retail society, then under the presidency of Amos Mann of the Church of Christ community, also 'proved sympathetic'.[39] By all accounts, despite an early struggle, Equity soon prospered and new steam-powered premises were erected in Bede Street in 1889. Equity specialized mainly in high-quality men's boots, a strategy which gave them a secure niche in the market provided by the 'stores'. Profits were divided by the following formula: 15 per cent to share capital; 35 per cent to workers; 20 per cent to customers; 12 per cent to the committee; 10 per cent each to a provident fund and to share capital; 5 per cent to a social and education fund, and 3 per cent to remunerate members for special services.[40] Profits averaged out over the first ten years of Equity's existence were over £1,000 per annum, and with such an apparently secure base the members embarked on a grandiose community building project.[41]

The top floor of the new works in Bede Street contained a large hall for educational and social uses. Lloyd noted that the hall 'will seat two hundred and fifty people. There are newspapers, games, a piano of coopera-tive make, a library, portraits of prominent cooperators and cooperative curtains and windows.'[42] The 'brotherhood of workers' did not stop at the factory gate. Several building societies were formed amongst the workers and 60 dwellings erected. One street of these buildings which runs from Narborough Road towards the Bede Street factory was named Equity Road 'in honour of the works'. The houses which cost on average £400 each were far higher in quality and certainly larger than typical working-class housing. Lloyd noted that they 'contained four bedrooms, bathroom, parlour, dining-room, kitchen and scullery. There are marble mantels, attractive woodwork and gas fixtures.'[43] Plate 5, reproduced from his book, of an Equity worker proudly standing in the wrought-iron gateway to his imposing home certainly lives up to Lloyd's description.

Not surprisingly the Equity became a beacon of hope for the local Labour movement. J. T. Taylor, a worker at Equity and one of the founding members of the ILP, encouraged some of his fellow congregationalists at the Church of Christ to start up a similar venture specializing in children's footwear.[44] The tightly knit shoemaking community of the Church of Christ did not take much persuading. As well as Taylor the congregation had another notable cooperator, Amos Mann, amongst their membership. Again help was given from the local retail society and the Equity traveller carried samples from the new cooperative, called the Leicester Anchor Boot and Shoe Productive Society, when production commenced in 1893. The 'Anchor' men were even more community minded than their 'Equity' mentors. The rules of the Anchor were broadly similar to those drawn up by Greening for Equity. The members soon embarked upon plans to build their own 'garden city' on 28 acres of land at Humberstone.

In the same year that the Anchor society began production, a group of workers from the Glenfield district 'sought the advice of the Bede Street Society' about starting a society of their own.[45] This mushrooming of productive societies naturally attracted trade union interest. As we have already observed, relations between NUBSO and the CWS were anything but cordial and the union had no qualms in backing potentially rival undertakings. Capital was invested in Equity from branch funds and even William Inskip, who could be extremely hostile to cooperative schemes, had a deep admiration for the Bede Street factory as well as being a personal investor in the society.[46] The socialist trade unionists, however, especially Richards and Curley, were even more enthusiastic in their support for such a project. Indeed what differentiated the socialists from Inskip on the question of supporting cooperative schemes was the former's plan to commit union funds to launch new enterprises. The successful genesis of the Equity works had spurred Richards and Curley into believing that similar ventures were possible and that the growing funds of NUBSO should be used for them. Indeed Curley went so far as to oppose Richards during the anti-arbitration campaign, arguing that union finances expended on strikes would be better used to start cooperatives.[47]

The concept of cooperative production touched a nerve that ran to the heart of young socialist trade unionists during the early 1890s. The main tenets of this idea hinged upon the fact that where socialism did exist in Britain during the 1890s it tended to be intensely local. Conflict and struggle occurred within specific communities and socialist solutions, if they were to have any popular currency, had to be dressed in local garbs. Thus while a cursory glance at NUBSO's conference and monthly reports from the period show that the Leicester socialists spent most of their energy pursuing cooperative aims, these aims were the core of the emerging local socialist programme.

Yet, as we have seen, existing societies in Leicester were already heavily influenced by the Neale – Greening school of cooperation. Indeed this group of cooperative theorists had formed the Cooperative Productive Federation in 1882 to act both as a pressure group inside the Cooperative Congress, advocating the 'bonus for labour', and to give assistance to new societies.[48] The upsurge of interest in the late 1880s led to a renewal of the debate on labour that had dominated the mid-1870s.[49] The new Leicester societies became the van of the new producers' movement and Greening

---

LEICESTER CO-OPERATIVE

HOSIERY MANUFACTURING SOCIETY Ltd.

TO TRADE UNIONISTS.

How can the Workers obtain a larger share of the wealth produced? By Trade Unionists and Co-operators working shoulder to shoulder, and thus obtain direct control, year by year, of a larger amount of the Trade of the Country.

The Leicester Co-operative Hosiery Society employs only Trade Unionists under conditions which are commended by Trade Union Leaders. The aim of all workers should be to give a fair chance to honourable employers, to spend less in striking against bad ones, and by associated industry take their places.

You can help in this movement by purchasing your Stockings, Socks, Cardigans, and Woollen Underclothing, from the Leicester Hosiery Society through the Tailoring and Drapery Departments of the Co-operative Society, High Street.

Fig. 3   Advertisement for the Leicester Cooperative Hosiery Manufacturing Society Ltd, 1894 (Leicester Trades Council Annual Report, 1894: courtesy London School of Economics and Political Science Library)

and D. F. Schloss, the civil servant at the Board of Trade and spare-time advocate of producers' societies, gave the local enterprises much attention.[50] Thus the socialist cooperators of the early 1890s had to work within an existing ideology. While new socialist-inspired ventures could be more forthright about their ultimate aims, caution was needed in dealing with established societies. The hosiery cooperative is a good illustration of this point. The manager, George Newell, had been with the society since its birth in the late 1860s and over the years had developed a close affinity with Greening and Neale, eventually becoming a major spokesman for the Producers' Cooperative Federation.[51] By the early 1890s, however, the LAHU, which still had a presence on the board, became involved in the socialist cooperative movement. Both Holmes and Chaplin, the union's most senior officials, were ILP members and brought socialist ideas to the cooperative. Figure 3, an advertisement from the Trades Council report of 1894, shows both their influence and the persistence of Christian Socialist class collaborationism. Thus the language of 'direct control' becomes mixed with Christian Socialist pleadings for fairness to 'honourable employers' and the evils of strike action. This ambiguity was to remain within the older societies.

The centrality of the cooperative ideal to Leicester socialism did not mean that the socialist commonwealth was to be achieved by everyone becoming an employee of the store. The self-managing workshop was to become the main form of industrial organization in all areas of local activity. Burgess, the ILP parliamentary candidate, outlined this vision in relation to the local footwear industry in a lengthy *Clarion* article in the midst of the 1895 lock-out. Rooting his analysis in Marx's writings on machinery and relating this theory to the turmoil in the boot trade, Burgess claimed that the local cooperatives, which were unaffected by the dispute, offered the only solution to the problem. The question was how were the cooperatives to be generalized? Burgess replied that this could only be achieved by 'the nation boldly socialising the means of production', which in turn would be handed over to the workers to run on cooperative lines.[52] But before such a grandiose solution could be achieved the workers had to show that such a mode of organization was possible, and it was this aim which inspired the socialist activists of the period.

The ideal was not to be confined solely to manufacturing industry. We have already observed, in the previous chapter, the prominence given by socialists in their municipal programme to the extension of cooperative principles to diverse forms of municipal activity. The town council was to play the initiating role in democratizing other areas of production that lay beyond the established municipal undertakings of gas and water. Item seven of the Leicester ILP's municipal programme called for 'The establishment of Coal Yards, Bakeries, Farms, etc.', a tactic not unique to Leicester.[53]

During the last decade of the nineteenth century the state continued to

144

perform a relatively minor role in the economy. Thus while socialists subscribed to the somewhat abstract belief in the nationalization of the means of production, more often than not the idea of 'common owner-ship' took local form. The state did, of course, ultimately have a major legislative role to perform as Burgess's *Clarion* article highlights. Yet if the local community was to democratize both local industry and services, and if the immediate role of socialists was to help in laying down the found-ations of the new industrial commonwealth, how were they to escape the very circumstances that were causing havoc in private industry, this side of the legislative revolution?

To a certain extent the retail societies provided a vital lifeline by selling the goods made by the Leicester cooperatives. But even this market was to cause problems. The main obstacle facing footwear societies was that they had to operate within the shadow of the CWS works. Butcher had been none too happy when part of his workforce left to form the Equity. 'It was a creation', he declared angrily, 'of an aristocracy of labour.' It was even claimed that the CWS brought pressure upon several leather suppliers in an attempt to cut off supplies of raw material to the infant cooperative.[54] Moreover, the new boot societies had to face the threat of competition from the CWS during a period when Butcher was equipping the new Wheatsheaf works with modern machinery in order to stave off com-petition from private manufacturers.[55] This development, together with the new branch factory at Enderby, brought widespread condem-nation from the local Labour movement. Jimmy Holmes, in a letter to *Commonweal*, attacked these developments and claimed that one of Butcher's objectives in his modernization programme was to 'smash the Equity'.[56]

Undoubtedly many of the workers who established the Equity thought that the new factory would provide good working conditions similar to those enjoyed at the nearby hosiery cooperative. The producers' move-ment was closely linked to and indeed was largely a product of, the structural changes that were taking place in the private sector. Obstinate opposition to the introduction of machines was inevitable. But the pro-ducers' societies were highly selective in the machines they used. Lasting machines were, of course, frowned upon as were some of the newer finishing devices. With outmoded plant and a high element of hand work, together with competition from the CWS, life inside the Equity was no bed of roses. Certainly this worker, described by Greening, had little time, nor probably energy, to sing hymns:

> One man was stamping out those ornamental figures they put round the tops of ladies boots, 'gimping' I think they call it, by swinging round an immense level; and he was swinging it round at a tremendous rate. He never stopped all the time I was talking to him. I said 'You are working very hard, don't you stop that all day?' He said, 'No! in the Wholesale Society they have got a steam engine to do this work, and I have got to get as many dozens a day

done by this machine as their steam engine turns out, so I can't stop until I've got my number.'[57]

NUBSO were not unaware of this problem. Nor were the Leicester socialists when launching the union-funded St Crispin Society in 1893. This cooperative was started with £1,000 of capital, given by both local branches without interest.[58] In order to distance the new society from CWS competition the union decided to market the cooperative's products in their own shop rather than through retail societies. Ninety per cent of St Crispin's profits were to be devoted entirely to expanding the factory, and the society was run on self-managing principles. The majority of the committee were elected from the workforce. Clarkmead, Curley and Richards lobbied vigorously for more union funds in order to extend the scheme. At the union's 1894 conference they proposed

> (1) that £3,000 from union funds be set aside to provide a market for the sale of goods by Cooperative Societies directly connected with the Union.(2) to be used as follows: by opening retail shops in various parts of the country, say Bristol, Nottingham, Northampton, Kettering, Leeds and Leicester, with a distributive depot in Leicester. All to be under control of a committee of five and a manager; the committee to be elected by Union Vote, and the manager to be appointed by the Committee. (3) The Committee to have power to purchase goods only from Union Societies.[59]

Clarkmead asserted that this would be a notable advance by the Union. 'It would ultimately lead to the Union getting the benefit of the whole industry.' These proposals were rejected when it was disclosed that the St Crispin shop in Leicester 'had been a miserable failure. The members had failed to show their sympathy with the principle in an effectual way. They had very few members who had paid up more than one share. Such was their interest in Cooperative Production.' Clearly the workers in Leicester were not willing to invest their own capital, while the wider public's anticipated interest in St Crispin cooperative boots had been overestimated. This is not surprising: finding share capital must have been difficult for workers during an unsettled period, while the public were probably reluctant to buy the more expensive St Crispin boot.

It was hard going at both the Equity and the Anchor. Both societies were eventually forced by the competition to consider the troublesome question of machinery. The matter was so controversial that, despite Equity being given special dispensation to pay below statement wages by the union in 1893, the claim that new technology would bring a rise in wages was rejected by a considerable section of the workforce. The committee was also divided on this issue, but the plain fact that the survival of the cooperative was at stake resulted in the eventual mechanization of the plant.[60] Circumstances were no brighter at the Anchor, even though children's footwear generally involved more hand work. Mann remarked that 'there was a good deal of controversy at this time concerning this matter of the introduction of power'.[61] Again the committee was split over the issue and 'the then Committee did not see their way clearly to carry it out'. The Anchor soldiered on without machinery but in 1896 'a sub-committee was appointed to ascertain the cost of a gas engine' which was installed later that year.

The remaining years of the 1890s were primarily concerned with survival. The optimism of earlier years had dissipated. No new shoe societies were formed and those that remained often had to resort to distasteful measures. Equity became increasingly reliant upon professional managers, who were paid four times the rate of the average worker, to chart the society's path through the increasingly complicated world of shoe production. The education fund was steadily reduced and the retail societies were constantly demanding a higher return on their sales to equal that paid by the CWS.[62] Things were little better at the Anchor, whose members had to cancel their annual paid weekly holiday.[63]

Outside the shoe trade it was not quite so bad. The hosiery society expanded during the 1890s and employed over 300 workers. Capital investment reached nearly £40,000 in 1897.[64] Meanwhile a few out-of-work engineers, including T. Carter, the ASE delegate to the Trades Council and future treasurer of the local ILP,[65] formed a small engineering cooperative which, after an early struggle, became profitable in 1897.[66] Building workers also participated in the movement. A small society was set up in the early 1890s and appears to have been mainly employed in construction work for other cooperatives.[67]

The most important new addition to the growing family of producers' cooperatives was undoubtedly the Cooperative Printing Society. This enterprise first appeared in 1894 and after a few months its future was assured when Richards, opposed vigorously by Inskip, secured the NUBSO printing account for the society.[68] Problems faced by typographers over the introduction of the Linotype machine closely resemble those caused by the lasting machine in shoemaking.[69] As we saw in the previous chapter, the Leicester members of the Typographical Association were close allies of the NUBSO militants in the Burgess by-election of 1894. Like shoemakers, typographers had a long tradition of cooperation which, in the early 1890s, was closely linked by militant printers to trade unionism and socialism. This society prospered, winning many contracts from the Labour movement, and indeed still survives.

Yet these new enterprises, like the trades that they performed, were limited to the service sector of an economy that was dominated by footwear. When the tide turned against boot cooperatives in the mid-1890s cooperation as an alternative political economy which could be made by the voluntary actions of working people was no longer viable. We should not be too unsympathetic when we judge the energy and idealism of the young men who attempted to create the commonwealth from 'the bottom up'. While we can point to many flaws in their strategy, particularly a strong element of blind faith, which accounts for their misjudgment of ordinary working people's willingness to pay for the experiment, we must remember that for a short period cooperation did appear to work. Between 1889, when the hosiery society moved to larger premises, and 1895, when the St Crispin venture collapsed, an increasing number of local people had found a haven of employment in the producers' movement.

Most of the societies survived, but at a price. Greening had imposed a rule in the Equity constitution which forbade political activity by the cooperative.[70] This may partly explain the departure of Taylor, the ILP treasurer, to the Anchor, which had a similar constitution to Equity but appears to have ignored the political embargo.[71] Similarly Equity was only allowed to operate within the limits laid down by the retail societies. When the society opened up a retail shop in Huddersfield, where the local society refused to sell their shoes, retailing cooperatives with shares in Equity insisted on the shops' closure.[72] These difficulties, however, pale in comparison to the events that occurred at the hosiery cooperative early in the new century. Under pressure from the investing stores the cooperative was forced to sell out to the CWS. Despite earlier assurances, the latter organization promptly closed down the Leicester works and removed the machinery to a country village.[73]

During these years the Cooperative Productive Federation, which along with its sister organization, the Labour Association, was the remnant of the Vivian–Greening–Neale Christian Socialist school, moved its headquarters to Leicester. This was largely an acknowledgment of the fact that the 19 cooperatives in and around Leicester constituted one-third of the movement's membership.[74] Yet, as Cole has pointed out, this body was little more than a rump of its former glory.[75] Its days of influence in the wider world of cooperation were at an end. Certainly in Leicester the movement had peaked in 1895. Cooperative production in the town was impelled forward during the early years of the 1890s by the troubles that accompanied the structural changes within the footwear industry. After the victory of the manufacturers in the 1895 lock-out new ventures were impossible. Producers' cooperatives had to face the reality of the market which was dominated by machine-made products from both Massachusetts and the native industry. The major factor which caused many Leicester shoe workers to resort to cooperation was the deep-rooted desire either to dodge the machine or to use it on the workers' terms. Both the capitalists' victory of 1895 and Butcher's technocratic regime at the Wheatsheaf were the negation of this dream. Few had the prescience of Beatrice Webb who noted in her diary in December 1890: 'visiting production societies roundabout Leicester (in bitter cold weather). Sad these efforts which are doomed to failure.'[76]

If machines, and people's reluctance to buy the cooperatives' goods, conspired against the strategy of cooperative production as a means of restructuring society, what were the implications for the local Labour movement? After 1895 Richards and Curley stopped delivering their lectures to trade union branches on the 'Industrial Cooperative Scheme'. The demands of branch administration undoubtedly increased during the following five years as membership declined and the cause of the unemployed shoe workers came to the fore. In fact the victory of the shoe machines was also to produce changes in the politics of the Labour movement. The socialists could no longer take for granted the leadership of skilled shoe workers, whose autonomy at work and craft status were under threat from mechanization. The reality, after 1895, was of a semi-skilled workforce paid by the day and paced by the machine companies. Moreover, as we shall see in the next chapter, many of those whom the socialists had championed during the first part of the decade, especially the lasters, were now facing long-term unemployment thanks to the 'strong youth' and the lasting machine. Thus poverty was to replace worker autonomy as the dominant theme in Leicester socialism.

11 The Rise of James Ramsay MacDonald and the Consolidation of Class Politics, 1895–1906

In the eleven-year period between the boot-trade lock-out and the general election of 1906, major changes occurred in local working-class politics. At the beginning of the period local socialism was largely an expression of fear and uncertainty experienced by certain skilled sections of the working population threatened by structural changes in the organization of work. The class antagonisms aroused by mechanization gave birth to a form of socialism that was designed to secure the material well-being of those workers. Thus despite the fiery rhetoric of the young socialist lasters, Cotton's patents operatives, engineers and typographers, the new doctrine was as much concerned with preserving existing status relations within the workforce as it was in providing answers to the growing problem of poverty and the interests of the working class in general. By the early years of the present century, however, this emphasis upon the problems of the skilled man at work had given way to a new concern over the reality of the unemployed skilled man. As in the first half of the 1890s, the footwear workers, particularly the lasters, were to be the central actors in the changing scene of working-class politics. If the socialism of the first half of the 1890s can be characterized as radical sectionalism, the socialism of the subsequent decade can be described as aggressive reformism, as questions of worker autonomy were replaced by the necessity of finding palliatives to ease the burden of the growing army of Leicester's unemployed. This change in political focus is also illuminated by a change in socialist parliamentary candidates. Joseph Burgess, the ex-editor of the *Workman's Times*, was an ideal spokesman for an embittered skilled workforce grasping for radical solutions during a period of upheaval. The appeal of James Ramsay MacDonald, on the other hand, has to be seen partly as an expression of growing local concern over the problem of poverty and the need to employ the agency of the state to alleviate working-class misery. The word partly is used here because the division between the old and new forms of working-class politics was never clearly separate during the period. Elements from both were to remain intermingled for many years, a situation which was often made more complex by Labour politicians choosing to give emphasis to either 'old radicalism' or new 'social reformism' to suit the demands of particular electoral circumstances.

By following closely the process of structural change within the Leicester working class in the period under review, and the attendant shifts in socialist politics, this chapter will attempt to answer two sets of questions both of which have a wide currency in contemporary Labour historiography. First, how do we explain the arrival and subsequent rise to power of MacDonald, the exemplar *par excellence* of compromise and the 'softly softly' approach of political reform, as the champion of a local Labour movement with a deeply ingrained militant, radical tradition? Secondly, to what extent had independent working-class politics become a viable, electorally successful movement by the end of the period?

The events of 1895, in particular the April lock-out, proved to be a watershed in local Labour politics. The imposition of the employers' 'Seven Commandments' effectively curtailed the militants' area of activity and took the steam out of Leicester's socialist movement. In other footwear centres, most notably London, the fortunes of local socialist trade union officials were totally eclipsed as a cowed labour force, fearful of retaliation from the manufacturers' federation, declined to follow their erstwhile leaders on new campaigns.[1] Richards, however, by far the most calculating of the young socialists, sensing the changing mood of the membership, dropped the politics and rhetoric of the class struggle and concentrated his energy on the immediate practical problems that faced his branch.

Uppermost amongst the difficulties faced by Leicester shoe workers was growing unemployment as American imports continued to erode the local trade's markets and manufacturers restructured the workforce and production methods to make Leicester shoes more competitive.[2] How extensive was unemployment in Leicester and what groups of the workforce were affected? It is impossible to answer this question with precision. Labour statistics were notoriously inadequate during the period and no union branch records with details of out-of-work payments survive.[3] The problem is further exacerbated by the wealthy No. 1 Branch helping members who failed to pay subscriptions and levies.[4] Yet by 1900 the membership of the branch had slumped by over two-and-a-half thousand to 8,732 compared with the 1895 figure of 11,375 members.[5] Moreover, the 1900 membership return does not equal the number of trade unionists in work. Indeed in the early years of the present century the No. 1 Branch was paying out large amounts to unemployed members.[6]

Paradoxically, employment in the footwear industry in Leicester had increased by over 2,000 in the decade 1891–1901 to 26,561 workers.[7] Several factors explain the decline in union membership. Older workers, unable to cope with the new work rhythms of the team system, were forced out of the trade. Even Day, the editor of the *Shoe and Leather Record* and no friend of the union, noted in his 1903 essay that 'there had been some hardship among the older men unable to learn how to operate the new machines'.[8] Victimization of previously militant members also took place but it is impossible to say how extensive this was.[9] Female employment also increased during the decade from 7,320 workers in 1891 to 8,791 in 1901, but this is probably an indication of the general growth of the industry during the decade rather than a manifestation of female substitution.[10] The union never complained of dilution in the period and there is no evidence that women were as yet employed outside their traditional domain of the 'closing room'. Apathy amongst members after the 1895 lock-out may also have had an effect, but while this has a certain intuititive appeal it must be remembered that most trade unionists had an important material stake in the union's welfare functions and were unwilling to lose these benefits by forgoing membership in what was an extremely difficult period. The major factor in explaining the decline in union membership, and the one validated by contemporaty comment from both sides of industry, was the substitution of young for old labour. The spectre of the strong youth which had haunted union officials since the demonstration of the lasting machine in the Northampton showroom in 1889 became a reality in the years immediately after the lock-out. Day candidly admitted that 'younger men have had to be drafted into the factories and considerable displacement of labour has been inevitable'.[11] This process was largely centred on the lasting branch of the trade which had formed the core of the union's strength. Lasters were not only displaced by lasting machines. The lasting shops had traditionally performed various preparatory functions and sole attachment as well as lasting. In the years after the lock-out the reorganization of production involved removing the preparatory work to the notoriously ill-paid rough stuff department and the new, easy-to-operate, Goodyear welting machine replaced the more cumbersome Blake stitcher.[12] Thus the autonomy enjoyed by workers in the lasting shops prior to 1895 was finally broken. The terms of the 1895 settlement imposed both a system of day-work wages and a major restructuring of the labour process. The proud lasters, many of whom had paid their apprentices' premium, were either being replaced by youths or were having to adapt themselves to the rigours of semi-skilled assembly line methods of production.

The young socialists at the No. 1 Branch under Richards's guidance responded quickly to the new industrial situation. Unlike their London counterparts they realized that the second part of the 1890s required caution. The rhetoric of class-struggle socialism may have had an appeal to their members in the first half of the decade, but what was now required were palliatives and first aid treatment to a dejected workforce. The first response of both the union generally and the socialists was to encourage work spreading by limiting output. An element of piece work, linked to day rates, had been retained in the 1895 settlement and the union was partly successful in persuading members to limit output in order both to provide work for unemployed colleagues and to slow the pace of production to a speed manageable by older workers. Furthermore, the union was able to gain overtime payments at time and a quarter of normal rates in order 'not so much to obtain time and a quarter as ... to do our best to abolish overtime, and thus secure more continuous employment to our members'.[13]

Another strategy, this time initiated by Richards, designed to ease the growing problem of unemployment, was the campaign to persuade smaller employers to introduce the 'hand team' system. This method of work organization involved the production of footwear with the minimum use of machinery. The majority of the work was done by hand workers organized on an extreme form of subdivision. The hand-team system, however, met the staunch opposition of the machine companies who often managed to persuade employers not to give work to those workers who had been employed in hand work.[14]

Perhaps the most interesting development in the NUBSO survival strategy was their efforts to use existing local political institutions to assist their rearguard action. In 1896 the union requested the Trades Council to lobby the town council on the plight of out-of-work shoemakers. The council complied with this request and the town clerk was instructed to write to local manufacturers suggesting that they 'should equally share the work among their various employees'.[15] The council had, of course, intervened in previous periods of local distress but the 1896 plea to employers was to be highly significant as it introduced a new era of local political struggle over social questions. The council could no longer play a neutral role in issues between employers and workers, despite its desire to remain outside these disputes. The days of the early 1890s when the good offices of the mayor were opened to the two warring factions of local society to sort out their disputes were over. The Labour movement, despite their poor local electoral performance, was pushed by circumstances towards a realization that the municipality could help. The socialists saw that the struggle for local reforms could provide the stepping-stones towards the fulfilment of their municipal programme. Thus the Trades Council successfully badgered the corporation into establishing a temporary labour bureau for the registration of unemployed workers. It was reported in January 1897 that 1,500 people had recorded their names as totally unemployed. In view of the scale of the problem the corporation was forced to set up an unemployment committee and funds were raised to relieve the distress. £670 was raised by public subscription, and although the relief afforded to the unemployed and their 4,100 dependants must have been slight, the precedent of assistance without the usual penalties incurred by going to the Guardians was slowly being established.[16] Furthermore, socialist agitation was carried out alongside these developments. Figure 4, a page from the Trades Council report of 1896, bears the hallmark of Richards's campaigns inside the council chamber as the champion of the municipal employee as well as his earlier use of the town council officers' salary question in his battle with Inskip.[17]

TO WORKING MEN VOTERS.

FACTS NOT TO BE FORGOTTEN AT THE MUNICIPAL ELECTIONS.

DEBT OF THE BOROUGH £2,250,000.

To Refund Capital and Interest a Sum amounting to **£24,000** per annum is levied to pay off old debts.

During the Unemployed agitation the Council were asked to pay 5½d. per hour to the Unemployed who were worth it. This was refused, only nine supporting it.

Look how the Capitalist Party sweat their Working Men Employes, and yet raise their Favourites' Salaries

Fifty Labourers at Leicester Corporation Gas Works struck for an advance of One Halfpenny per Hour. This was refused, men turned adrift, and their places filled up by, guess—

When the overpaid Officials ask for a rise, what is the result. The following:—

		£	£
Gas Engineer	raised from	750 to	1250
Magistrates' Clerk	,, ,,	1000 to	1250
Borough Surveyor	,, ,,	700 to	1000
Waterworks' Engineer	,, ,,	500 to	600
Borough Accountant	,, ,,	400 to	500
Curator of Museum	,, ,,	200 to	300
Chief Constable	,, ,,	400 to	500
Librarian	,, ,,	180 to	220
Abbey Park Manager	,, ,,	160 to	200
Town Clerk's Assistant	,, ,,	180 to	200
Conveyancing Clerk	,, ,,	130 to	135
Cashier	,, ,,	150 to	160
Borough Surveyor's Assistant	,, ,,	250 to	300
Sewage Works' Assistant	,, ,,	180 to	200

The above will show to you that whilst some servants of this noble ancient borough are receiving 4½d. per hour upon which no man can live decently, others are receiving 10s. per hour. Compare the above Table with the Trades' Council's Maximum Wage of £500 per year.

Fellow Workers, this can be remedied by united action, the power is in your hands, use it with all the force your intellect can command.

Fig. 4 Independent Labour Party local government election advertisement, 1896 (Leicester Trades Council Annual Report, 1896: courtesy London School of Economics and Political Science Library)

Figure 4, which appeared in the report as an ILP advertisement, was obviously designed to inject an element of class into local politics and suggests that while the NUBSO militants, who dominated the ILP, were drawing in their horns in the industrial arena, much of their rhetorical talent was being channelled into new areas. Yet lobbying and rhetoric were limited given the Labour movement's inability to increase their independent presence inside the council chamber. Despite the ILP's impressive start, relative to other areas of England, the Leicester branch was still organizationally weak and unable to translate growing working-class discontent into electoral success.

The problem faced by the new party was essentially one of political organization. It is true that in a large measure the Trades Council had been won over to their cause, but in electoral terms the ILP lacked machinery outside Richards's power base in the Wyggeston ward. Before 1898, what ward organization that did exist was located in the neighbourhood coffee and cocoa houses established by middle-class patrons during the temperance fervour of the late 1870s.[18] What record remains of this early ward structure tends to confirm that local groups concentrated on informal gatherings and discussion circles rather than party building.[19] The ILP was therefore forced to rely upon *ad hoc* assistance from the Trades Council. This assistance took two forms. First, the Trades Council could use its traditional function as the local voice of labour to recommend socialist candidates to working-class electors. This approval and recommendation was highly important in the politics of the period. For example, the Liberals spent much energy in trying to gain approval from the Trades Council for their parliamentary candidates.[20] Second, the Trades Council could assist with the election expenses of working men candidates.

Trades Council funding helped secure Banton's return as Richards's fellow representative in the Wyggeston ward in 1896. This ward, claimed to be densely populated with shoemakers, and sending three councillors to the town hall, became a bastion of local socialism during the period. With much fanfare the ward eventually became completely represented by the ILP in 1898. It is worth retelling Richards's account of the election of Slater, the leader of the local tailors' union, for the ward in that year:

> We set to work and our opponents say we do work. We paraded the ward with a home made lantern three feet square and set upon two poles, with mottoes on each side, and a naphtha lamp inside, and accompanied by our I.L.P. brass band ... More canvas, more votes, and whilst we are canvassing we are making Socialists, which is our principal object and we insist upon a good energetic canvass. Whilst one person is doing this and addressing circulars, the agitators are holding fifteen to twenty meetings, and we make a point of holding a meeting in each street of the ward, and often four or five upon a good central spot.
> On polling day we see that all vote and give them no peace until they do.[21]

Despite a strong element of working-class self-help Slater's campaign was expensive. The Trades Council awarded him £45 11s. 4½d. to cover his costs, in addition to the £7 granted to Chaplin in his successful fight to be the ILP's fourth councillor in the Aylestone ward and the £8 7s. 10d. expended on Carter's unsuccessful attempt to win a seat on the Guardians.[22]

This expenditure of over £50 placed a great strain on the Trades Council. The balance in hand the previous year had been over £41 and at the end of 1898 this had been reduced to 17s. 2d. The problem was that electoral funds had to compete with other Trades Council activities such as assisting the local infirmary and making grants to workers on strike. George Green, the Trades Council secretary, lamented the poor state of the Council's finances, caused by the election expenses, in his annual report and went on to call for a 'Federation of local trades', linked to a national federation, to superintend and finance working-class candidates. Thus at a local level the need for a new organization, distinctly geared to political activity, financed by trade unions for the return of independent Labour candidates, was finding expression. To meet this demand the Leicester ILP embarked on two courses of action. First, key local activists, especially Richards, threw their energy into campaigning for a national party based upon an alliance of trade unions and socialist groups. Second, local party organization was streamlined and improved.

Richards, along with Barnes of the ASE, spent much of the following year touring Britain with J. Ramsay MacDonald, lecturing to Trades Councils, union conferences and local labour groups on the need to win TUC support for a Labour Party.[23] Just when MacDonald first came into contact with the Leicester Labour movement is unknown. He would have almost certainly met Richards at ILP national conferences in the late 1890s, especially as Richards was often a candidate for a place on the party's council.[24] Banton had also been a delegate to the national conference and in 1897 attempted to win a seat on the council.[25] Indeed in subsequent years Banton was to establish close bonds with MacDonald.[26]

Several factors help to explain MacDonald's eventual parliamentary candidature for the ILP in Leicester. His staunch opposition to the SDF must certainly have endeared him to the Leicester ILP. Ever since the defection of the Leicester SDF into the ILP camp in 1894, local socialists had suffered a good deal of criticism in *Justice*.[27] On the other hand, the more moderate section of the Leicester ILP, particularly those such as Banton and Chaplin who had previously been Liberal Party activists, probably saw MacDonald as the ideal candidate to overcome Liberal opposition in future parliamentary elections.[28] This is supported by the warm reception which greeted his eventual candidature in the local Liberal press.[29] MacDonald's reputation as a socialist intellectual, with copious theoretical publications and his editorship of the *Ethical World*, widely read in secularist circles, must have appealed to the more studious members. The financial independence which he gained via marriage may

156

also have been a further attraction.[30] His circumstances were certainly much more favourable than those of Joe Burgess, whose previous candidature had sorely taxed both branch and national party funds.[31]

Above all, MacDonald's position as a major figure in the party leadership both flattered the local branch and helped to bolster his popular appeal. Moreover, he possessed the good looks and the skills of oratory to complement his office. The Leicester branch was certainly not slow in exploiting these attributes. In the parliamentary campaign of 1900, threepenny tickets bearing MacDonald's photograph proved to be a useful money-spinner.[32] MacDonald's populism was certainly infectious. The anonymous poet, A.C.B., who tells the reader of his secularism and socialism and his joy at working at the Leicester printing cooperative in his autobiographical poem, was moved to write a sonnet in dedication to MacDonald, which also conveys something of his charismatic appeal:

> A refuge from the storms of life
>   These walls for years have stood;
> Long may they stand till human strife
>   Find rest in brotherhood.
> He who loves Honour hates the tortuous tricks
> Which constitute the game of Politics;
> Therefore, though Labour's cause claims my support,
> In fields of party strife I find no forte,
> Save with a song of sympathy to assist
> The side where stands the strong protagonist.
> Thus, to my mind, Ramsay MacDonald seem'd
> Destin'd to shape those ends of which we dream'd
> We visionaries, looking for the day
> When Falsehood, Force, and Fraud shall pass away.
> No mindless mob can guide us to the goal,
> Calmness of judgement, fervency of soul,
> Must lead us on; two qualities united
> In him for whom this sonnet was indited:[33]

Short-term political factors also aided MacDonald's emergence as the ILP candidate. The clouds of war in South Africa gathered ominously during the summer of 1899, which coincided with the months between his proposal as candidate by Richards to the Trades Council in June and his eventual nomination in October.[34] When hostilities began MacDonald found that the Leicester ILP shared his deep distaste for the war. 'On three different occasions prior to the outbreak of hostilities resolutions were passed at the Corn Exchange meetings protesting against war in South Africa.'[35] Furthermore, Leicester liberalism had deep radical roots. Chamberlain's defection in 1886 had had little local impact.[36] There was thus a staunch body of local Radical Liberal opinion that preferred MacDonald's stand against the war to the vacillation of Hazell, one of the local MPs.[37]

Another factor which was to add to MacDonald's local appeal was the re-emergence of the 'land question' as a major element in local Labour politics at the turn of the century. The complexities of this issue will be discussed below but at this point it is worth noting that MacDonald's personal background gave him the capacity fully to exploit this issue. Born into the north-east of Scotland fishing and agricultural community of Lossiemouth, MacDonald soon developed the 'good honest hatred the Scotsman has for Landlords'. Land nationalization had been the subject of an early essay,[38] and his knowledge of the issue was to provide useful capital during his first years in Leicester.

The strength of Leicester liberalism was also being sapped by the growth of conservatism amongst local manufacturers. This expansion of local Toryism was not caused by defections from liberalism, but by new manufacturers, businessmen and professionals, who emerged during and after the 1880s, joining the Conservatives rather than the Liberals. This process, according to Freer, was a product of the different social background of the new rich. Many came from farming and country stock, and found Leicester's Tory county society more congenial than the rather arid nonconformity of the indigenous elite.[39] Thus by 1900 the Liberal Association in Leicester was no longer the undisputed political expression of the local middle class. Indeed, despite the continuity of nonconformist Liberal radicalism the war undermined the unity of the Association. Sir Israel Hart, the Association's president, became a staunch imperialist. Although the imperialist faction was to be outflanked by Edward Wood, the leader of the moderate Gladstonians, it would not have required much political foresight on the part of MacDonald to realize that when the war was over, Leicester liberalism would be a mere rump of its former self.

MacDonald stood as candidate for the Labour Representation Committee in the 1900 general election in what turned out to be an extremely acrimonious local campaign. The Conservatives, as elsewhere, capitalized to the full on the war, while the fact that the local regiment had been under siege at Ladysmith added piquancy to the proceedings.[40] MacDonald, however, tried to divert attention from the war towards social issues. He intended to fight the election 'upon Leicester rather than Johannesburg, upon London rather than Pretoria ... upon the problems which faced the wage earners rather than upon the problems of the capitalists who did their mining for gold and diamonds in South Africa by black labour'.[41] His campaign concentrated upon the nationalization of the mines, the taxation of land values to finance old age pensions and the provision of low-interest loans to municipalities to improve working-class housing.[42] MacDonald failed to better the vote cast for Burgess in 1895, but his 4,164 supporters added to the rising Tory fortunes whose candidate, Rolleston, beat Hazell by nearly 1,500 votes. The Leicester Liberal Association subsequently undertook an intense internal examination in the light of their first parliamentary setback in 40 years. The Labour movement, on the other hand, were undoubtedly pleased by MacDonald's performance. He had retained their share of the vote in circumstances that were unfavourable to Labour and his stand on South Africa both pleased ILP militant activists and helped to split the Liberal camp.

If the Leicester Labour movement gained advantages from having MacDonald as their candidate, what were the attractions in Leicester for MacDonald? As we have already seen, a potentially favourable local political realignment must have figured in MacDonald's calculations. Furthermore, he soon developed a close personal and political relationship with the emerging leader of local liberalism, Edward Wood. Indeed Wood was persuaded to put money into the *Leicester Pioneer* when MacDonald was assisting the restructuring of the newspaper.[43] Wood also had good contacts with established Labour figures, especially Banton, having for many years worked with Trades Council officials on the administration of the local infirmary, while his annual 'Labour Dinner' helped to cement these ties.[44] Thus local circumstances appeared to favour future electoral negotiations with the Liberal Association. His candidature in Leicester also assisted MacDonald in winning NUBSO support for the proposed LRC.[45] Richards played a crucial role in mustering support amongst the branches for union affiliation in what was a period of waning NUBSO fortunes and political disaffection amongst the membership. In a very low poll the No. 1 Branch voted 295 for and 227 against joining the LRC, while the No. 2, Clickers', Branch, voted 91 for, 118 against. Affiliation, of course, also involved subscriptions which made the task of winning support even more difficult, but with the help of Freak in London and other local activists a narrow majority in favour of joining was secured.[46] MacDonald welded his position with the union by attending the 1900 union conference where in his address he declared 'that the time has now come for labour to take up an independent position upon all labour matters in the House of Commons'.[47] Richards and Freak were the two NUBSO delegates at the Farringdon Hall inaugural conference earlier in the year and upon his return Richards informed his members that

> It [the L.R.C.] will bring together the toiling masses . . . It will bring together the kindly disposed people who believe in humanity and will mark the period of the oppressed as against the oppressor . . . There was every indication there of this when you take some of the extreme Socialists of a few years ago, who have not abandoned their hope of nationalising everything, yet still feel sure that they cannot hope to succeed without joining hands with those who are not so extreme, viz. the steady plodding Trade Unionists[48]

The first part of this statement, with its references to morally motivated people and crude historicism, could almost have been penned by MacDonald, while the remainder indicates the distance travelled down the path of reformism by the NUBSO militants from the mid-1890s.

The Trades Council, as we have seen, affiliated at the inauguration of the LRC and other local unions soon joined the new organization.[49]

MacDonald undoubtedly had the solid support of local labour organizations but what type of political machine was he inheriting? The need to coordinate the political activities of the Trades Council, ILP ward organizations and the *ad hoc* parliamentary arrangements was apparent and being discussed in 1898.[50] Indeed this need was a major factor in the attraction of MacDonald to the local Labour movement. The Trades Council's call for a political federation of all trades in 1898 foreshadowed the emergence of a local LRC in early 1903, but in the years between these two dates activists had begun to establish a more structured organization.

The colourful local election campaign in Wyggeston in 1898 could not be undertaken in every ward, but this type of intense community-based activity did establish precedents for political organization in other working-class areas. Efforts were made to establish a network of supporters each responsible for propaganda, canvassing and registration work in their individual street. Even more novel was the post of 'workshop captain' established during this period. The 'workshop captain's' role was the same as that of the street organizer but based in the factory rather than the neighbourhood.[51] This system caught the imagination of MacDonald and Henderson who recommended its virtues in their handbook on party and electoral organization. Not only was it potentially highly effective, but also did away with the need for paid full-time party workers. It could be claimed that this system of political organization was similar to the Liberal caucus machine perfected three decades earlier in Birmingham. More relevant, however, was the precedent of local trade union organization. Until recent years Leicester's industry, based primarily on outwork, produced a form of trade union organization that leaned heavily on neighbourhood activists to collect subscriptions and pass on information to a workforce that was based in the community rather than the factory.[52]

Despite this high element of voluntary work the improved political structure still required money if Labour was to improve its electoral performance. Here MacDonald was to play a key role. As author of the Leicester Labour Representation Committee constitution MacDonald was anxious to set a precedent for the movement nationally.[53] The management committee of the Leicester LRC was composed of five Trades Council delegates, five from the ILP and three from the Building Trades Council, while trade unions and cooperatives were allocated one delegate per hundred members. Each delegate had to contribute one pound and the trade unions and cooperatives were also charged one penny for each of their members.[54] Given the fact that NUBSO, the LAHU, the elastic web weavers and many smaller unions joined the local LRC, together with the retail cooperatives and two producers' cooperatives, the financial position of Labour's political organization must have been a vast improvement on the situation of the 1890s.[55]

The formation of the Leicester LRC coincided with the Gladstone–MacDonald negotiations on a future Labour–Liberal electoral pact. The

160

coincidence was also geographical, the more crucial aspects of the agreement being finalized at MacDonald's bedside in the Leicester isolation hospital where he was committed with a feverish infection.[56] The negotiations had, however, been held up by another local incident, this time in the ranks of the Leicester Liberal Association. After the defeat of Hazell in 1900 the Association quickly dropped him as their future candidate. They first tried to replace him by a politician of national stature, Asquith being one of many whom the Association contacted.[57] Asquith declined the invitation, and as the need to check the ILP had been cited as a major consideration in choosing a new candidate, the Association offered the vacancy to Wood, the local 'friend of labour' and the sitting mayor. Wood, however, had the foresight to see that Labour's fortunes were rising after the arrival of MacDonald and turned down the offer.[58] The situation was further complicated when Sir Israel Hart, the leader of the Liberal Imperialist faction, offered himself as Broadhurst's partner. Hart's possible candidature was attractive to certain quarters of the Liberal establishment, who clung tenaciously to a belief that the two seats should continue to represent both moderate and radical Liberal opinion. Thus as Broadhurst was, in the eyes of many Liberals, the heir of Taylor and subsequent Radical members, many believed that Hart was only claiming the moderate's birthright. The problem was, of course, that the local political contours were rapidly changing. For example, Hart had offended the Labour movement and alienated himself from an important section of local liberalism over his stand against increased municipalization of local services,[59] while the South African war had also created new fissures inside Leicester liberalism.

Wood outlined the options available to the Association in a future parliamentary election as follows: (1) nominate only Broadhurst; (2) nominate Broadhurst and make arrangements with Labour so that the Liberals could support MacDonald; (3) nominate Broadhurst and Hart.[60] Wood favoured the second option and MacDonald's refusal to complete the agreement with Gladstone until the Leicester situation was resolved undoubtedly brought the pressure of the national party to bear upon the Leicester Association.[61] The *Post*, firmly siding with Wood, told Leicester Liberals that 'the paramount and pressing duty of every Progressive worthy of the name is to "go" for the only working political union that can enable Leicester to throw off its minority member'.[62] Hart's candidature was heavily defeated at the annual meeting of the 'Liberal thousand' which endorsed the Broadhurst–MacDonald ticket, while another local claimant to the seat, this time the popular leader of the moderates, Tudor Walters, was hastily found a safe seat in the Sheffield division of Brightside.[63]

Thus with an agreement between the Liberals and the local LRC Leicester politics in late 1903 appeared to have found a new stability. Indeed the new political situation seemed to be the model of the electoral arrangements envisaged by MacDonald and Gladstone. The pairing of

Broadhurst with MacDonald may have shown an uncommon bias towards Labour but as Wood candidly told the assembled 'thousand' in September, 'Labour M.P.s could be relied upon to vote with the Liberals.'[64] More importantly, Labour locally appeared to have abandoned the political style and language of the class struggle that distinguished the mid-1890s and had joined hands with the Liberals in the great 'progressive cause'. Even Richards, the erstwhile class warrior, had availed himself of the opportunities afforded by the electoral pact, by accepting LRC nomination for the Wolverhampton West constituency, one of the seats earmarked in the Gladstone–MacDonald arrangement, where he was reported to be wooing the electorate with his 'attractive personality, pleasing voice ... and great fairness and moderation'.[65]

For several months Leicester appeared to be the quintessential heartland of the Lib-Lab pact. The *Post* noted with pleasure the opposition of the ILP in Dewsbury to SDF local government candidates as an endorsement of the electoral arrangement's potential: 'Happily this new and most promising departure is already bearing fruit.'[66] Indeed it was generally assumed that the parliamentary pact should have a local dimension. The first test of the goodwill between both parties came in the November 1903 local government elections.

During the run up to this poll the term 'progressive' was employed by the Liberal press to describe both the Liberal and the two Labour candidates contesting for municipal office, the latter being given a free run against the Conservatives. At both Labour ward election meetings prominent Liberals shared the platform with Labour men. Peacock, the Labour candidate for St Margaret's ward, told the assembled audience of Liberal councillors, Association officers and ILP members that 'he was much obliged to the Liberals who had supported him that week. Although he did not believe that the Liberals and Labour men would become one political party he thought the time would come when the old political names would change ... let them unite solidly so as to make a great progressive force.'[67] Similar feelings were expressed by Alderman T. Smith, secretary of the Liberal Association, who chaired Chaplin's pre-election meeting in the Aylestone ward. 'The chairman said it no doubt seemed rather an anomalous thing for an alderman of the borough to be occupying the chair at that meeting when he remembered that one of the strongest points in Mr. Chaplin's programme was the abolition of aldermen. (hear, hear). This was, however, one of the sacrifices that Liberalism had to make for Labour when it was necessary for the two parties to unite.'[68]

To the Tories' anger, the alliance candidates romped home, gaining almost 70 per cent of the votes cast. The Liberal *Post* was ecstatic over the great progressive victory and looked forward to the next general election with enthusiasm.[69] The Liberal *Leicester Chronicle's* rather condescending prophecy, made at an early ILP intervention into local politics in 1895, appeared to be realized: 'they cannot do any harm, of course, but if they take their share of the work, and are willing to be guided by experience, their ideas will be broadened. For the present they represent a body of opinion that should not be ignored, though it is crude and ill-informed.'[70] This success, however, was to be the high-water mark of Labour–Liberal cooperation in local politics. Within four months the Liberals were crying foul when Labour, without consulting their erstwhile partners, fielded 13 candidates in the Guardian elections. Why this sudden change in electoral tactics on the part of Labour? A possible explanation could be that Labour was goaded into adopting an independent electoral stance by the constant stream of criticism levied against them by Sir John Rolleston, the Tory parliamentary victor of 1900, and the local Conservative press. This explanation seems plausible. Rolleston and Hubbard, the secretary of the LRC, carried out a long and acrimonious correspondence in the local press on the question of Labour's independence, which suggests that Labour felt the issue to be of some importance.[71] This line of reasoning, however, cannot satisfactorily explain the timing of Labour's abandoning the alliance. Furthermore, it ignores the fact that the Guardian elections of 1904 were conducted over specific issues, especially unemployment, a problem which divided and ultimately smashed the short-lived political alliance.

Previous local government elections were distinguished by the lack of public interest. In March 1901 the main issues were the time-honoured ones of vaccination and costs. The ILP fielded only three candidates, one of whom was elected, on a very low poll. Similarly in November 1902 the *Post* noted that the municipal elections presented 'no particular burning questions of a local character'. As expected the 1903 'alliance' elections concentrated on the lowest common denominator between the two parties, free trade and religious education.[72] This period of political calm came to an abrupt end with a rise in unemployment during the winter 1903–4.

As we have seen, unemployment in Leicester arose from the displacement of adult males from their traditional skilled tasks by machinery operated by youths and women. Both major industries had traditionally experienced seasonal unemployment, as was the norm in most clothing trades. Lack of work in the early years of the present century was, however, becoming profoundly different in character with the arrival of long-term structural unemployment disproportionately affecting the main breadwinner of the working-class family. The problem had been accumulating for several years. Richards and Banton had tried to move a resolution authorizing the council to borrow funds in order to undertake public works to employ those out of work. Their attempt failed because not enough councillors were present to form a quorum.[73] Discontent was already being expressed at the 'alliance' elections in 1903. The *Pioneer*, the local Labour weekly, noted the increasing complaints by those men on the 'test' over the allegedly 'unsympathetic' and 'inhuman' attitudes of the Liberal-dominated Board of Guardians.[74] By January 1904 feelings against the Guardians were so strong that the LRC decided to field 13 candidates at the March elections. Unfortunately there is a gap in the surviving copies of the *Pioneer* between October 1903 and January 1904, and from February 1904 until December 1904, so that it is impossible to outline accurately the changing attitudes of organized labour towards the progressive alliance. We can, however, pick out the main economic developments that were under way during the winter of 1903–4 and relate these to the political upheavals of the following spring.

Increased mechanization, particularly in the shoe factories, wrought profound upheavals in the lives of working-class families. The most important aspect of this development was the changing social composition of the poor law recipients. The Guardians were no longer dealing with a clientele that was largely composed of the traditional poor and social misfits. Instead they were being swamped by applications from skilled and semi-skilled adult male shoe workers. One Liberal Guardian, a member of the 'Test Yard' Committee, admitted that the majority of applicants for the test 'were workmen who had been thrown out of work by the introduction of machinery'.[75] Two weeks later it was noted in the *Post* that 'the labour test men are dissatisfied ... These men are mainly composed of shoe hands. They are trades unionists ...' Over the previous decade the number of inmates of the workhouse had risen from 700 to 1,100 and those on outdoor relief from 1,600 to 3,900. The number of shoe workers admitted to the workhouse increased by nearly 50 per cent in the four years between 1901 and 1905.[76] It is not too difficult to locate the source of dissatisfaction with the administration of relief, the issue upon which Labour fought the 1904 election. The Guardians, faced with an ever-growing influx of applicants at the test yard, were forced to rely upon the time-honoured occupations of stone breaking, okum picking and wood chopping, tasks which naturally were found degrading by once proud shoemaking artisans. Furthermore, renumeration was poor, often as low as 10d. per day, with a 4s. 0d. per week maximum being paid to those on outdoor relief.[77] It was not only the monotonous hard work of the test yard and the pitiful level of remuneration that caused dissent; the loss of self-respect and charges of shirking that met their protests tended to galvanize the men into action and organization.[78]

No doubt the men had used their previous trade union experience to bring their case to the attention of the organized Labour movement. Those fragments of the *Pioneer* that are available are full of grievances from the 'test' men.[79] Moreover, with the major local trade union, NUBSO, hamstrung by the Taff Vale decision, and the continued displacement by young labour, the reality of the 'test' loomed in all shoe workers' minds.[80] Indeed local manufacturers began to gloat over their success. One footwear manufacturer claimed that 'some of the businesses have produced veritable gold mines'. 'It is the result of keener supervision, better organization in the factories, the most approved equipment, and good management generally.'[81] By March the casualties of this success had organized themselves under the capable leadership of George White, a young unemployed laster, and were actively engaged in both the press and the Guardian election campaign.[82]

Leicester liberalism was deeply grieved by Labour's new-found independence. One Liberal Guardian, seeking re-election, called Labour's intervention 'a kind of civil war', while another claimed that 'some of the most respected leaders of the Labour Party were just as discouraged and disappointed as members of the Liberal Party'.[83] There may have been an element of truth in the latter claim; both Chaplin and Banton emphasized the point that Labour were fighting because they were under-represented on the Board, a far more moderate position than that adopted by George Bibbings, the Labour candidate for Newton Ward, whose active supporters included George White. His aim was 'relief without pauperisation'.[84] In the weeks leading up to the election lines hardened between the parties with attention being increasingly focused upon policy. Bibbing's programme involved increased payments for those on out-relief, a more humane regime for the workhouse, and the provision of useful, reasonably paid employment. This policy, however, found the chink in liberalism's progressive armour and the ensuing debate took on the complexion of the classic 'economist' versus 'improver' controversy. 'Labourites seem to be more concerned to persons who are really undeserving than to the unfortunate or struggling ratepayer', thundered one Liberal candidate, while the *Post* warned against large increases in payments to the test men for fear that they would 'remain on the test when they might, could, and should obtain work in the ordinary channels of industry.'[85]

The thesis that the Labour Party came into existence because liberalism refused to make more representative offices available to working men has often been employed by historians.[86] The argument could be used to explain the intervention of Labour in the 1904 Leicester Guardians election. The statements of Banton and Chaplin on representation, noted above, could be cited in support. Where the thesis falls short, however, is in the area of policy. The Labour candidates wanted increased representation, according to Martin Curley, the president of the LRC, in order that 'the policy of the Board of Guardians should be altered and if it were to be altered they must alter the representation on the Board'.[87] In the pages which follow an alternative argument for explaining the consolidation of the Labour Party in Leicester will be proposed. It will be argued that Labour dramatically improved its local electoral performance in the two years prior to the 1906 general election because the new party was successfully able to exploit rising working-class concern over poverty and unemployment. The proposed solutions to this social problem forwarded by Labour breached the parameters of the local Lib–Lab alliance and irreversibly peeled off a large section of Liberal working-class support. Furthermore, this haemorrhage of working-class voters from the ranks of Leicester liberalism had far-reaching effects upon local Liberal organization. By 1906 the Liberal party machine had virtually collapsed in most working-class areas.

The divisions between the two parties on the question of social policy were essentially ones of degree and cost. Labour's demands for more municipal employment was not a radical departure from current practice and a far cry from the reforms proposed in their municipal programme, but their insistence that this work had to be paid for with acceptable wages was anathema to liberalism. Well-paid employment provided by the community was a demand that both touched the nerve of the ratepayer, whose cause the Liberals had traditionally championed, and threatened the smooth working of the local labour market. Indeed the issue became so important locally that it drained the goodwill from the electoral alliance so noticeable at the previous autumn's municipal poll. The gulf between the two parties became so wide over this issue that even the middle ground of working-class Lib-Labism disappeared.[88] Similarly the notion of the land as a solution to the problem of structural unemployment was espoused by both parties. Some years previously the Leicester Guardians had acquired several fields at nearby Gilroes and Crown Hill farms for cultivation by those on relief. Wages were equivalent to those paid in the 'test yard' and there were frequent complaints from the men over the long walk to work and the lack of shelter.[89] Labour was eager to take up the offer of Joseph Fels, the Georgite millionaire, to part-fund a Guardian-run land colony similar to his Hollesey Bay scheme. The Liberals were also interested in the plan but balked at the prospect of the large initial outlay demanded by Fels, although the Guardians did authorize the renting of an additional 35 acres to supplement their existing smallholding.[90]

Some Labour activists, on the other hand, were far more committed to the belief that land colonies offered the most efficient solution to both urban unemployment and rural depopulation. MacDonald told a Leicester audience that 'there must be two types [of land colonies], one penal for rogues and vagabonds and one educational for honest men ... a gateway back to the land, a means by which our population may be redistributed over England'.[91] Agriculture became an *idée fixe* with some Leicester ILP members which was to persist for many years.[92] In the 1907 Guardian elections, for example, one Labour candidate advocated the abolition of stone breaking to be replaced by land schemes in order to 'get the men on the land, and give them a healthy useful training which would be valuable to them when the state provided for the acquisition of smallholdings'.[93] The Labour advocates of land colonies were naturally infuriated by the Liberals' unwillingness to place the existing schemes on a sound footing. A long walk, perhaps through inclement weather, with the prospect of spending a day digging a wet field without facilities or shelter was probably an even worse prospect than stone breaking. Banton, motivated by a sense of frustration and anger that the Labour vision was being killed at birth, spoke out furiously against conditions on the Guardians' allotments.[94] Yet how realistic was Labour's vision of land colonies solving all the great problems of the day? More importantly, did these plans carry popular support? The Leicester unemployed shoemakers appear to have shown little interest in the various schemes on offer. Significantly when the question of what to do with the money given to the men who took part in the June 1905 unemployment march by well-wishers was discussed, the marchers turned down the plan advocated by two of their leaders, Sherriff and the Rev. F. L. Donaldson, to use all the funds to launch a land colony.[95] Nevertheless the land question, one of the most potent elements in nineteenth-century working-class radicalism, took on new life in the early years of the present century. The attraction of land reform to Labour politicians during the period was that it could both harness deep-rooted opinion on the subject and be presented as a simple, easily understood answer to the problems of poverty and unemployment. Indeed Leicester was a most fertile setting for the revival of the land campaign. Rural labour, either by migrating into Leicester or by producing goods in the villages that had previously been made in Leicester, had been a constant problem for the local Labour movement. Thus the age-old oppositon of town and country was again revived, this time to compete with a programme of social welfare reforms in the formulation of Labour ideology.

Labour activists were not, however, united around the policy of agricultural undertakings as a solution to unemployment. Most noticeably Bibbings, a spiritualist lecturer elected as a Guardian in 1904, Richards and White preferred to concentrate on the policy of relief without pauperization.[96] This division within Labour's ranks over policy contrasts strongly with the staunch support of cooperative production which unified the movement during the early and mid-1890s. The failure to formulate a clear-cut socialist programme, relevant to local needs and economic structure, largely explains the ascendancy of land reform and welfare palliatives in the early years of the present century. This is not to argue the simplistic formula that socialism consists only of ideas. Rather the social relations of production in the Leicester footwear and hosiery industries were at a particular stage of development. The rise of a young semi-skilled workforce who differed fundamentally from the skilled workers of the 1890s, saw little appeal in the socialism of the artisan producers' cooperative variety. The increasingly disorientated skilled craftsmen who filled the ranks of the unemployed witnessed with despair the triumph of the machine and the irrelevance of their old cry for industrial self-management. They stumbled forward in their demand for welfare palliatives, and harked back to nineteenth-century radicalism with the old shibboleth of land reform. Land and welfare reforms were the lowest common denominators amongst an increasingly divided Labour movement that had lost the certainty of direction that was so apparent in the first five years of the 1890s.

Yet despite this confused policy situation we can still discern the interplay of themes that had been central to Leicester socialism and Labour movement politics for nearly two decades. Land reform, more than old radicalism, continued to haunt working-class politicians. This was a continuing concern amongst Labour leaders, recently expressed both by cooperative production schemes and by the ILP municipal programme, to check and curtail the reserve army of labour. We must not, however, lose sight of the other major aspect of Labour policy. Palliatives, welfare measures, 'relief without pauperisation', all these were new elements in the Labour package and for their origins we need not search the excess baggage of radicalism. These policies were the product, however imperfectly developed, of the growing notion of economic equality, an idea which emanated from socialism.

The policy of reformism was implemented locally when in March 1904 the Trades Council persuaded the mayor to set up a Citizens' Aid Society (CAS) in order to distribute Trades Council funds and local charities to those out of work who were not in receipt of relief from the Guardians. This humble device, which was never a success, did further the principle, locally, of relief without disenfranchisement.[97] The *Post* carried a somewhat abbreviated report on the society's formation, noting only that the organization's aim was to cut out charitable overlaps. This apparent lack of interest by the *Post* is significant both of the Liberals' vexation at Labour's new-found assertiveness and the increasing 'economist' position being adopted by the erstwhile party of progress. Moreover, the concession by the mayor of the need for a second tier of relief confirmed that unemployment was far worse than the Guardians' statistics suggested. This was a potentially dangerous reflection upon a political party which was still largely identified as the party of the manufacturer, boasting nine footwear factory owners as members of the town council.[98]

Ill feeling continued up to the elections. The disclosure that the Guardians had deliberately voted the two ILP members off key committees incensed the Labour movement.[99] The gulf between the former political partners became unbridgeable. 'They [the LRC] were opposing not Liberals and not Tories, but the party of the capitalists and the employers', Hubbard, a Guardian candidate, told his audience, while Curley, the president of the LRC, laid down the party's new policy: 'The Labour Party would continue its propaganda in November next. They did not exist for one man, and whether Mr. MacDonald was returned to parliament or not they would go forward independent of the Liberal and Tory Parties.'[100]

Go forward they did, and in fine style. Their 13 candidates gained one-third of all the votes cast for the 36 seats, which gave Labour 11 members on the new Board. This election was to be even more significant for local politics than the 4,000 votes cast for Burgess a decade earlier. Labour, as Table 10 shows, had finally established a real electoral presence. Furthermore, with the LRC carrying out a coordinating function between the various sectors of the Labour movement the ILP was able to concentrate on education and propaganda work. In short, Labour now possessed both votes and a party machine that was the equal of the two major parties. Moreover, Labour had enlarged and consolidated its position by engaging in conflict with established liberalism over an issue which was of deep concern and importance to the working class and not by playing the role of junior partner in the progressive alliance. Labour's new-found strength in Leicester was based upon the expression of class-based politics that originated from the angry shoemakers forced to suffer the imposition of the 'test'.

Table 10   Labour candidates returned to the Board of Guardians, 1902–7.

1902	1904	1907
2	11	16

Source: Guardian Minutes

Yet the election of March 1904 was only the first stage in the process of Labour's consolidation in Leicester. As Curley promised the propaganda continued in November when Labour fielded six candidates at the municipal elections, four of whom were successful. Again, as in March, the dominant issue was unemployment. The November elections in many ways were of equal significance to the earlier Guardian poll. Five Labour candidates fought contests in November. Only the Westcotes contestant was unopposed. Furthermore, these five Labour candidates were opposed by only a single candidate each. In short, Labour in Leicester was faced with a Liberal–Conservative pact in November 1904.[101] In two wards the Conservative candidates were given a clear run against Labour, the other three being straight Liberal–Labour contests. Despite this handicap there was a marked general increase in the Labour vote, a fact which alarmed the *Post*, which commented with a touch of despair that 'After all this shows not the stream of the tendency but the force of the current.'[102]

Table 11   Labour councillors returned to the town council, 1902–6.

1902	1903	1904	1905	1906
2	4	7	11	11

Source: Leicester Council minute books

Clearly major developments were under way within Leicester liberalism. The 'progressive' experiment had been smashed on the rocks of unemployment and the party was forced to adopt a new local electoral strategy. As early as February 1904 the Liberal Association was seriously discussing the parliamentary situation in the light of Labour's intervention at the Guardian elections.[103] By April 1904 the Liberal St Margaret's ward committee, a previous bastion of Lib-Labism, whose past municipal representatives had included the general secretary of NUBSO requested 'a reconsideration of parliamentary arrangements in the light of the organized attack against Liberal candidates throughout the town'.[104] The conclusion that Leicester liberalism was forced to tolerate the parliamentary pact at the behest of the national party is inescapable. More ominously for the Liberals, there were increasing danger signs that the local party machine was in need of major repair. Those wards that faced Labour candidates found that their existing organization could not cope with the electoral pressures and were forced to seek help from the executive committee.[105] As Labour contested seats in predominantly working-class areas the Liberal machine in those wards faced two major problems, the recruitment of party workers and the collection of funds.

The working-class Liberal wards had in the past a fair proportion of working-class leaders on their committees. George Banton, for example, sat on the Westcotes ward committee in 1892, Jabez Chaplin on the Latimer ward committee and the Woolley brothers, both NUBSO officers, were also members of ward organizations.[106] The formation of the Leicester ILP, however, in 1894 produced a haemorrhage of working-class activists from liberalism. Banton and Chaplin were perhaps the most notable of those working-class Liberals who joined the ranks of the ILP. Paradoxically the 'progressive' election of 1903 assisted in the further alienation of working-class Liberals. The electoral pact of November 1903 could not accommodate all the old Lib-Lab candidates, so that J. H. Woolley lost his municipal seat when his ward organization was forced to accept an orthodox Liberal candidate.[107] Needless to say Woolley stood again several years later for the Labour Party. The process was also generational with many of the old guard of working-class Liberals such as Inskip, the general secretary of NUBSO, and Potter, the president of the Leicester Cooperative Society, passing away. Perhaps of most importance, the old connection between Leicester liberalism and the national executive of NUBSO was finally severed by Inskip's death in 1899. No future general secretary was to sit in the council chamber as the Liberal representative for St Margaret's ward, that seat being filled in 1904 by Charlie Freak, the union's general president and member of the national LRC. Leicester liberalism failed to fill the vacuum created by desertion and death in its working-class ranks. No satisfactory replacement for T. Smith, another former NUBSO general secretary, could be found when he retired from the key position of secretary to the Liberal Association, and the small

170

group of three Liberal working-class councillors in 1902 were not re-placed when they left office.

The working-class Liberal wards underwent a period of financial crisis in the early years of this century, a crisis from which they failed to recover. To field a candidate against a Labour contestant placed the working-class Liberal ward under severe pressure. The problem could only be solved by the Liberal Association imposing a levy of £10 on those Liberal candidates who were contesting seats where there was no Labour opponent.[108] By 1907 the Association's minute book noted the difficulty in finding candi-dates to fight the forthcoming Guardian elections, while the municipal elections in November of that year placed the party machine under such strain that the entire ward organization of the town had to be subordi-nated to the executive committee.[109] Even this measure was not a success, the executive having to bail out the Castle ward to the sum of £15 after the election.[110] During the following year Leicester liberalism reached a new low when the municipal election subcommittee reported that 'a vigorous electoral campaign will bring reprisals by our rivals and even safe seats would prove expensive to defend'.[111]

When a political party in the early years of the present century lost members it experienced other adverse effects apart from financial ones. In particular all those aspects of political life which can be broadly cate-gorized as social and educational began to suffer. Regular ward meetings became formal rather than lively and local organizations appear to have ceased their social and propaganda functions. Such atrophy during a period when local political organization was highly dependent upon multifarious activities in order to hold together its activist members in the periods between elections could only spell disaster. The executive of Leicester's Liberal Association was naturally worried about the decline of ward activity. In November 1905 the Association's minute book expressed 'concern over the condition of ward organisation and the lack of interest shown in political work by various committees'. During the following month the Association resolved 'that ward committees arrange more meet-ings of a social educational and political nature'.[112] By May 1908 a certain desperation can be detected in the Association's decision to combat Labour's propaganda campaign by holding outdoor meetings, a method previously frowned upon by Liberals.[113] These efforts to bolster their flagging organization, however, appear to have borne little fruit. Labour continued to gain seats on both the Board of Guardians and in the council chamber, while liberalism became increasingly dependent on an alliance with the Tories in their attempt to stem the Labour tide.

The Liberals' concern with the decline of local organization and propa-ganda suggests that the opposite process was under way in the Labour camp. We have already seen that Labour was riding a crest of popular discontent over persistent unemployment, but to what extent was the party developing the accretions that are necessary to sustain a political organization when popular movements inevitably wane? What contemporaries called a 'political machine' was undoubtedly established by Leicester's Labour movement during the period under review but a survey of this organization has to encompass other aspects of the movement than the simple sketching of the party's anatomy by marking the lines of local headquarters and ward committees. The establishment of the Labour Party as a permanent political force in Leicester was achieved by the development of three distinct yet closely related areas of activity: propaganda, organization and socialization.

To a new political movement with few resources propaganda is the first and most necessary task for survival. The early socialists in Leicester were perhaps more fortunate than others in starting life in the local Secular Hall. Tom Barclay and the few other working-class secularists who formed the nucleus of the local branch of the Socialist League brought two essential attributes to the movement: the ability to hold lively controversial discussions and the willingness to utilize for propaganda purposes Leicester's time-honoured open air pitches, at the market place, Humberstone Gate and Russell Square, in use since the days of the Charter and beyond. Barclay was justly proud of his recruitment successes at these meetings. Many of Leicester's future Labour leaders' first experience of socialist doctrine was at these Sunday events. The tradition of the working-class stump orator continued up until the First World War in Leicester as an integral part of the Labour movement, perhaps reaching its apogee during the 1905 unemployment campaign.[114] Yet effective as outdoor campaigning could be it had serious limitations. Poor weather and a few dull speakers could combine to negate perhaps a year's hard work. Other means of getting the message across had to be found. The establishment of a local Labour press admirably filled this gap.

The *Pioneer* was probably one of the most successful of the early Labour weeklies. Started by Barclay in the early 1890s, it cost ½d. and claimed a circulation of 5,000 in 1895. Publication, however, appears to have been intermittent until 1899 when F. J. Gould, the full-time secretary of the Secular Hall and former journalist, devoted his energy and organizational talents to the paper.[115] As in the period of Barclay's editorship, the *Pioneer* was always well endowed with advertisements and under Gould's guidance began a more settled period of publication. The paper developed a lively journalistic style, not unlike the *Clarion*, aimed at mass appeal. A sports page with commentaries on local soccer and cricket matches, reviews of performances at local music halls and theatres, book reviews and the serialization of popular novels all helped to enliven the *Pioneer*'s other more mundane functions. Politics was given a central place in this Labour weekly. A page devoted to the national scene provided a useful left-wing contrast to the picture offered by the national and local orthodox press, while local politics were presented in what must have been a refreshing new dimension. The *Pioneer* also served as a notice-board for all the organizations involved in the Labour movement, from the women's auxiliary of the ILP to the Trades Council. Furthermore, the *Pioneer* offered the Labour movement the opportunity of engaging the attention of those members of the working class not formally active within the Labour movement, but who nevertheless sympathized with the socialist cause, a section of society characterized by Blatchford as 'the unattached'. It is of course notoriously difficult to gauge the efficacy of the Labour press in such areas as propaganda and recruitment, but allegations of corruption on the Board of Guardians certainly caused a minor storm amongst the members when they appeared in 1904,[116] while MacDonald, acutely aware of the role played by the *Pioneer*, devoted both time, in the form of articles, and money to the weekly.[117] Above all the *Pioneer* assisted in the building up of a sense of unity and community in the local Labour movement; it was their paper and all the various groups and institutions used it to the full.

The importance of this coordinating function brings us to our next element in the process of party building, establishing a physical organization. Gaining recruits and sympathizers during periods of industrial crisis or widespread unemployment is one thing; holding on to this new support and moulding it into a tangible phenomenon like a political party required different talents from those of stump rhetoric and cutting journalism. The new party could not compete with the salubrious offices of the Liberals and Conservatives but facilities were at hand within the existing Labour movement. An early example of cooperation between the industrial and political wings of the Labour movement was the location of the office at the Socialist League branch inside the headquarters of the LAHU. As we have seen, the ILP during the 1890s was based in the local Labour Club, but as this institution foundered the party headquarters moved along with the new LRC into the Trades Council Hall.[118] The formation of the Leicester LRC in 1903 provided an organizational lifeline to the ILP. The LRC took over the important functions of coordinating, financing and superintending electoral matters. The ILP was thus free to concentrate upon propaganda without the worry of having constantly to engage in fund-raising activities. Despite the presence of a few Lib-Labers on the Trades Council the LRC existed harmoniously alongside the ILP. The smooth operation of this political division of Labour can largely be explained by the dominant presence of NUBSO and the LAHU upon the Trades Council. Both these unions possessed socialist leaders. Indeed most of the leading officers of the LRC were long-standing members of the ILP, men like Martin Curley. The LRC president was T. F. Richards, chief assistant in the industrial and political struggles of the early 1890s, a fact not lost upon Leicester's Liberals whose Association minute book acidly notes the decision to 'refer in future to the Labour Party as the I.L.P.'.[119]

Liberated from electoral worries the ILP concentrated its energies upon building up a strong network of ward organizations. Again the reorganized Labour movement was bequeathed a structure that had been first laid down in the early 1890s. The initial ward organization of the mid-1890s based in the neighbourhood coffee and cocoa houses was replaced by a more formal system holding regular meetings usually in school rooms. The new ward organizations were from the beginning extremely active in propaganda work and in bringing their respective communities into the party structure. Up until 1903, however, this ward organization was probably skeletal and only functioned in those districts, such as Richards's base in Wyggeston, which had a tradition of electoral activity. The unemployment campaign of 1903–5 breathed life into the existing district committees as well as expanding their numbers.[120] With the growth of Labour's appeal the wards faced the task of socializing the new members into the party. This process took the form of women's circles, summer picnics, bazaars, children's activities and guest lectures.[121] The role of political discussion and education naturally took on a new significance and importance against the backcloth of the unemployment campaign and to meet this need many of the wards developed their own Labour churches based in the district committee rooms.

The first reference to the Labour church movement in Leicester appeared in 1903 some years after the collapse of Trevor's organization. By 1905 there were four churches in the town. It is all too easy to exaggerate the role of religion in the early Labour movement, placing the party on a continuum that stretches back to Victorian nonconformity. The reports on the Sunday meetings of the four Leicester Labour churches that appeared in the *Pioneer*, presumably compiled by persons attending the gatherings, rarely mention any religious aspects apart perhaps from an occasional visit from a *Clarion* choir.[122] The churches were invariably a winter phenomenon and appear to have been a substitute for Sunday outdoor campaigning. This suggests that the Labour church in Leicester was primarily a ruse to allow for indoor socialist lectures on a Sunday without offending sabbatarian sentiments, especially amongst those responsible for hiring the publicly owned meeting rooms.[123] The leading figures in the movement came from a variety of religious backgrounds. Banton was a noted nonconformist, Gould a leading secularist, Bibbings a spiritualist lecturer, Sherriff a lapsed salvationist, while many others appear to have had no religious affiliations. Above all, the meetings were political, favourite topics being the cure for unemployment, the land question and socialist themes. The churches continued until 1910 when interest began to wane. Throughout the period they were an integral part of the wards' social and educational activities.

The possession of a broad-based party machine could, however, present problems for the leaders of Leicester's Labour movement. In particular the LRC was now vulnerable to policy initiatives emanating from the wards. The first signs of tension were, as we have seen, shown in the 1904

174

Guardian elections when some of the local Labour leaders were unhappy at the party's break from the progressive alliance. Problems increased during the following years as the unemployment movement gathered momentum. The new Guardians elected in 1904 included a number of men who differed in social background from the full-time trade union officials who had previously dominated Labour's elected representatives. This new generation of Labour leaders were often men who had emerged through propaganda work and ward organization rather than from a trade union milieu. Paradoxically the strength of the Leicester trade union movement and its staunch support for Labour had facilitated, by the creation of the LRC, the progress to office of socialists who were not themselves trade union leaders, in contrast to the years before the formation of the LRC, when only Trades Council delegates were given election funding by that body. Furthermore, they came to office as the champions of the unemployed. Three of these Guardians, Bibbings, Harris and Sherriff, assisted White in the leadership and organization of the local unemployed demonstrations and processions that began in the winter of 1904–5. These activities culminated in the June 1905 march of 470 unemployed shoemakers to London headed by Sherriff, the local purveyor of the Clarion bicycle, White and F. L. Donaldson, a high church Anglican vicar (see plate 10).

These processions, which were designed partly to bring local attention to the plight of the unemployed and partly to raise money for the workless by street collections, started in the winter of 1904–5. The initial impetus for the processions began in October when the corporation, under pressure from Labour councillors, opened up a labour bureau for the registration of the unemployed, possibly in anticipation of the government extending the local works programme initiated by Chamberlain some years earlier.[124] Resentment, however, was aroused amongst the thousand men who attended the opening of the bureau over footballers and bandsmen being given preference for corporation employment.[125] George White, the young crippled laster who had previously campaigned in the press and lobbied the Guardians for better treatment for those on the 'test', seized the initiative afforded by the lengthy queue of workless outside the Town Hall and led them on a march around the major thoroughfares.[126] This local exercise in street drama caught the attention of a number of the newly elected Labour Guardians. Three of these Guardians, Bibbings, Sherriff and Harris, assisted White in the subsequent daily organization of the processions and usually addressed the gathered unemployed when the walk ended in the market place.

By May the daily gatherings of the unemployed were dominating the local press and the Trades council was warning of the potentially riotous behaviour of the marchers.[127] The local press was certainly concerned by these events and a distinct softening of their previous tough attitude on unemployment relief can be detected in the *Post*. For example, the newspaper's editorial of 5 March 1904, cited above, warning against making life easier for the unemployed for fear of upsetting the local labour market, when contrasted with the warm reception given by the *Post* to the news in May 1905 that the mayor was convening the council's unemployment committee to find new ways of assisting those on relief, shows how much the attitudes of local liberalism had changed over the previous year.[128]

A striking departure in the local unemployment campaign was initiated by the news in May that James Gribble, the full-time NUBSO official in Northampton and leader of that town's formidable SDF organization, was embarking upon a march of striking shoemakers from the village of Raunds to London. This march was designed to lobby Whitehall to impose 'fair wage clauses' upon village manufacturers who had a notorious reputation for sweating their workers employed on army contracts.[129] The Leicester and Northampton socialists had been keen rivals for some time. Gribble, in particular, was a fierce critic of Richards's recently acquired reformism.[130] The successful outcome of the Raunds march, when the government gave way to the strikers' demands, was widely reported in the local press, together with the warm reception given to the marchers in London.[131] An element of one-upmanship was certainly present when Sherriff told the daily meeting of the unemployed on 10 May that plans were being drawn up for a march of unemployed Leicester shoemakers to London.[132] An extra element of topicality was added when Sherriff announced that the march was not to lobby Parliament, but to petition the king, taking as his precedent not Gribble but Gapon and the recent unrest in Russia.[133] Needless to say the local Trades Council and prominent Labour figures were embarrassed by and opposed to Sherriff's scheme. Feelings were heightened when Sherriff told the crowd on 29 May that 'He turned away from a cruel and heartless Parliament and his object was to go and see the King.' '. . . the unemployed in England were suffering under the same conditions as the Russian peasantry; and if the King did not see them then the press of this country would no longer be able to throw stones at the Russian Monarch'.[134]

Two days later the Trades Council condemned the proposed march. Chaplin noted that 'it was not likely that uncle Ted would leave his cosy room to meet them outside Buckingham Palace'. Richards, his youthful militancy making a temporary comeback, supported the march and added that 'the men were acting spontaneously and not on the advice of their leaders'.[135] The Trades Council voted 31 to 22 not to support the march.

This set-back to the marchers was soon reversed. Local interest snowballed and by the time the marchers left the market place singing 'Lead kindly light', 80,000 people had gathered to see their departure.[136] The intervention of F. L. Donaldson, a popular local ritualist vicar, helped to boost support for the march. Dressed in his surplice and academic hood, Donaldson frequently addressed the unemployed in the days before the march. On 1 June he spoke to the gathered crowd telling the men the value of processions and the ancient right of Englishmen to petition the king.[137] When the marchers, mostly shoemakers, left the square headed by Sherriff and White they were joined by their erstwhile opponents Banton and Chaplin, while Donaldson, overcome by the occasion, agreed to accompany the marchers to London as their Father Gapon/John Ball.[138]

The march itself was relatively uneventful. The monotony of the long walk was punctuated by a hymn-singing session orchestrated by Donaldson outside Bunyan's cottage in Bedfordshire.[139] Their time in London was in many ways a disaster, the two-day stay being marred by relentlessly heavy storms. It was reported that Buckingham Palace was surrounded by armed guards, but the weather was so inclement that the men abandoned their march up the Mall.[140] A large meeting, addressed by MacDonald who had been in charge of the London arrangements, was held in Trafalgar Square before the men started their long trek back to Leicester.

MacDonald, who had allegedly 'half killed himself' in organizing and coordinating the marchers' activities in London, presided over the Trafalgar Square meeting. He did not make a speech, choosing instead to give a short introduction in which he claimed that the purpose of the march was to show solidarity with the unemployed of the metropolis. Jabez Chaplin, who, along with other Leicester Labour leaders, had taken the train down to London for the event, was more specific. He noted that the main cause of the march was unemployment in the footwear trade caused by mechanization and concluded that 'in a properly organised system of industry the improvements in industry would simply mean shorter hours and better labour conditions for the workers'. Although involved in the march, MacDonald did not view the rising national unemployment movement as enthusiastically as did Keir Hardie. The movement, claimed Hardie, would force the government to pass the Unemployment Relief Bill and thus establish the principles of (1) moving responsibility on to the community to find work for the unemployed; (2) the cost of this would be a public charge and not a charity; (3) relief would not involve the loss of the rights of citizenship.[141] MacDonald, on the other hand, claimed that the bill was fraught with pitfalls and concluded that it required so many amendments that its passing was unlikely.[142]

The event was not, however, a total failure. A large sum of money, the organizers would never disclose how much, had been collected from well-wishers and its subsequent distribution must have brought some relief. In wider terms the attention raised by the Leicester men helped to stimulate growing agitation against unemployment in other localities. Indeed Brown has argued that the sharp rise in demonstrations, often violent, that followed the Leicester march, forced the government to pass the bill.[143]

The march was also significant in other respects. It can be seen as the swan-song of the radical shoemaker, the death-throes of a working-class cultural tradition being hastened by rapid mechanization and new forms of work organization. The strong element of street theatre that so distinguished the local daily processions and the march itself looks back to the noisy era of artisan agitations. On the other hand the march was the first genuine unemployment march of the modern period and set precedents which others would follow. These events also show that the socialist debate on strategy carried out in the late 1880s had not entirely killed the belief that extra-parliamentary agitation was a useful form of working-class political activity. In this respect the march both looks back to the demonstrations of the 1880s and forward to the unrest of the years before the First World War.

The unemployment agitation in Leicester dissipated in the weeks after the march. Perhaps the organization demanded by the event drained the energy of local activists. In the months of midsummer a sense of both anticlimax and anticipation of the outcome of the Unemployment Bill became the dominant feature of the local Labour movement. Employment prospects also began to improve markedly. Hosiery, which had not suffered from unemployment during the first years of the present century, was employing nearly 6 per cent more workers in November 1905 than it had been in the previous November.[144] More importantly the Leicester footwear trade was at long last increasing levels of employment, so much so that the *Labour Gazette* noted an improvement of 6.7 per cent in employment figures in December 1905 in comparison to the previous December.[145]

Despite this marked improvement unemployment remained the key issue in the November council elections. Labour contested three wards and won two. G. O. Kenny, the victor of the Aylestone contest, was reported to have 'appealed to the voters because he is in favour of finding work for the workless, decent housing, and the feeding of starving children'. The other successful Labour candidate, J. Riley, had 'campaigned strongly on the right to work'. A fourth Labour candidate was given a clear run in the Wyggeston ward. In their summary of these results the *Post* commented bitterly that 'the Labour Party took up the position that any understanding which may exist between them and the Liberals applies only to the Parliamentary elections and claimed three more seats on the council'.[146]

The 1906 general election campaign was, in contrast to the recent local government contests, a low key affair. Both Broadhurst and MacDonald focused attention on land reform in their local pre-election meetings. The Conservatives, somewhat taken aback by this sudden appearance of unity, refused to attend the meeting arranged by the mayor to discuss the fixing of the polling day.[147] The Conservatives were not the only body upset by apparent collusion between Broadhurst and MacDonald. The Trades Council meeting on 2 January was dominated by misgivings over the prospect of MacDonald sharing the same platform with Broadhurst. Many delegates expressed their concern over such a public abandonment of the principle of Labour independence and a fierce debate followed. The discussion, however, was concluded by Chaplin pointing out to the meeting that no matter how distasteful they might have found the campaign, independence had to be sacrificed in order to reverse the Taff Vale decision.[148]

The Conservatives attempted to make tariff reform the main issue but as elsewhere the threat of a 'stomach tax' proved stronger than the vague promise of increased employment.[149] Broadhurst initiated the Lib-Lab campaign by emphasizing the importance of land reform in his first election meeting. The land question was the key issue in 1906, according to Broadhurst, as it was the only way to 'prevent the migration of labourers from the country into the great centres of industry'. MacDonald began his campaign three days later with a crowded open meeting at the Temperance Hall. Flanked by Sir Edward Wood and George Banton, MacDonald told the audience that he supported the Liberal government's proposals on Chinese labour and their amendments to the Unemployment Act. He continued with an outline of his own policies on such matters as three-yearly parliaments, female suffrage, the payment of members and the abolition of the House of Lords. He concluded this section of his speech by noting that he was, however, 'Quite content to support such instalments of reform as he could get'.[150] This was followed by his elucidation of his own social policies which were 'the elevation of the family, drastic land legislation, training colonies, the taxation of unearned income, and the rights of local authorities to acquire land'.

There was little in this programme which differed from Broadhurst's policy. The 'elevation of the family', for example, was MacDonald's term for ending female industrial labour. There was nothing new in this idea, indeed Broadhurst had proposed the same policy locally in the late 1880s.[151] 'Men were being supplanted by women ...', MacDonald told the audience, 'they were brought in not to be economically independent but to undersell man's labour. This was fundamentally wrong. (Cheers).' Similarly his ideas on land reform display the hallmark of nineteenth-century radicalism. He 'believed in drastic land legislation, in reviving peasant industries ... in the revival of agricultural security and village recreations ... unemployed farms should be made colleges of agriculture so that men and women could be taught the arts and mysteries of growing fruit and vegetables'.[152] Such ideas no doubt would have sounded equally at home if they had been expressed in Lossiemouth but MacDonald was not out to inspire in January 1906. He was being extremely cautious so as not to alienate the Liberal vote from the progressive alliance.

Away from the large, much publicized, town centre meetings MacDonald placed less emphasis upon land reform. This was especially the case in the wards where he could frequently be faced by a more critical audience. At one of these venues he was accused of 'hobnobbing with the bosses', a reference to his appearance on the platform with Wood, the chairman of

Freeman, Hardy and Willis. He met this particular accusation with the riposte that he 'did not hobnob with anyone' and then went on to discuss the need for housing reform.[153] Yet even at these engagements MacDonald was ever cautious. For example, at the Willow Street meeting his late arrival gave his wife, Margaret, the opportunity to address the audience on the need for factory legislation and shorter working hours. When MacDonald finally arrived he took over from his wife, promising the audience that he intended to fight for a major redistribution of income. This reform, however, was to be achieved by 'not so much a detailed programme as a certain tone of mind'. The spiritualists found him equally reticent when he addressed a meeting at their hall in Silver Street, chaired by Chaplin, the call for housing reform being the high point of his speech. The following day's meeting at Oxford Street School found MacDonald more forthcoming when he spoke on the need for the provision of school meals.[154] This cautious approach paid handsome dividends. MacDonald polled only 60 votes less than Broadhurst, a good indication of the Labour candidate's appeal to Leicester Liberals.[155]

There is a danger of overemphasizing the degree of potential criticism that could be levied at MacDonald from the ranks of the Leicester Labour movement. We must keep in mind the point that MacDonald's local popularity reached new heights in January 1906. This fact is well illustrated by the *Pioneer*'s account of his adoption meeting at the Temperance Hall:

> As the speaker [MacDonald] led them through the many intricate subjects with which he dealt they seemed to follow him with an almost breathless eagerness. As he added fact to fact, and little by little completed the sequence of a practically faultless argument, one could almost feel the pent-up excitement of the audience: and when the final climax came and the speaker had added the last link to his chain, there was such a round of cheers as could only have come from the throats of the British working men.[156]

David Marquand has warned the present-day writer of the danger of anachronism in assessing the political theory of MacDonald during this period. 'His theory was produced in and for the 1900s, not for the 1920s and still less for the 1950s or the 1970s.'[157] Marquand buttresses his argument by pointing out that the heart of MacDonald's theory, a staunch belief that idealism not class was the motive power of history, was shared by many other socialists and radicals of the period. The *Pioneer*'s account of his adoption meeting perhaps further underlines Marquand's point, in as much as it suggests that MacDonald's philosophy had wide popular currency. Yet if we move our focus away from the carnival atmosphere of the general election to the more mundane setting of the town council chambers and the Board of Guardians, do we not find Labour representatives motivated by different forces from those of 'progressive idealism'? This is not to argue that the Labour representatives who gained office in local government after 1903 were hardened Marxists with a clear-cut programme for social change. Far from it. They shared much of MacDonald's ambiguity and confusion on how socialism was to be achieved. These councillors and guardians were, however, the product of a local expression of a class-based political movement which had tested and rejected the policy of collaboration with progressive liberalism. It is therefore of little wonder that MacDonald proved to be so testy over charges of abandoning Labour's independence, for between the two poles of parliamentary and local elections lay two opposing conceptions of both the structure and style of working-class politics.

This contradiction between 'class' and 'idealism' remained below the surface, apart from the few acid comments expressed at ward meetings, during the election campaign. Several factors explain this particular squaring of the circle. Taff Vale undoubtedly worked in MacDonald's favour as it effectively silenced the Trades Council, the most powerful potential source of opposition. Indeed MacDonald fully utilized the acquiescence of organized labour to the idea of the Lib–Lab pact. At the Temperance Hall meeting he told his audience that 'He was on no account going to ask them to plump on polling day. The Trades Council advised everybody influenced by the Labour movement to vote for Mr. Broadhurst and him.'[158] Populism was another factor fully exploited by MacDonald. His remarks on the South African war and Chinese labour display his skill in appealing to the working man's sense of indignation over the loss of employment opportunity:

> They were told it [the war] was going to plant the Union Jack upon the land of the free. But the echoes of the muskets had hardly died out on the battlefields, the ink on the treaty was hardly dry, before the men who plotted the war began to plot to bring in Chinese slaves. (Cheers). They could talk about their gold; their gold is tainted. (Hear Hear). They could talk about employing white men; it was not true, and even if it were true, was he going to stand and see his white brothers degraded to the position of yellow slave drivers? No, he was not. (Loud and continuous cheers).[159]

If we project forward to the period immediately after the scope of this book it is interesting to note that virtually the same set of circumstances was to work in favour of the Lib–Lab pact. For example, the need to reverse the Osborne decision over the payment of members firmly tied Labour to the Liberal tail in the elections of 1910.[160] MacDonald's local appeal remained of such a scale that his threatened resignation from the Leicester seat resulted in the abandonment of Leicester Labour Party's plan to field their own candidate at a by-election when the Liberal member resigned in 1913.[161]

Labour politics in Leicester after 1895 shifted away from a concern over the sectional interests of the more skilled male workers towards an emphasis on the problems created by poverty and unemployment in the wake of major industrial changes, particularly in footwear. The growing unemployment movement stimulated party organization while the issues that unemployment created reintroduced the element of class into local politics shortly after the signing of the progressive alliance. The subsequent local elections witnessed the demise of class collaboration in parochial politics and the consolidation and growth of Labour's electoral performance. In order to check the rising tide of Labour's electoral success the Liberals formed a tacit alliance with the Conservatives in local government campaigns. Class collaboration had been abandoned by Labour but the movement continued to lack a sense of direction in terms of policy. Thus old palliatives such as land reform became intermingled with the more modern socialist notions on equality. MacDonald was able to exploit this ambiguity in local Labour politics which together with short-term factors, especially Taff Vale, assured him of a submissive Labour movement in his joint campaign with Henry Broadhurst.

Despite this 'progressive' victory the golden age of Leicester liberalism was at an end. The backbone of Leicester liberalism had been the coalition between the working and middle class, an alliance assiduously cultivated by John Biggs and sealed with the election of P. A. Taylor in 1862. This class alliance had been welded in a period dominated by artisan forms of production. The inescapable fact behind the break up of the alliance was that by the early years of the present century the artisans had been replaced by semi-skilled factory operatives. The material base of radical Leicester had vanished in the two decades that separate the retirement of Taylor and the election of MacDonald. Liberal Party organization was in serious decline in most working-class areas and after 1906 the Liberal presence in local elections became increasingly dependent upon terminal nursing care dispensed by the Conservatives.

Conclusion

By comparing the Leicester of 1906 with that of the 1860s we can detect both change and continuity. The first and most notable difference is that of size. The population increased three-and-a-half fold during the period. The local economy also underwent a thoroughgoing transformation, especially with the growing importance of footwear. Yet the economy was not, unlike that of other similar towns, experiencing the advantages of a diversified manufacturing base. Hosiery and footwear employed 37.3 per cent of the workforce in 1861 and 53.9 per cent in 1901. Leicester in 1901 still awaited the benefits of new metal-based industries; this sector of the economy employed 7.2 per cent of the workforce in 1861, and 6.1 per cent in 1901. Despite the continuous importance of these two trades to Leicester major changes had occurred in the production of footwear and hosiery. If a stockinger or riveter from the 1860s could have toured a hosiery or footwear factory in the early years of the present century he would have been astounded by changes in the production process. First and foremost of these changes would be the actual location of production. Gone were the workshops, garrets and domestic-based units, to be replaced by steam-powered factories. Inside the factories noisy machinery had replaced the hand frames and lasting benches. The workers who operated the new devices were, in hosiery, largely female, and in footwear, predominantly male, but younger semi-skilled operatives, relentlessly paced by the mechanized teams.

Such profound changes in the world of work altered the cultural and political disposition of the workforce. The informal milieu of workshop production had provided the ideal environment for nurturing an artisan life style. Observance of St Monday, a physical and material distancing from the ultimate employer, autonomy over the production process, and for those who had a taste for such things, participation in a lively radical political culture, were real benefits which coexisted with the many curses of such a mode of industrial organization. In contrast the hosiery and footwear workers of the early 1900s experienced the routinized reality of modern factory life. Hosiery production was becomingly increasingly dominated by female labour while the descendants of the stocking frame knitters, the Cotton's patent operatives, were doggedly fighting to retain their place in this production process via the policy of 'one man, one frame'. The changes in footwear were equally noticeable. The mechanized 'team system' had become virtually universal in the Leicester factories, while the pace of production was now fixed not by custom but by the American machine company. Moreover, de-skilling had been carried out on a wide scale, and those workers who had previously considered themselves craftsmen would be fortunate if they still had work, albeit as semi-skilled machine operatives. Indeed the restructuring of the British footwear industry had become the model for those sections of the business community that still retained a strong faith in the ultimate virtues of free trade.[1]

This thoroughgoing transition was not achieved without disturbance to social and political life. This is not to argue that these areas of life were unchanging before the arrival of factory production. The major expansion in local industry which had earlier occurred was accompanied by a considerable influx of migrant workers. Such growth of what was a highly inefficient form of industrial organization enhanced and reinforced old cultural and working patterns. It is hoped that the discussion on religion has highlighted at least one major shift that was under way in working–class culture during the apparently stable decades between the 1860s and the 1880s. Manufacturers in Leicester during the 1880s and 1890s were therefore faced with what was a peculiarly obdurate workforce, and the process of centralization and mechanization was destined to have fundamental social and political consequences for the local community.

Employers in Leicester since the days of the reformed corporation had dominated local politics. The connections between class and political allegiance were brought to the fore as workers wrestled with manufacturers who formed the spine of local liberalism. The political upheavals which accompanied the economic ones were not, however, simply a matter of workers becoming disenchanted with liberalism because that happened to be the party of the bosses. This is not to deny that the identity of interest between employers and liberalism was not brought into question by elements of the Labour movement. The rhetoric of the socialist shoemakers during the early 1890s and the language of class that was utilized during the 1894 by-election highlight the importance of this factor. The argument that has been posed in this study is that liberalism was questioned and ultimately rejected by a large section of the Leicester working class because it was both the manufacturers' doctrine and also highly unsuitable in dealing with the problems of poverty and unemployment created by economic dislocation.

Even the above formulation is incomplete. Socialism required more than propitious local circumstances and national advocates. A layer of local activists rooted in the community was required to build and sustain the movement. Leicester was unusually well served in this vital area. The virile artisan political culture of the town provided a group of young men well versed in the art of controversy and with the audacity both to espouse and to propagate new radical ideas. Of perhaps equal importance were the people who listened to the socialist propaganda and related the new theory to their own circumstances. In particular the trade union officers and Trades Council delegates who formed the bulk of the Leicester ILP upon its formation in 1894 selectively harnessed ideas propagated by members of the Socialist League and the SDF in the production of a political ideology tailored to local circumstances.

Thus the socialism of the Leicester ILP was an expression of indigenous working–class traditions, contemporary circumstances and socialist ideas. The Labour movement that the new party was attempting to lead and shape both looked back to what increasingly appeared to have been a golden age of workshop production and forward to the collective solution of poverty. The ILP succeeded in winning a substantial section of working-class electoral support because it could draw strength from both facets of this apparent ambiguity.

The themes pursued in this book are manifestly central to the debate currently being waged over the rise of independent Labour politics and the decline of liberalism. One group of historians has argued that the rise of Labour was inevitable, although they differ over the factors which created Labour's inexorable growth.[2] A second group has pointed to the tenacity of liberalism: surviving on its traditional links with nonconformity in Wales, reinvigorated by 'New' liberalism in Lancashire, or sustained by a combination of 'Old' and 'New' Liberalism in the North–East of England.[3] The evidence presented in this study clearly supports the first group. Continuities can obviously be discerned between liberalism and Labour in Leicester but grand generalizations on the subject lose sight of particularity, context and the drama of the historical process as it shaped, and was being shaped by, the activities of seemingly unimportant people.

Appendix 1   Population growth 1851–1901 (Leicester)

	1851	1861	1871	1881	1891	1901
Males	28,691	31,766	44,973	57,720	82,441	99,014
Females	31,893	36,290	50,247	64,656	92,183	112,565
Total	60,584	68,056	95,220	122,376	174,624	211,579

Source: Census reports, 1851–1901

Appendix 2 Industrial employment 1851–1901: percentages (Leicester)

	1851	1861	1871	1881	1891	1901
Agriculture	3.4	3.6	3.1	1.1	1.8	1.3
Mines and quarries	1.7	1.8	1.9	1.5	1.2	0.4
Metals, etc.	4.0	7.2	6.0	4.6	6.2	6.1
Precious metals, etc.	0.2	0.1	0.3	0.3	0.3	1.0
Building, etc.	5.6	6.8	10.8	10.2	6.6	9.7
Furniture, etc.	3.7	2.4	6.2	1.0	1.1	2.2
Bricks, etc.	1.7	1.4	0.9	0.7	1.0	0.4
Chemicals, etc.	1.1	0.7	0.9	2.9	2.2	2.1
Skins, etc.	0.7	0.7	0.8	0.7	0.8	0.9
Paper, etc.	0.3	0.2	0.3	0.9	1.2	3.9
Textiles	51.9	44.6	31.5	32.2	27.0	23.5
Dress	25.7	30.5	37.3	43.9	50.6	48.5
	100.0	100.0	100.0	100.0	100.0	100.0
HOSIERY	38.5	26.4	20.7	22.2	21.5	17.1
FOOTWEAR	6.2	10.9	21.6	33.4	41.0	36.8

Source: Census reports, 1851–1901

Appendix 3 Industrial employment 1851–1901: numbers (Leicester)

	1851	1861	1871	1881	1891	1901
Agriculture	757	906	733	413	1,035	920
Mines and quarries	392	436	450	604	725	298
Metals, etc.	904	1,803	1,431	1,798	3,634	4,368
Precious metals, etc.	38	28	60	114	168	710
Building, etc.	1,260	1,700	2,569	3,998	3,874	7,010
Furniture, etc.	839	591	1,470	396	663	1,593
Bricks, etc.	377	351	200	280	604	272
Chemicals, etc.	258	188	226	1,153	1,274	1,524
Skins, etc.	157	182	196	252	444	679
Paper, etc.	62	57	58	342	715	2,844
Textiles	11,643	11,128	7,488	12,575	15,944	17,004
Dress	5,769	7,611	8,862	17,178	29,857	35,029
Total	22,456	24,981	23,743	39,103	58,937	72,251
HOSIERY	8,652	6,602	4,923	8,699	12,667	12,389
FOOTWEAR	1,396	2,741	5,103	13,056	24,159	26,561

Source: Census reports, 1851–1901

Appendix 4   The employment of male and female labour in the hosiery and footwear industries

	1851	1861	1871	1881	1891	1901
Hosiery						
Numbers:						
M	5,759	4,153	3,037	3,391	4,286	3,282
F	2,893	2,449	1,886	5,308	8,381	9,107
	8,652	6,602	4,923	8,699	12,667	12,389
Percentages:						
M	*66.6*	*62.9*	*61.7*	*39.0*	*33.8*	*26.5*
F	*33.4*	*37.1*	*38.1*	*61.0*	*66.2*	*73.5*
Footwear						
Numbers:						
M	1,071	1,897	3,714	9,173	16,839	17,770
F	325	844	1,389	3,883	7,320	8,791
	1,396	2,741	5,103	13,056	24,159	26,561
Percentages:						
M	76.7	69.2	72.8	70.3	69.7	66.9
F	23.3	30.8	27.2	29.7	30.3	33.1

Source: Census reports, 1851–1901. The number of females employed, particularly in the hosiery industry, is likely to be underestimated during the early decades; the figures for 1871 are for persons over 20 only.

Appendix 5   Estimated immigration 1851–1901: percentages (Leicester)

	1851	1861	1871	1881	1891	1901
London	5.8	8.5	5.2	7.0	5.5	9.7
S.E. counties	2.4	3.2	3.3	3.2	4.5	8.9
S. Midland counties	18.8	19.4	25.6	19.8	17.9	14.7
E. counties	3.8	3.0	3.4	2.9	4.6	6.5
S.W. counties	2.4	1.7	3.5	2.5	2.9	1.1
W. Midland counties	19.4	29.1	22.3	23.8	17.8	18.2
N. Midland counties	28.9	20.0	18.4	23.8	22.5	12.3
N.W. and N.E. counties	12.4	7.5	9.3	10.3	14.3	18.3
N. counties	.9	1.0	1.4	1.2	1.2	2.2
Elsewhere	5.2	6.6	7.6	5.5	8.8	8.1
	100.0	100.0	100.0	100.0	100.0	100.0
Northamptonshire	13.8	13.2	16.5	12.6	8.9	8.9
Warwickshire	11.5	21.4	9.3	11.2	5.0	4.0
Nottinghamshire	8.3	7.2	5.3	9.1	5.6	3.6
Staffordshire	3.2	3.8	6.9	8.6	7.0	6.9
Lincolnshire	10.9	3.9	5.7	5.8	8.2	3.9
Derbyshire	3.9	5.7	3.7	5.2	5.9	6.0

Source: Census reports, 1851–1901

Appendix 6 Trade union membership (Leicester), boot and shoe industry

	NUBSO		
	National	*Leicester*	
		No. 1	*No. 2*
1874	4,204	1,397	Nil
1891	30,046	10,000	1,700
1893	41,274	11,200	2,000
1900	27,960	11,000	1,900
1910	30,197	11,000	2,463

Source: NUBSO Annual Registers

Notes

NOTE: Places of publication are given only for works published outside the United Kingdom.

Introduction

1 R. McKibbin, *The Evolution of the Labour Party 1910–24* (1974), ch. 3.
2 W. Lancaster, 'The tradition of militancy in the Leicester I.L.P.' (M.A. dissertation, University of Warwick, 1979).
3 P. F. Clarke, *Lancashire and the New Liberalism* (1971), 6.
4 McKibbin, *op. cit.*, ch. 2, *passim*.
5 H. Pelling, *The Origins of the Labour Party* (1966 edn), 222.
6 See especially A. E. Musson, 'Industrial motive power in the United Kingdom, 1800–1870', *Economic History Review*, 29 (1976) and his subsequent work *The Growth of British Industry* (1978). See also R. Samuel, 'The workshop of the world, steam power and hand technology in mid-Victorian Britain', *History Workshop Journal*, 3 (1977).
7 W. H. Fraser, *The Coming of the Mass Market 1850–1914* (1981), chs. 2 and 5.
8 See Appendices 1 and 2.

Chapter 1

1 E. J. Hobsbawm's 'The labour aristocracy in nineteenth-century Britain' in *Labouring Men* (1964) is the classic statement on this topic. J. Foster, *Class Struggle and the Industrial Revolution: Early Industrial Capitalism in Three English Towns* (1974) has been the most influential work on the 'labour aristocracy' in recent years. For a review essay that covers most of the contemporary material on the 'labour aristocracy' debate see H. F.

Moorhouse, 'The Marxist theory of the labour aristocracy', *Social History*, 3 (1978). See P. Joyce, *Work, Society and Politics: The Culture of the Factory in Late Victorian England* (1980) on the subject of paternalism and factory community.
2 F. A. Wells, *The British Hosiery and Knitwear Industry: Its History and Organisation* (1972).
3 G. Henson, *The Civil, Political, and Mechanical History of the Framework Knitters* (1831).
4 W. Felkin, *An Account of the Machine-Wrought Hosiery Trade: Its Extent and the Condition of the Framework Knitters*; being a paper read in the statistical section, at the second York meeting of the British Association, 1845.
5 Returns of Factories under Inspection: Steam and Water Power; Persons employed (1862); Returns of the Number of Cotton, Woollen, Shoddy, Worsted, Flax, Hemp, Jute, Rope, Horsehair, Elastic, Hosiery, Lace and Silk Factories, subject to the Factories Act, 1867–8.
6 Felkin, *op. cit.*, 10.
7 Return showing the boroughs and districts in which the Workshops Regulation Act has been enforced (1870), 15.
8 Musson, *op. cit., passim*.
9 Return of the Number of Manufacturing Establishments in which the hours of work are regulated by any act of Parliament (1871), 140.
10 Return of Factory Inspectors Salaries, etc. (1887), 5.
11 Royal Commission on Framework Knitters (1845), minutes of evidence, q. 91.

12 Felkin, *op. cit.*, 10–11.
13 RC on Framework Knitters (1845), minutes of evidence, q. 127.
14 *Ibid.*, q. 135.
15 When wide machines were introduced into the trade at Harwick, female knitters had to be replaced by men, a point that lends colour to the stockingers' view that the operation of wide frames was 'man's work'. B. Drake, *Women in Trade Unions* (1920), 133.
16 J. Dare, *Report of the Leicester Domestic Mission* (1853).
17 SC on Stoppage of Wages (Hosiery) (1855), qq. 2–14.
18 *Ibid.*, q. 363.
19 *Ibid.*, qq. 391–2, 455.
20 *Ibid.*, q. 2,417.
21 *Ibid.*, qq. 1,198, 1,206, 1,238.
22 RC on the Truck System (1871), q. 41,652.
23 C. W. Webb, *Corah's of Leicester* (1948), 16–18.
24 RC on the Truck System, q. 41,665.
25 *Ibid.*, qq. 41,673–4.
26 *Ibid.*, q. 42,855.
27 *Ibid.*, q. 41,732 and SC on Stoppage of Wages (Hosiery), q. 186.
28 W. T. Rowlett, 'The hosiery trade in Leicester', Leicester Chamber of Commerce Yearbook (1911).
29 Wells. *op. cit.*, 119–21.
30 See C. W. and P. Cunnington, *The History of Underclothes* (1951), chs IX and X on the growing importance of undergarments in the dress of the period and the important fad for Jaeger Sanitary Woollen underwear.
31 RC on Depression of Trade and Industry (1886), Appendix II, q. 4,715.
32 *Ibid.*
33 Willkomm was the director of the Hosiery School at Chemnitz.
34 Wells, *op. cit.*, 149.
35 *Ibid.*, 129–30.
36 RC on the Factories and Workshops Acts (1876), qq. 7,602–7.
37 *Ibid.*, q. 7,608.
38 I have been unable to locate any sources on the LHMA, but as Angrave and Harris were prominent members of the Chamber of Commerce, which spearheaded the campaign for technical education in hosiery, the LHMA may have been a subcommittee of the Chamber during this period.
39 Mundella told the RC on Trades Unions 1867–8 that it was the policy of hosiers to select the most skilled hand frame knitters to operate the new technology. RC on Trades Unions (1867–8), Tenth Report, q. 19,464.
40 Wells, *op. cit.*, 158.
41 RC on Factories and Workshops Acts, q. 7,213.
42 RC on Labour (1892), minutes of evidence, qq. 13,773–7.
43 Wells, *op. cit.*, 156.
44 *Ibid.*
45 LAHU monthly report, April 1888.
46 Wells, *op. cit.*, 160.
47 RC on Labour, minutes of evidence, Part II, evidence of J. Holmes, qq. 12,734–7.
48 B. and S. Webb, *History of Trade Unionism* (1901 edn), 40.
49 Wells, *op. cit.*, 88.
50 R. Hall, *An Appeal to the Public, on the Subject of the Framework Knitters Fund* (1820); and R. Hall, *A Reply to the Principal Objections Advanced by Cobbett and Others against the Framework Knitters' Friendly Relief Society* (1821).
51 Hall specifically called the society a 'union' in his pamphlets which is an interesting early appearance of the term.
52 Quoted in Wells, *op. cit.*, 63.
53 See A. T. Patterson, *Radical Leicester. A History of Leicester, 1780–1850* (1954), chs 7 and 8 on this interesting period. Also Leicester Poll Books 1826 on the stockingers' franchise.
54 William Jackson, 'An address to the frame-work knitters of the town and county of Leicester' (1833).
55 J. F. C. Harrison, 'Chartism in Leicester', in A. Briggs (ed.), *Chartist Studies* (1959), 100.
56 Patterson, *op. cit.*, 298–300.
57 Harrison, *op. cit.*; Patterson, *op. cit.*, chs 15, 16.
58 RC on Framework Knitters, qq. 8, 9, 31, 126.
59 Patterson, *op. cit.*, 381; Felkin, *op. cit.*, 10–11.
60 RC on Framework Knitters, qq. 30–8.
61 Hobsbawm, *Labouring Men*, 273.
62 William Biggs in *Leicestershire Mercury*, 3 April 1841.
63 Felkin, *op. cit.*, 19–20.
64 RC on Framework Knitters, qq. 121–7.
65 *Ibid.*, qq. 111, 125.
66 Leicester Poll Books (1826); also see R. W. Greaves, 'Roman Catholic relief and the Leicester election of 1826', in *Transactions* of the Royal Historical

Society (1946) on the importance of local factors in the 1826 election.

67 Leicester Poll Books (1857).
68 RC on Framework Knitters, q. 129.
69 Dare, *op. cit.*, Webb Collection, Section A, 120, 126. There is of course a debate on the question of rising living standards for the period 1850–70. What evidence there is suggests that wages did indeed rise in Leicester hosiery during these years. For a summary of this debate see R. A. Church, *The Great Victorian Boom 1850–1873* (1975).
70 RC on Framework Knitters, q. 55.
71 Cunnington, *op. cit.*, chs 7, 8, 9.
72 See the tables on wages in Miscellaneous Statistics, Part IV (1862), 256; Miscellaneous Statistics, Part IV (1866), 280; Miscellaneous Statistics, Part X (1879), 399; Miscellaneous Statistics, Part XI, (1883), 418. All the above tables are subdivided into Plain, Fancy, and Under Clothes sections.
73 RC on the Truck System, qq. 821–2.
74 Webb Collection, Section A, 121, 141.
75 See RC on Trades Unions (1867–8), evidence of A. J. Mundella, q. 19,342 on the lock-out that led to the instigation of the Nottingham Arbitration Board. Also J. H. Porter, 'Wage bargaining and conciliation agreements, 1860–1914', *Economic History Review*, 33, 3 (1970).
76 RC on the Truck System, q. 840.
77 Webb Collection, Section A, 126.
78 RC on Children's Employment (1863), 264, evidence of A. J. Mundella.
79 G. Willkomm, *Technology of Framework Knitting* (1885), 252.
80 Quoted in Drake, *op. cit.*, 14. The Rev. J. Page Hopps of the Unitarian Great Meeting seems to have been the main instigator of this move, Hopps being an active member of the league, *ibid.*, 17.
81 *Women's Union Journal*, July 1878.
82 RC on the Factories Acts (1876), qq. 7,808–10.
83 Drake, *op. cit.*, 14–16.
84 RC on the Factories Acts, q. 7,804.
85 Wells, *op. cit.*, 158.
86 A. Fox, *A History of the National Union of Boot and Shoe Operatives* (1958), 309. This time the propaganda came from the suffragettes.
87 Drake, *op. cit.*, 14.
88 B. L. Hutchins and A. Harrison, *A History of Factory Legislation* (1903) still offers the best account of the complexities of the nineteenth-century Acts.
89 RC on the Factories Acts, qq. 137–8.
90 Webb Collection, Section A, vol. 34, 2.
91 It is extremely difficult, because of the diversity of products, to furnish precise figures for wage rates. This is further hampered by the lack of data on this subject. The nearest reliable information that is available was published in Miscellaneous Statistics, Part XI (1883), 418, which show that earnings for male power frame knitters in the plain branch of the trade were 30s. 0d. per week in comparison with 24s. 0d. for hand frame men.
92 C. W. Webb, *op. cit.*, 33. The firm also did much business manufacturing football kits.
93 *Leicester Illustrated*, 1891, 36–7.
94 RC on Labour (1892), Part II, qq. 12,729–34.
95 E. Royle, *Radicals, Secularists and Republicans. Popular Freethought in Britain 1866–1915* (1980), 20.
96 *Commonweal*, 24 March 1888.
97 D. W. S. Higgins, 'For the socialist cause: Rowland Barrett: a biography, 1877–1950' (M.A. dissertation, University of Warwick, 1980), 137.
98 Leicester Hosiery Union Minutes, 14 August 1911.
99 Drake, *op. cit.*, table II.
100 T. J. Chandler, 'The Leicestershire hosiery trade 1844–1954', *Hosiery Trade Journal* (April 1955).
101 Wright's *Leicester Directory* (1888).
102 RC on Labour, Part II, qq. 12,723–7.
103 For an account of these riots see the issues of the *Leicester Chronicle and Mercury* for February 1886.
104 Wright's *Leicester Directory* (1888).
105 LAHU monthly report, April 1886.
106 *Ibid.*, October 1888.
107 *Ibid.*, November 1890.
108 RC on Labour, Part II, q. 12,789, evidence of J. Holmes.
109 Leicester Trades Council Annual Report, 1897.
110 LAHU monthly report, January 1890.
111 *Ibid.*, October 1891.
112 *Leicester Advertiser*, 20 February 1886. Letter from J. H. Cooper, director of N. Corah and Sons, and Cooper.
113 Webb Collection, Section A, vol. 34.
114 *Ibid.* Letter from Jabez Chaplin of the LAHU executive committee which related how this was already happening

in Nottingham, where one adult male 'overlooked' four frames typically operated by women and youths. Chaplin's major complaint was against similar development in Leicester where the union had been forced in several instances to allow adult males to 'overlook' two frames each, operated by youths.

115 Printed in the LAHU monthly report, April 1888.

116 RC on the Factories Acts, q. 7,213, evidence of D. Merrick.

117 Willkomm, *op. cit.*, 324–5.

118 RC on Labour, part 2, qq. 13,773–6.

119 LAHU monthly report, April 1888.

120 *Ibid.*, May 1889 and January 1890. The efficiency and versatility of these machines was so great that even the union-backed Leicester Cooperative Hosiery Society, a producers' cooperative, was tempted to introduce the steam-powered automatic 'Griswolds', see T. Blandford and G. Newell, *A History of the Leicester Cooperative Hosiery Manufacturing Society Ltd.* (1898), 53.

121 Webb Collection, Section A, vol. 34.

122 LAHU monthly report, February 1890.

123 Drake, *op. cit.*, table II.

124 LAHU monthly report, February 1890, June 1888, January 1891.

125 In 1885 there were 800 female members to 600 males – Annual Report of the Chief Labour Correspondent on Trade Unions.

126 Drake, *op. cit.*, 17.

127 Webb Collection, Section A, vol. 34.

128 Wells, *op. cit..*, 164.

129 RC on Labour, part 2, q. 12,835.

130 In the late 1890s the Leicester Cooperative Hosiery Manufacturing Society employed over 300 LAHU members and Holmes was both a member of the management committee and a leading figure in the society.

131 LAHU monthly report, April 1888.

132 The LAHU in November 1890 organized a meeting of all trades in Leicester, at the Bond Street Working Men's Club, with the object of increasing union membership amongst female workers. The only female speakers who appeared in the report of this meeting were Miss Abrahams (Lady Dilke's secretary) and Mrs Briant of the Nottingham Cigar Makers Society. LAHU monthly report, November 1890.

133 RC on Labour, part 2, q. 12,806.

134 LAHU monthly report, November 1889.

135 LAHU monthly report, November 1890, November 1889, August 1889.

136 *Commonweal*, 24 March 1888.

137 RC on Labour, part 2, q. 13,626.

138 8,652 were recorded as being employed in hosiery in the 1851 census, 12,667 in 1891. During the same period industrial employment rose from 22,456 in 1851 to 58,937 in 1891.

139 See the letter of J. Holmes to the *Leicester Daily Post*, 30 November 1889.

Chapter 2

1 Census reports 1851–1901.

2 See Appendices 1 and 2.

3 A. T. Patterson, *Radical Leicester. A History of Leicester, 1780–1850* (1954), 388. J. Simmons, *Leicester Past and Present* (1974), II, 2–5.

4 *Ibid.*; V. W. Hogg, 'Footwear production', in *Victoria County History of Leicester*, IV (1958), 314–19.

5 Hogg, *op. cit.*, 314.

6 *Ibid.*

7 White's *Directory of Leicester* (1846), 143.

8 *Ibid.*, 172–4.

9 The method had been applied during the Napoleonic Wars, but had subsequently disappeared from use. See J. H. Clapham, '*Economic history of Great Britain*', Vol. 2 '*Free Trade and Steel*' (1963 edn), 94.

10 *Hiltons 1869–1969: S. Hilton & Sons Ltd* (1969), 6.

11 Spencer's *New Guide to Leicester* (1888), 191.

12 RC on Children's Employment, 2nd Report (1864), 165.

13 *Ibid.*, 3rd Report (1864), 125.

14 Crick's was the only Leicester boot firm to furnish specific data to the RC on Children's Employment.

15 Drake's *Directory of Leicester* (1861), 74–5; C. W. Webb, *Corah's of Leicester* (1948), 40.

16 H. Hartopp, *Roll of the Mayors of the Borough and Lord Mayors of the City of Leicester, 1209–1935* (1935), 211–12.

17 J. Dare, *Report of the Leicester Domestic Mission* (1875).

18 RC on Children's Employment, 2nd Report, 166. Evidence of Mr Johnson,

Crick's foreman, 'Some employers let out sewing machines just as the old stocking frames were let out for hire. I believe they pay about 1s. 6d. per week.'

19 *Ibid.*, 165.

20 See above, Chapter 1.

21 *Stead and Simpson Centenary, 1834–1934* (n.d.), private print, unpaginated.

22 Hogg, *op. cit.*, 316.

23 RC on Children's Employment, 3rd Report, 130.

24 J. Schumpeter, *Business Cycles* (1939), I, 391.

25 National Union of Boot & Shoe Operatives, Monthly Report, December 1890.

26 *Hiltons 1869–1969*, 10, 12.

27 Hartopp, *op. cit.*, 254–5.

28 *Leicester Illustrated* (1891), 58–9.

29 P. R. Mountfield, 'The location of footwear manufacture in England and Wales' (Ph.D. thesis, University of Nottingham, 1962), 286.

30 Clapham, *op. cit.*, 95.

31 RC on Children's Employment, 2nd Report, 247.

32 *Ibid.* 165.

33 *Leicester Illustrated* (1891), 83–5.

34 J. T. Day, 'The boot and shoe trade,', in H. Cox (ed), *British Industries under Free Trade* (1902), 237.

35 D. F. Schloss, '*Bootmaking; Life and Labour*' (1889), 237.

36 E. J. Hobsbawm and J. W. Scott, 'Political shoemakers', *Past and Present, 89* (1980), 94–5.

37 G. B. Sutton, *C. and J. Clark 1833–1903. A History of Shoemaking in Street, Somerset* (1979), 67.

38 H. C. Hillman, 'The size of firms in the boot and shoe industry', *Economic Journal, 49* (1939), 283.

39 Talents which well accord with More's concept of 'genuine skill'. See C. More, *Skill and the English Working Class 1870–1914* (1980), ch. 1 *passim*.

40 Quoted in A. Fox, *A History of the National Union of Boot and Shoe Operatives, 1870–1957* (1958), 20.

41 *Ibid.*, 21.

42 Miscellaneous Statistics, Part VI (1866), 293.

43 Fox, *op. cit.*, 21.

44 Of the ten firms visited by the reporter who compiled the accounts of footwear factories for *Leicester Illustrated* (1891), the clicking rooms contained on average 10 per cent of the workforce.

45 RC on Children's Employment, 2nd Report, 165.

46 *Ibid.*, 247.

47 RC on the Factories and Workshops Acts (1876), q. 7,140.

48 Miscellaneous Statistics, Part VI (1866), 293; *Ibid.*, Part X (1879), 406.

49 V. A. Hatley, 'Monsters in Campbell Square. The early history of two industrial premises in Northampton', *Northamptonshire Past and Present, 4, 1* (1966–7). R. A. Church, 'Labour supply and innovation, 1800–1860: the boot and shoe industry', *Business History, 12* (1970).

50 RC on Children's Employment, 2nd Report, 167.

51 *Shoe and Leather Record*, 22 November 1890, quoted in Fox, *op. cit.*, 22–3.

52 Dare, *op. cit.* (1862).

53 See also Appendix 5 which highlights the growth in numbers of immigrants from Staffordshire during this period.

54 T. F. Richards, 'How I Got On', *Pearsons Weekly*, 26 April 1906.

55 RC on Children's Employment, 2nd Report, 167.

56 Miscellaneous Statistics, Part X (1879), 406.

57 Dare, *op. cit.* (1865).

58 NUBSO monthly report, March 1891.

59 Factory Inspector's Reports (1863), 39; Dare, *op. cit.* (1865).

60 Richards, *op. cit.*

61 Dare, *op. cit.* (1875).

62 NUBSO monthly report, September 1883.

63 See Appendix 2.

64 The census figures probably understate the number of employees in the industry. Given the fact that the trade was highly seasonal there was a large reserve of labour in the town, mainly women and children, who were often recruited to cope with periods of high demand.

65 The 1891 and 1901 figures include the clickers' No. 2 Branch, who joined the union in 1891.

66 RC on the Factories and Workshops Acts (1876), qq. 7,560–75, 7, 090, 7,135–6.

67 The Unitarian's spokesman, J. Dare, had persistently denounced workshop production in the pages of his annual reports.

68 RC on the Factories and Workshops Acts (1876), qq. 7,516–18.

69 Day, *op. cit.*, 237.

70 Schumpeter, *op. cit.*, I, 391.

71 Dare, *op. cit* (1872).
72 M. H. Dodd, 'Marlboro Massachusetts and the shoe workers strike of 1898–1899', *Labor History, 20*, 3 (1979). See also J. T. Cumbler, *Working-Class Community in Industrial America* (Westport, Conn., 1979), 13–17 for a survey of the development of the shoe industry in Lynn, Massachusetts.
73 Sutton, *op. cit.*, 150–2.
74 H. A. Silverman, *Studies in Industrial Organisation* (1946), 204–9 surveys regional diversification in footwear production. See also *Leicester Illustrated* (1891), 51 on the importance of football boots to Walker and Kempson's factory.
75 Silverman, *op. cit.*
76 Sutton, *op. cit.*, 25.
77 Schloss, *op. cit.*, 254. Schloss noted that 'men's men can only make a lady's boot with difficulty and cannot make a lady's slipper at all; and vice versa'.
78 P. Head, 'Boots and shoes', in D. H. Aldcroft (ed.), *The Development of British Industry and Foreign Competition 1875–1914* (1968), 160.
79 Wright's *Directory of Leicester* (1880), 13.
80 NUBSO monthly report, June 1887.
81 *Labour Gazette*, 1893–1900.
82 Head, *op. cit.*, 159.
83 Fox, *op. cit.*, 89.
84 NUBSO monthly report, November 1888.
85 *Shoe and Leather Record*, 17 November 1888.
86 Up until 1891 the greater proportion of Leicester shoe workers worked 'outdoors'. RC on Labour (1892), Group C, part 2, q. 16,019, evidence of W. Inskip.
87 RC on the Factories and Workshops Acts (1876), q. 7,573.
88 NUBSO monthly report, April 1881.
89 Inspectors of Factories Returns. Showing names, dates of appointment, salaries, etc. (1887), 4.
90 RC on the Factories and Workshops Acts (1876), q. 7,403.
91 NUBSO monthly report, September 1883.
92 *Ibid.*, June 1880.
93 *Ibid.*, September 1883,
94 Head, *op. cit.*, 171.
95 B. and S. Webb, *History of Trade Unionism* (1919), 163.
96 See G. Thorn, 'The early history of the "Amalgamated Society of Boot and Shoemakers (Cordwainers)"', *Bulletin* of the Society for the Study of Labour History, *39* (1979) on the lack of source material on this organization.
97 Fox, *op. cit.*, ch. I.
98 This brief account is largely based on Fox, ch. I *passim.*
99 The union's name was changed to NUBSO in 1880.
100 B. and S. Webb, *Industrial Democracy* (1898), 10–11. The Webbs noted that in Leicester the general meetings were often attended by 'thousands with results that are often calamitous to the union'.
101 Fox, *op. cit.*, 34.
102 Where he subsequently played an important role in Leicester affairs.
103 NUBSO monthly report, November 1880.
104 Fox, *op. cit.*, 70–1.
105 In September 1877 he was elected as a Liberal to the Leicester school board. His candidature was nominated without opposition by W. Walker of Walker and Kempson's shoe firm. NUBSO monthly report, September 1877.
106 NUBSO monthly report, October 1877.
107 *Ibid.*, April 1878.
108 *Ibid.*, December 1882.
109 *Ibid.*, May 1878.
110 *Ibid.*
111 *Ibid.*, October 1881.
112 *Ibid.*, April 1885.
113 *Ibid.*, November 1888.
114 B. and S. Webb, *Industrial Democracy*, 402.
115 RC on Labour (1892), Part II, q. 16,019.
116 Dare, *op. cit.* (1862).
117 NUBSO monthly report, December 1878.
118 *Ibid.*, December 1882.

Chapter 3

1 The material on this concept is, to say the least, copious. The following are some of the main texts on the subject. E. J. Hobsbawm, *Labouring Men* (1964), ch. 15; R. J. Harrison, *Before the Socialists* (1965); J. Foster, *Class Struggle and the Industrial Revolution* (1974); J. Hinton, *The First Shop Stewards Movement* (1973); R. Q. Gray, *The Labour Aristocracy in Victorian Edinburgh* (1976); H. Pelling, 'The concept of the labour

aristocracy', in *Popular Politics and Society in Late Victorian Britain* (1968); and A. E. Musson, *British Trade Unions 1800–1875* (1972) offer a critical appraisal of the subject. See also H. F. Moorhouse, 'The Marxist theory of the labour aristocracy', *Social History, 3,* (1978) for a review of the debate.

2 P. Joyce, *Work, Society and Politics: The Culture of the Factory in Late Victorian England* (1980). For a particularly useful critique of Joyce's work see N. Kirk, 'Cotton workers and deference', *Bulletin* of the Society for The Study of Labour History, 42, 1981.

3 Hobsbawm, *op. cit.,* 273.

4 During the period neither group formed trade unions nor participated in labour and working-class politics.

5 Joyce, *op. cit.*; G. B. Sutton, *C. and J. Clark 1833–1903. A History of Shoemaking in Street, Somerset* (1979), 154–9 has useful material on Clark's more robust paternalistic regime in Street, Somerset.

6 The main benefactors of the mission in 1875 included Brewin, Coltman, Charlesworth, Fielding, Johnson, Paget, Rowlett, Riley, Simpson, Stokes, Stone and Whetstone. All of these apart from S. Stone, the town clerk, either owned, or were connected with, hosiery and footwear manufacturing. J. Dare, *Report of The Leicester Domestic Mission* (1875).

7 *Ibid.* (1853).

8 *Ibid.* (1857).

9 *Ibid.* (1853).

10 *Ibid.* (1864).

11 *Ibid.*

12 Joyce, *op. cit.,* 74.

13 RC on Children's Employment, First Report (1863), 293.

14 *Ibid.*, 2nd Report (1864), 166.

15 Dare, *op. cit.* (1875). The overall effect of pre-board school education in Leicester must have been minimal. The town was 7,000 places short in 1867 and the average attendance was 18 months. *Ibid.* (1867).

16 The middle-class-run Mechanics Institute provided similar temporary accommodation for 'infidel artisans' in the 1830s. F. B. Lott, *Story of the Leicester Mechanics Institute* (1935), 5.

17 Local Tories were, however, highly suspicious of the club's potential political influence, see *Leicester Journal,* 4 May 1866.

18 Quoted in R. N. Price, 'The Working

Men's Club movement and Victorian social reform ideology', *Victorian Studies*, 15 (1971), 127.

19 Dare, *op. cit.* (1866).

20 By 1882 the club had 500 members; George Sedgewick and William Inskip, both NUBSO officers, held the president's and secretary's post at the club. Wright's *Directory of Leicester* (1882), 278.

21 *The Pioneer*, 18 November 1905.

22 Dare, *op. cit* (1864).

23 *Ibid.*

24 When the firm opened the St Margaret's works in 1886 one of the employees composed a poem to commemorate the event entitled 'The Warehouse Opening'. One of the verses ran as follows:

> Here may the hand that's willing
> Find ever work to do;
> Here may the earnest hearted
> Work on with purpose true.
> May Workers and Employers
> Each for the other care,
> And in a generous spirit,
> Each other's burdens bear.

Cited in C. W. Webb, *Corah's of Leicester* (1948), 41. The firm also fielded its own cricket team in 1877 (*Leicester Chronicle*, 22 September 1877), and organized a workers' 'Choral Union' in 1883. C. W. Webb, *op. cit.,* 44.

25 M. Elliott, *Victorian Leicester* (1979), ch. 6 contains a useful survey of nineteenth-century Leicester housing, including a discussion of the Freehold Land Society.

26 Joyce, *op. cit.,* 227.

27 SC on Stoppage of Wages (Hosiery) (1854/5), qq. 374–80.

28 RC on the Truck System (1871), qq. 41,665–711.

29 NUBSO monthly report, October 1877, April 1878.

30 Kirk, *op. cit.*

31 G. Stedman Jones, 'Class struggle and the industrial revolution', *New Left Review*, 90 (1975), 35–71.

32 R. Samuel, 'The workshop of the world. Steam power and hand technology in mid-Victorian Britain', *History Workshop Journal, 3* (1977).

33 K. Marx, *Capital*, I (Moscow, 1970), ch. XV.

34 S. Pollard, *The Genesis of Modern Management* (1965), 160, 166.

Chapter 4

1 See E. J. Hobsbawm and J. W. Scott's survey of shoemakers in the nineteenth century, 'Political shoemakers', *Past and Present*, 89 (1980).

2 E. Royle, *Victorian Infidels. The Origins of the British Secularist Movement 1791–1866* (1974); and E. Royle, *Radicals, Secularists and Republicans. Popular Freethought in Britain 1866–1915* (1980).

3 F. J. Gould, *History of the Leicester Secular Society* (1900), 4.

4 A. T. Patterson, *Radical Leicester. A History of Leicester, 1780–1850* (1954), ch. 6 *passim*, for a survey of early nineteenth-century radical movements in Leicester.

5 *Ibid.*, 288. See also Royle, *Victorian Infidels*, 295.

6 Even after this date the records are not particularly revealing. For example, the occupation of members is not given. Shareholders' lists of the Secular Hall Company, however, do give this information, but this is not representative of the membership as only the few better-off members could afford the £5 shares.

7 T. Barclay, *Memoirs and Medleys. The Autobiography of a Bottlewasher* (1934). Barclay, 1852–1933, was a working-class member and socialist agitator. F. J. Gould, as well as writing an early history of the society, also relates much useful information on Leicester in his *Life Story of a Humanist* (1923). S. A. Gimson, the son of Josiah and president of the society from 1888 until 1937, produced two unpublished typescripts, 'Random Recollections of the Leicester Secular Society with Digressions', vols I and II, which are contained in the society's archive.

8 Both the Royle volumes include material on the Leicester society.

9 Royle, *Victorian Infidels*, 310–11.

10 In 1877 Gimson and the Leicester society joined Holyoake in the formation of the anti-Bradlaugh organization, the British Secular Union. Royle, *Radicals, Secularists and Republicans*, 18. Gimson himself was a firm advocate of cooperative production: in 1872 he introduced a profit-sharing scheme into his own factory. Report of the Board of Trade on Profit-Sharing (1891), 42–3. See also G. J. Holyoake, *Secular Prospects in Death, an Address at the Funeral of J. Gimson* (1883).

11 O. Chadwick, *The Victorian Church*, (1966), I, 391–8.

12 *Ibid.*, 396–7.

13 All were large shareholders in the Secular Hall Company. Perhaps this schism may have been an element in Dare's frequent attacks on infidelity.

14 Gould, *History of the Leicester Secular Society*, 8, 10–11. See J. F. C. Harrison, 'Chartism in Leicester', in A. Briggs (ed.), *Chartist Studies* (1959) for Seal's chartist activities. E. P. Thompson's *William Morris. Romantic to Revolutionary* (1977 edn), 279–80 contains information on Sketchley's post-Chartist activities.

15 Gould, *History of the Leicester Secular Society*, 8.

16 M. Quin, *Memoirs of a Positivist* (1924), 48.

17 Gould, *Life Story of a Humanist*, 85.

18 Gould, *History of the Leicester Secular Society*, 14.

19 List of shareholders of the Leicester Secular Hall Company, LLRO 1068/15.

20 Gould, *History of the Leicester Secular Society*, 14.

21 *Ibid.*, 28; list of shareholders of the Leicester Secular Hall Company.

22 His family-owned firm set aside a trust fund to yield £100 per annum for the upkeep of the hall. Gould, *History of the Leicester Secular Society*, 11, 28, 35

23 For a stimulating discussion on the influence of Comte on Holyoake see Royle, *Radical Infidels*, ch. 3.

24 Quin, *op. cit.*, 43.

25 Gimson, *op. cit.*, I, 19; Quin, *op. cit.*, 43–4.

26 Which brought down the wrath of Bradlaugh's 'National Reformer', Royle, *Radicals, Secularists and Republicans*, 138.

27 Gould, *History of the Leicester Secular Society*, 33–4.

28 Royle, *Radicals, Secularists and Republicans*, 134.

29 Quin, *op. cit.*, 27–8.

30 F. J. Gould was then full-time secretary of the society and had taken over Findley's mantle. Gould was also an active member of the ILP and town councillor. Relations between Gould and Gimson soon deteriorated to the extent that Gould and the positivists left the society to form a Church of Humanity in Highcross Street in 1908.

Gimson's parting words to the positivists were 'Well my friends you can hardly expect us to turn our Secular Society into a Positivist Society and Labour church.' Gould, *Life Story of a Humanist*, 108.

31 *Ibid.*, 85.
32 Royle, *Radicals, Secularists and Republicans*, ch. 3 *passim*.
33 *Ibid.*, 32. Royle has also noted the brief appearance of a rival NSS branch in Leicester during the BSU period. *Ibid.*, 56.
34 Gould, *History of the Leicester Secular Society*, 22.
35 Barclay, *op. cit.*, 41–6.
36 *Ibid.*, 122.
37 Gould, *History of the Leicester Secular Society*, 43.
38 NUBSO monthly report, October 1883.
39 This was especially so during the 1886 riots in Leicester. See *Leicester Chronicle and Leicestershire Mercury*, 13 February 1886.
40 Royle, *Radicals, Secularists and Republicans*, 232.
41 Gimson, *op. cit.*, I, 25.
42 *Ibid.*, 20–3. One of Morris's early converts was Sydney Gimson's young brother Ernest, who became a leading member of the Arts and Crafts movement. For an interesting account of Ernest Gimson's subsequent career see R. Gradidge, *Dream Houses. The Edwardian Ideal* (1980), 163–72.
43 See Barclay, *op cit.*, 66–8 for a comprehensive list of speakers.
44 *Commonweal*, December 1885.
45 P. Redfern, *Journey to Understanding* (1946), 29.
46 Royle, *Victorian Infidels*, ch. 1.
47 S. Gimson noted that 'Our secularism is not intermittent, alternating grand revivals with seasons of sloth, we keep steadily at work month after month, year after year.' Quoted in Royle, *Radicals, Secularists and Republicans*, 57.
48 Royle, *Victorian Infidels*, 310.

Chapter 5

1 J. Vincent, *The Formation of the Liberal Party, 1857–1868* (1966), 65–76.
2 E. J. Hobsbawm, *Labouring Men* (1964), 372–3.
3 H. Pelling, *The Origins of the Labour Party* (1976), ch. 7 *passim*.
4 D. Clark, *Colne Valley: Radicalism to Socialism* (1981), 192. E. P. Thompson, 'Homage to Tom Maguire', in A. Briggs and J. Saville (eds), *Essays in Labour History*, I (1960), 289.
5 D. M. Thompson, 'The Liberation Society', in P. Hollis (ed.), *Pressure from Without in Early Victorian Society* (1974), 214–15.
6 D. M. Thompson, 'The 1851 religious census: problems and possibilities', *Victorian Studies, 11*, 1 (1967).
7 Census of Great Britain, 1851. Religious Worship, cxxix.
8 J. Dare, *Report of the Leicester Domestic Mission* (1846).
9 For example, the General Baptists had 1,424 free seats in comparison with 2,005 appropriated. See Census reports 1851, cclxi. Although of course it must be remembered that not all appropriated seats were rented for money.
10 Dare, *op. cit.* (1846).
11 *Ibid.* (1857). This trend has also been found to occur in present-day Britain, see M. Stacey, *Tradition and Change. A Study of Banbury* (1960), 71.
12 *Victoria County History of Leicester*, IV (1958), 393.
13 *Ibid.*, 390–4.
14 See D. Freer, 'Business families in Victorian Leicester' (M. Phil. thesis, University of Leicester, 1975), ch. 9 *passim*; Dr Clark has noted a similar pattern in the Colne Valley which led to the area being a relatively weak centre of nonconformity by 1900. See Clark, *op. cit.*, 192.
15 *Hiltons 1869–1969: S. Hilton & Sons Ltd* (1969), 3–6.
16 Freer, *op. cit.*, 271–2.
17 *Illustrated Leicester: Its History and Commerce* (1895), 39.
18 George Banton, the first president of the Leicester ILP, future mayor and MP for the town, was a prominent lay preacher at this church. See his obituary in the *Leicester Evening Mail*, 19 April 1932.
19 See below, p. 78.
20 *Victoria County History of Leicester*, IV, 394.
21 J. E. Hextall and A. L. Brightman, *Fifty Years of Church, Men, and Things at St. Paul's Leicester* (1921), 19.
22 *Ibid.*, 16.
23 *Church Times*, 9 October 1901.
24 See B. Webb, *Our Partnership*, ed. B. Drake and M. Cole (1948), 205–10

for a brief biographical account of Creighton.

25 L. Creighton, *The Life and Letters of Mandell Creighton* (1904), II, 25.

26 See in particular D. Bowen, *The Idea of the Victorian Church: A Study of the Church of England 1833–1889* (Montreal, 1968).

27 On the role of Christian Socialism in the Leicester producers' cooperative movement see below, Chapter 10.

28 Hextall and Brightman, *op. cit.*, 60.

29 Freer, *op. cit.*, 271–4.

30 Sir Samuel Faire, Sir Edward Wood and Sir Thomas Wright were all knighted in the late nineteenth century. Many in fact made such a transition, the Corahs and Pagets being the most notable. Indeed it was a descendant of T. T. Paget who became Master of the Quorn Hunt later in the century.

31 E. Atkin, *The Vaughan Working Men's College 1862–1912* (1912) is an interesting early history of the college. See also A. J. Allaway, *Vaughan College Leicester 1862–1962* (1962).

32 Atkin, *op. cit.*, 52, 66.

33 Census of Great Britain, 1851, Religious Worship, cxxix.

34 For an interesting discussion of the Mormons in Victorian Britain, see D. J. Davies, 'Aspects of Latter Day Saint eschatology', in *A Sociological Yearbook of Religion in Britain*, 6 (1973). See also P. A. M. Taylor, '*Expectations Westward': The Mormons and the Emigration of Their British Converts in the Nineteenth Century* (1965).

35 Includes Union Church, Society of Friends, Unitarians, Calvinists, Gospel Hall, Brethren, Christians, Hellelujah Band and the Catholic Apostolic Church.

36 Church of Christ.

37 Although there were sufficient emigrants from Leicester to enable the founding of New Leicester in Utah.

38 It is highly unlikely that the Quakers, Unitarians and Calvinists, which was probably the isolated congregation in 1851, could account for much more than their combined total of 828.

39 H. Davies, *Worship and Theology in England*, IV (Princeton, NJ, 1968), ch. VI *passim*.

40 *Ibid.*, 139–43.

41 J. F. C. Harrison, *The Second Coming. Popular Millenarianism 1780–1850* (1979), 184.

42 *British Millennial Harbinger* (1859),

467; (1860), 254; (1861), 572; (1875), 217; (1866), 147. The Grafton Street Chapel also had an educational building. A. Mann, *Democracy in Industry* (1914), 6.

43 Amos Mann, the leader of the church, became a town councillor in 1896. He was joined in later years by another member of the sect, J. T. Taylor, who was also treasurer of the ILP. Mann was also president of the Anchor Boot and Shoe Cooperative, and Taylor was manager. The two were also largely responsible for setting up the church's 'garden city' at Humberstone. See Mann, *op. cit.*, for the history of the church and their subsequent activities.

44 Davies, *op. cit.*, 168.

45 St J. Ervine, *God's Soldier: General William Booth* (1934), I, 377–8, 389–90. One of the dissatisfied salvationists in Leicester, Amos Sheriff, left the Army in the early 1880s and later associated himself closely with F. L. Donaldson, the local Christian Socialist vicar and high church ritualist. Sheriff was a founding member of the ILP, leader of the 1905 unemployment march and Mayor of Leicester in 1922.

46 Although the Catholic Apostolic Church had its roots in a small congregation of 'Irvingites', a millenarian sect, which met in Cank Street. White's *Directory of Leicester* (1877), 308.

47 Dare, *op. cit.* (1859).

48 L. Barrow, 'Socialism in eternity. The ideology of plebeian spiritualists, 1853–1913', *History Workshop Journal*, 9 (1980), 38.

49 It was not until the 1880s that spiritualism was able to establish a national movement. *Ibid.*, 39.

50 Dare, *op. cit.* (1865).

51 *Spiritualist*, 23 July 1875.

52 White's *Directory* (1877), 308.

53 Barrow, *op. cit.*, 63. Similarly, leading members of the Lancaster ILP were also spiritualists. See N. Todd, 'A history of Labour in Lancaster and Barrow-in-Furness' (M. Litt. thesis, University of Lancaster, 1976), 57.

54 *Freedom*, August 1892.

55 *Leicester Trades Council Trade Union Congress Leicester 1903. Official Souvenir* (1903).

56 J. Holmes was a prominent Leicester secularist before his conversion in 1881. *Medium and Daybreak*, 4 February 1881.

57 Holmes reported a debate in which he was involved with local secularists, including Gimson, soon after joining the spiritualists. Holmes referred to his erstwhile colleagues rather scornfully as 'atheists and sceptics', which suggests that for Holmes, at least, spiritualism involved a 'leap of faith' similar to other religions, and beyond the ken of the hardened rationalist. *Medium and Daybreak*, 4 February 1881, 75.

58 K. S. Inglis, *Churches and the Working Classes in Victorian England* (1963), 322–36; J. Obelkevich, *Religion and Rural Society* (1976), 328; G. Kitson Clark, *The Making of Victorian England* (1962), ch. 6.

59 P. Joyce, *Work, Society and Politics: The Culture of the Factory in Late Victorian England* (1980), 240–1.

60 R. Moore, *Pit-men, Preachers, and Politics. The Effects of Methodism in a Durham Mining Community* (1974), 81–2.

61 Obelkevich, *op. cit.*, 13.

62 Hextall and Brightman, *op. cit.*, 61 on Mason's role as arbiter in footwear disputes. Creighton, *op. cit.*, 127–8 on Creighton's activities in the 1895 shoe lock-out. See below, Chapter 11 on Donaldson and the 1904–5 unemployment campaign.

63 The minister referred to here was the Reverend Bellow. I am indebted to Lord Brockway for this information. For a discussion of Campbell and 'The New Theology' see P. d'A. Jones, *The Christian Socialist Revival 1877–1914* (Princeton, NJ, 1968), 421–6.

64 Inglis, *op. cit.*, 72. See also ch. 2 *passim* for a useful discussion of major trends in nonconformity during the period.

65 *Ibid.*, 66.

66 Clark, *op. cit.*, 192.

67 For the social and economic structure of Birmingham, See A. Briggs, *The History of Birmingham*, II (1852); for Nottingham, R. A. Church, *Economic and Social Change in a Midland Town: Victorian Nottingham* (1966).

68 Barrow, *op. cit.*, 43.

69 See Kitson Clark, *op. cit.*, 192 and ch. VI *passim*.

Chapter 6

1 R. H. Evans, 'Parliamentary history since 1835', *Victoria County History of Leicester*, IV (1985), 222–3ff.

What follows draws extensively on this essay.

2 See 'John Biggs 1801–1871', Leicester Museums Pamphlet (n.d.) for a useful summary of Biggs's political career.

3 SC on Stoppage of Wages (Hosiery) (1854/5), qq. 374–80. Biggs in this period was also fearful of the prospects of a possible Conservative–working class coalition, especially after Sir Henry Halford, the Tory MP for South Leicestershire, tried to pass a bill outlawing frame rent in 1847.

4 This description of Taylor is largely based upon his entry in the *Dictionary of National Biography* compiled by the young James Ramsay MacDonald.

5 A view held by Marx; see *Minutes of the General Council of the First International 1870–71* (Moscow, 1964), 165, 277.

6 Evans, *op. cit.*, 223.

7 J. Vincent, *The Formation of the British Liberal Party 1857–1868* (1966), 228. *Leicester Chronicle and Leicestershire Mercury*, 25 February 1865 on the local importance of Gladstone.

8 Harris, 2,295; Taylor, 2,199; Heygate, 1,945.

9 Evans, *op. cit.*, 223.

10 *Leicester Chronicle and Leicestershire Mercury*, 12 October 1867.

11 Evans, *op. cit.*, 226–8. The April 1880 general election result was: Taylor, 10,675; McArthur, 10,438; Winterton, 4,185; Warner, 3,820.

12 *Leicestershire Chronicle and Leicestershire Mercury*, 10 June 1874, quoted in Evans, *op. cit.*, 226.

13 *Ibid.*, 4 March 1871.

14 Merrick (1821–88) was the first working man to be elected to the town council, became president of the Trades Council upon its formation in 1872 and was nominated as a JP in 1886. See his obituary in *Leicester Daily Post*, 21 February 1888. Merrick does not appear to have been an active Chartist but his short book *The Warp of Life* (1876) offers a vivid account of the period. See J. F. C. Harrison, 'Chartism in Leicester' in A. Briggs (ed.), *Chartist Studies* (1959), 126–7.

15 *Leicester Chronicle*, 4 March 1871, 1 June 1872.

16 Evans, *op. cit.*, 226.

17 B. Harrison and P. Hollis, 'Chartism, liberalism and the life of Robert Lowry', *English Historical Review*, 82 (1967).

18 K. Tiller, 'Working class attitudes and

organisation in three industrial towns, 1850–1875' (Ph.D. thesis, University of Birmingham, 1975).

19 Vincent, *op. cit.*, 111.
20 Evans, *op. cit.*, 222.
21 Harrison, *op. cit.*, 130.
22 *Midland Workman and General Advertiser*, 12 October 1861 – 17 February 1862.
23 J. Hales, the secretary of the International, was an elastic web weaver. See *Minutes of the General Council, op. cit.*, 92–4.
24 *Archive of the International and British Federal Council* (Jung Collection), International Institute of Social History, Amsterdam, 676/9, February 1873, Hill to Jung.
Ibid., 677/12, February 1873, Hill to Jung. This was also a period when the International was receiving a bad press and commanded a certain notoriety. See H. Collins, 'The English branches of the First International', in A. Briggs and J. Saville (eds.), *Essays in Labour History, I* (1960) for the best account of the British participants in the International.
26 Jung Collection, 912/1, 19 February 1873, Randle to Jung.
27 *Ibid.*, 924/1, 12 March 1873; original spelling and punctuation.
28 Collins, *op. cit.*, 248, 272.
29 Jung Collection, 923/1, 19 February 1873, Randle to Jung; original spelling.
30 The Commune was celebrated for many years after in Leicester, see above, p.22.
31 Hill, the secretary of the Republicans, persuaded Randle to relinquish his secretary's post of the Leicester Internationalists and hand over duties tò the Republican leadership in anticipation of the alliance. After the visit of Mottershead, Hill effectively disbanded the Leicester branch by supporting Hales in the latter's feud against Marx and the General Council. See *ibid.*, 926/1, 21 May 1873, Randle to Jung.
32 W. H. Fraser, 'Trades Councils in England and Scotland 1858–1897' (Ph.D. thesis, University of Sussex, 1967), 570.
33 Evans, *op. cit.*, 227.
34 Fraser, *op. cit.*, 78.
35 Evans, *op. cit.*, 232.
36 *Leicester Mercury*, 26 March 1934 contains an obituary on Sedgewick.

For Kell see NUBSO monthly report, March 1891. A biographical entry on Smith is contained in H. Hartopp, *Roll of the Mayors of the Borough and Lord Mayors of the City of Leicester, 1209–1935* (1935). The presence of these three NUBSO officers on the school board may also indicate the wish of NUBSO to stem the flow of young under-age workers into the workshop sector of the shoe trade as well as the desire for political office.

37 J. Simmons, *Leicester Past and Present*, (1974), II, 17–19, 59; and S. M. Fraser, 'Leicester and smallpox: the Leicester method', *Medical History, 24* (1980). See also R. M. Macleod, 'Law, medicine and public opinion, the resistance to compulsory health legislation 1870–1907', *Public Law* (1967) for a survey of the movement nationally. What follows leans heavily on Fraser.
38 F. J. Gould, *The Life Story of a Humanist* (1923), 84.
39 Simmons, *op. cit.*, 59.
40 Fraser, *op. cit.*, 331.
41 Gould, *op. cit.*, 85. For the views of the secularists nationally on vaccination see E. Royle, *Radicals, Secularists and Republicans, Popular Freethought in Britain 1866–1915* (1980), 223–5.
42 Simmons, *op. cit.*, 19.

Chapter 7

1 H. Pelling, *The Origins of the Labour Party* (1966 edn), ch. 3.
2 *Freedom*, August 1890.
3 K. 757, Barclay to Mahon, 30 June 1885, Socialist League Archive, International Institute of Social History, Amsterdam (hereafter SL).
4 Probably individual membership as no branch existed in Leicester until the early 1890s.
5 Recently delivered at the Secular Hall. SL, K.758/1, Barclay to *Commonweal*, 19 July 1885.
6 R. Gradidge, 'Dream Houses'. *The Edwardian Ideal* (1980), 163–73. See also the Foreword by Sidney Gimson to T. Barclay, *Memoirs and Medley. The Autobiography of a Bottlewasher* (1934).
7 See especially E. P. Thompson's postscript to his 1977 Merlin edition of *William Morris. Romantic to Revolutionary*.

8 SL,K.763/1, Barclay to Socialist League, 20 November 1885.
9 SL, K.1120/1, Copeland to Socialist League, January 1887.
10 For example, there were frequent requests from the secretary to *Commonweal* to acknowledge subscriptions in the journal's columns in order to allay local suspicion.
11 SL, K.1445, Fowkes to Management Committee, 18 January 1888.
12 SL, K.1446, Fowkes to Socialist League, 23 October 1888.
13 SL, K.1447/1, Fowkes to Socialist League, 29 August 1887.
14 SL, K.603, Lecture and propaganda list for Autumn 1885.
15 Barclay, aged 33, was probably the oldest.
16 SL, K.974, Bunting to Aveling, 1 July 1885.
17 SL, K.976, Bunting to Mahon, 28 September 1885.
18 SL, K.763/1, Barclay to Socialist League, 20 November 1885.
19 SL, K.846/1–5, Billson to Socialist League (n.d.). See also Barclay's *Memoirs and Medleys*, 87.
20 *Freedom*, December 1891.
21 Barclay, *op. cit.*, 75, 84.
22 SL, K.3277, Yeoman to Morris, 8 November 1886; *Commonweal*, 25 December 1886.
23 Barclay, *op. cit.*, 76.
24 *Commonweal*, 1 January, 22 October 1887.
25 *British Labour History Ephemera* (1978), reel 33, items 309–14.
26 See above, p.20.
27 *Leicester Chronicle and Leicestershire Mercury*, 13 February 1886. The *Midland Free Press*, 20 February 1886, went so far as to claim that the strike and subsequent riots in which the majority of participants were female hosiery workers was orchestrated by 'Socialist . . . designing demagogues'.
28 The first issue appeared on 8 March 1886, a copy of which is in Leicester Record Office; three more issues, nos 22, 25 and 42, are kept in the International Institute for Social History periodical collection in Amsterdam.
29 Barclay, *op. cit.*, 81.
30 Barclay, *op. cit.*, 78.
31 *Commonweal*, 4 August 1888.
32 See the branch reports for 1888–9 published in *Commonweal*.
33 *Commonweal*, 12 March 1887.
34 *Ibid.*, 4 August, 1888, 27 July 1889, 12 August 1890.
35 Leicester Trades Council Annual Report (1892). In that year Warner's lonely vigil as the only anarchist on the Trades Council was relieved with the arrival of George Cores, a NUBSO delegate and leading member of the 'Freedom' group.
36 Barclay, *op. cit.*, 75–6.
37 Leicester Trades Council Annual Report (1893).
38 Thompson, *op. cit.*, 263–4, 571.

Chapter 8

1 What follows is largely gathered from A. Fox, *A History of the National Union of Boot and Shoe Operatives* (1958), 120–2.
2 NUBSO monthly report, July 1887, noted an unprecedented number of disputes over prices to be paid for the new season's samples.
3 NUBSO monthly report, May 1881.
4 *Ibid.*, March 1883. See, for example, Report of the Proceeding of the 1884 Union Conference, 10.
5 NUBSO monthly report, July 1886, January 1887.
6 *Ibid.*, April 1891.
7 Fox, *op. cit.*, ch. 18 contains a useful summary on the emergence of a national anti-arbitration movement in NUBSO.
8 J. H. Woolley, president of the Leicester branch, spoke in defence of arbitration at a heated mass meeting in the Temperance Hall in the following terms: 'The settlement of disputes by arbitration meant progress, while a recourse to the old methods of brute force . . . meant putting the clock back a quarter of a century.' NUBSO monthly report, October 1891.
9 See his autobiographical article, 'How I Got On', in *Pearsons Weekly*, 26 April 1906.
10 *Justice*, 30 April, 21 May, 8 October 1892.
11 NUBSO monthly report, October 1890.
12 They were all to be founder members of the Leicester ILP in 1894, Curley and Richards were later officers of the local LRC, Clarkmead having died in 1895.
13 J. Quail, *The Slow Burning Fuse: The Lost History of British Anarchism* (1978), 136, 235.

14 *Freedom*, October 1893.
15 B. and S. Webb, *Industrial Democracy* (1898), 11 has a useful account of NUBSO's tumultuous branch general meetings.
16 T. F. Richards, 'How I Got On', *Pearsons Weekly*, 6 April 1906.
17 NUBSO monthly report, March 1892, March 1890.
18 R. H. Evans, 'Parliamentary history since 1835', *Victoria County History of Leicester*, IV (1958), 232.
19 NUBSO monthly report, October 1889.
20 *Ibid.*, March 1891.
21 *Ibid*, October 1891.
22 *Ibid.*, January 1885.
23 RC on Labour, Part II, q. 16,019.
24 T. Barclay, for instance, frequently drifted from hosiery to boot factories, where he worked as a finisher. 'I was a boot finisher's sweater, and peeled osier-rods on a plantation close by St. Mary's Mount in the Newarke ... Finally I managed to learn something of the Hosiery Trade through being a Rotary Hand's helper.' Barclay, *Memoirs and Medleys. The Autobiography of a Bottlewasher* (1934), 14–15.
25 Richards, *op. cit.*
26 Sedgewick, the general secretary in expressing his opposition to the resolution to outlaw day work at the 1884 conference, pointed out that day work entailed indoor working, the net result of which would benefit the union as it would result in 'a closer connection between the men, and more united action.' 1888 Conference Report, 10.
27 NUBSO monthly report, December 1890.
28 *Ibid.*, January 1891.
29 *Shoe and Leather Record*, 19 January 1891.
30 Membership of the Leicester No. 1 Branch expanded from 8,478 in 1890 to 11,341 in 1892.
31 For example, Inskip chaired a meeting at the Leicester Working Men's Club in November 1890 where Miss Abrahams (Lady Dilke's secretary) spoke on the evils of sweating in the home. LAHU monthly report, November 1980.
32 J. Dare, *Report of the Leicester Domestic Mission* (1872).
33 *British Shoe Trades Journal*, 30 April 1892. Leicester Footwear

Manufacturers' Association Annual Report, 1892.
34 P. Redfern, *The Story of the C.W.S.* (1913), 52.
35 NUBSO monthly report, February 1892, October 1891.
36 The union argued that it was a deliberate policy to pick off the cream of the branch leadership and thus seriously weaken the union locally.
37 There is a full and interesting account of a particularly bitter strike at the local Cooperative Wholesale Society's factory over the behaviour of Lane, a new foreman and former secretary of No. 1 Branch, in B. Jones, *Cooperative Production* (1894), 228–30.
38 See above, P.00.
39 Griffin Ward, the chairman of the Leicester Footwear Manufacturers' Association, complained in 1892 that 'We find a great difficulty in keeping order in various establishments. The men have been used to working in their own homes, at their own pleasure, in their own way and doing what they liked in their own workshops and have grown up in habits which are perhaps somewhat difficult to eradicate. Sometimes there have been cases where men have set at defiance all regulations of the employers ... Leicester Footwear Manufacturers' Association Annual Report, 1892.
40 H. A. Silverman, *Studies in Industrial Organisation* (1946), 204–11.
41 G. B. Sutton, 'Shoemakers of Somerset. A history of C. & J. Clark 1833–1903' (M.A. dissertation, University of Nottingham, 1959), ch. VI, part IV. See also Sutton's *C. and J. Clark 1833–1903* (1979), ch. I, part 3.
42 Sutton, *C. and J. Clark 1833–1903*, 152.
43 See J. T. Cumbler, *Working Class Community in Industrial America* (Westport, Conn., 1979), 16–17 for the technological development of the Lynn, Massachusetts footwear industry.
44 H. C. Hillman, 'The size of firms in the boot and shoe industry', *Economic Journal*, 49 (1939), 280.
45 J. H. Clapham, *An Economic History of Great Britain* (1963 edn), III, 183.
46 J. T. Day, 'The boot and shoe trade', in H. Cox (ed.), *British Industries under Free Trade* (1902), 237–40.
47 *Shoe and Leather Record*, 27 March 1891.

48 Fox, *op. cit.*, 132.
49 NUBSO monthly report, April 1889.
50 *Shoe and Leather Record*, 19 February 1892.
51 P. Head, 'Boots and shoes', in D. H. Aldcroft (ed.), *The Development of British Industry and Foreign Competition 1875–1914* (1968), 169.
52 NUBSO monthly report, January 1890. *Labour Gazette*, May 1893.
53 NUBSO monthly report, May 1893.
54 *Labour Gazette*, August, September 1893, May 1894.
55 Head, *op. cit.*, 171.
56 NUBSO monthly report, December 1890.
57 Report of the Proceedings of the National Conference 1892, 45–6.
58 Award of the umpire on the limitations of boy labour 1892.
59 NUBSO monthly report, June 1892.
60 *Shoe and Leather Record*, 31 March 1893.
61 B. and S. Webb, *op. cit.*, 401–6.
62 Fox, *op. cit.*, 213–14.
63 To be fair to Fox, his subsequent theoretical works, particularly *Beyond Contract: Work, Power and Trust Relations* (1974), abandon the ideas of the 'Oxford school' of industrial relations that dominated his history of NUBSO and closely follow, at an abstract level, the interpretation taken in this chapter.
64 See the Webbs, *op. cit.*, ch. 8; Fox, *op. cit.*, ch. 22; E. Brunner, 'The origins of industrial peace: the case of the British boot and shoe industry', *Oxford Economic Papers*, nos 1, 2 (1949).
65 Brunner, *op. cit.*, 247.
66 H. Clegg *et al.*, *A History of British Trade Unions since 1889*, I (1964), 198–202.
67 In 1894 there were only 48 female NUBSO members in Leicester, 1,838 male members of the clickers No. 2 Branch and 10,965 members of the mainly lasters, No. 1 Branch. Source: NUBSO Annual Register, February 1894.
68 *Leicester Chronicle and Leicestershire Mercury*, 2 March 1895.
69 The dispute cost NUBSO over £56,000.
70 Louise Creighton, *The Life and Letters of Mandell Creighton* (1904), II, 127–8. Mandell Creighton may have gained some of his perception into industrial matters from his close friend Beatrice Webb.
71 For a full discussion of the 'Terms of Settlement', see Fox, *op. cit.*, 231–4. See also his appendix, 662–74, for a facsimile of the 'Terms of Settlement'.
72 *Freedom*, December 1893. The anarchist journal greeted this resolution with jubilation and dubbed its passing as the beginning of Leicester's 'reign of terror'. No evidence of its implementation has been found.
73 NUBSO monthly report, December 1895 includes a reprint of a *Midland Free Press* article on the subject.
74 NUBSO Conference Report, 1900, 66–73.

Chapter 9

1 SL,K.63/2, Barclay to Socialist League, January 1886.
2 Webb Collection, Section A, vol. 34.
3 J. B. Hendricks, 'The tailoresses in the ready-made clothing industry in Leeds, 1889–1899: a study in labour failure' (M.A. dissertation, University of Warwick, 1970). In particular Hendricks notes that most women perceived their working lives as short term, and episodic, being punctuated by marriage and child rearing, and thus felt little commitment to organization. Involvement in trade unions was also often seen as not respectable for women. See especially pp. 108–9.
4 *Freedom*, August 1890.
5 J. Quail, *The Slow Burning Fuse: The Lost History of British Anarchism* (1978) contains much information on these personalities.
6 In December 1891 Barclay criticized Creaghe's call for immediate revolutionary action and reiterated his own belief in the primacy of 'making socialists'.
7 *Freedom*, October, November, December 1891.
8 *Commonweal*, 6 December 1890.
9 Webb himself had spoken to a packed meeting at the Cooperative Hall in November 1889, the first of a series of Local Fabian Meetings. *Commonweal*, 2 November 1889, 8 February 1890.
10 *Freedom*, March 1892.
11 At least four of the seventeen members of the Socialist League mentioned by name, Holt, Chambers, Bent and Maclennen, joined the SDF during this period.

12 S. Yeo, 'A new life: the religion of socialism in Britain 1883–1896', *History Workshop Journal*, 4 (1977).

13 D. Clark, *Colne Valley: Radicalism to Socialism* (1981) concludes that the political and organizational success of the Colne Valley Labour League was due to local socialists who took a communal decision to reject the collective industrial approach (p. 186).

14 See R. J. Harrison's correspondence on the subject in *History Workshop Journal*, 5 (1978).

15 Attendances were often measured in thousands at the NUBSO No. 1 Branch.

16 *Commonweal*, 12 December 1891.

17 *Pioneer*, 3 January 1895.

18 The claim of Warner that the anarchists were more numerous than the ILP during this period was probably an exaggeration. Nevertheless, there were obviously enough of them to carry out disruptive activities in the club. The Rules of the Leicester Labour Club specifically limited membership to supporters of the ILP and SDF, while the 'objects' of the club laid emphasis upon 'constitutional action'. See Rules of the Leicester Labour Club, 1896.

19 *Pioneer*, 17 January 1895.

20 T. Barclay, *Memoirs and Medleys. The Autobiography of a Bottlewasher* (1934), 95.

21 Gorrie and the few remaining Socialist Leaguers continued on the fringe of the Leicester socialist movement for a number of years. In 1898 they re-formed under the name of the Leicester Socialist Society and claimed both support from the young dissident ILP members and political currency from the temporary re-emergence of the anti-vaccination campaign. This society disappeared after August 1898. See *Freedom*, July, August 1898.

22 The NUBSO conference of 1892 was dominated by the 'Stafford Resolution' which was a move to gain union backing for independent labour candidates locally and nationally.

23 In February 1892 the Leicester SDF was only able to announce outside venues and there is no mention for several months of branch meetings. See Branch Reports in *Justice*.

24 Along with Burnley, Northampton was the major provincial centre for social democracy. See P. A. Watmough, 'The membership of the Social Democratic Federation 1885–1902', *Bulletin* of the Society for the Study of Labour History, 34 (1977).

25 A. Fox, *A History of the National Union of Boot and Shoe Operatives* (1958), 102.

26 Census reports 1891. NUBSO Leicester Branch Annual Register, 1891. This is the nearest date on which figures are available for comparison.

27 E. Royle, *Radicals, Secularists and Republicans. Popular Freethought in Britain 1866–1915* (1980), 23–6, 53–6.

28 Note the striking similarities between the stance of the Leicester Owenites during the Chartist era and that of the Socialist Leaguers. The Chartist leader Thomas Cooper noted bitterly the cynicism of the Leicester Owenites towards the aims of Chartism. Does not the 'anti-statism' of the Owenites closely resemble the ideas of the League on this subject? See T. Cooper, *The Life of Thomas Cooper by Himself* (1872), 174.

29 Including attacking the mayor in the council chamber with the ceremonial mace while leading an unemployment demonstration. *Northampton Echo*, 14 August 1934.

30 E. J. Hobsbawm, *Labouring Men* (1964), 373.

31 For example, in 1892 the SDF were using the same outdoor pitches, Humberstone Gate and Russell Square, as the Anarchists. *Justice*, 2 January 1892.

32 H. Collins, 'The Marxism of the Social Democratic Federation', in A. Briggs and J. Saville (eds), *Essays in Labour History*, II (1971).

33 *Justice*, 29 August 1891.

34 J. Hill, 'Socialism and the Labour movement in Burnley', in J. Halstead and W. Lancaster (eds), *Socialist Studies* (forthcoming).

35 *Justice*, 21 May 1892. Hobart's lecture was later published by the Socialist Group of the London Society of Compositors as *Socialism and Trade Unionism* (1896).

36 See F. Engels, 'A working men's party', in *Labour Standard*, 23 July 1881. Engels was to give the newly formed ILP a glowing stamp of approval. See H. Pelling, *The Origins of the Labour Party* (1976), 123.

37 See above, p. 99.

38 NUBSO Conference Report, 1892, 11–13.

39 *Ibid.*, 1894, 39–41. Curley claimed that the 1892 resolution prevented two more Lib–Labers from sitting on Leicester council.
40 See Chapter 10.
41 NUBSO Conference Report, 1892, 56.
42 NUBSO monthly report, December 1892, February, July 1893.
43 Woolley, Inskip's erstwhile lieutenant, was the main speaker against the general secretary over this issue. NUBSO Conference Report, 1894, 53.
44 *Ibid.*, 35–42, 98–9 for what follows.
45 NUBSO monthly report, May 1894.
46 Leicester Trades Council Annual Report, 1900.
47 *Leicester Chronicle and Leicestershire Mercury*, 3 July 1886.
48 Leicester Trades Council Annual Report, 1891.
49 This amendment set an upper limit of 6,000 members for which societies could send delegates. The number of delegates above the first 1,000 was also drastically curtailed. See *ibid.*, 1893.
50 *Freedom*, June 1893. See also *British Labour History Ephemera* (1978), reel 20, items 209–12.
51 The Trades Council ruled that future May Day meetings were to be addressed only by bona fide trade unionists, a tactic designed to keep out itinerant anarchist speakers. See *Freedom*, June 1894.
52 Leicester Trades Council Annual Report, 1892. B. and S. Webb, *History of Trade Unionism* (1919), 426; H. Clegg *et al.*, *A History of British Trade Unions since 1889, I* (1964), 179–70.
53 *Leicester Chronicle and Leicestershire Mercury*, 13 May 1892.
54 *Freedom*, June 1893.
55 The best general account of Champion's activities during this period is H. Pelling's *The Origins of the Labour Party* (1976), 56–61. Recent Local studies have highlighted the creative role played by his followers in the emergence of independent labour political institutions, see especially T. Woodhouse, 'The working class', in D. Fraser (ed.), *A History of Modern Leeds* (1980). F. Reid's recent biography, *Keir Hardie. The Making of a Socialist* (1978), contains many references on Champion's relationship with the independent labour movement of the early 1890s.
56 ILP Conference Report, 1893.

57 J. Burgess, *Will Lloyd George Supplant Ramsay MacDonald?* (n.d., 1926?), 63. Field's hostility to Maltman Barry, Champion's colleague, may explain his friendship with Burgess. See *ibid.*, 74.
58 NUBSO General Council, May 1894, 39–41, 53.
59 Leicester Liberal Association Annual Report, 1892.
60 *Ibid.*; Barclay, *op. cit.*, 76, regarded Chaplin as 'one of my pupils'. Chaplin was also a leading member of the circle at the Silver Street Spiritualist Hall.
61 Leicester Liberal Association Annual Report, 1892.
62 *Freedom*, June 1893.
63 *Ibid.*, June 1894. The anarchists on this occasion were forced to mount their own rival demonstration. The Trades Council event was described by their leaflet at 'A Monster Demonstration'. Individual meetings were chaired by Curley, Woolley, Richards, Banton and Inskip. Despite the presence of Liberals the final meeting called for the nationalization of land and the instruments of production. The leaflets pertaining to this meeting are reproduced in the *British Labour History Ephemera, op. cit.*, reel 20, items 209–12.
64 *Leicester Chronicle and Leicestershire Mercury*, 17 March 1894.
65 *Labour Leader*, 2 June 1894.
66 A deliberate misprint by the *Leader*? 'Chatterbox' was probably Chatterton, the SDF Midlands organizer mentioned in *Justice*, 23 May 1896.
67 *Labour Leader*, 2 June 1894.
68 Francis Johnson Collection, correspondence file of the ILP, 1894/161, Richards to Hardie, 18 July.
69 *Ibid.*, 1894/179, Richards to Hardie, n.d.
70 Clark, *op. cit.*, ch. 4.
71 See A. E. Musson, *The Typographical Association. Origins and History up to 1949* (1954), ch. 15; *The Times*, 25 August 1894.
72 *Midland Free Press*, 1 September 1894.
73 *Ibid.*, 25 August 1894.
74 Burgess had worked in the Nottingham trade and had founded the local Nottingham labour newspaper *The Operative* in 1885. See J. Burgess, *John Burns* (1911), 3–4.
75 Francis Johnson Collection, 1894/187, T. Mann to John Lister, 29 August 1894.
76 *Leicester Daily Post*, 24 August 1894.

77 Quoted in *Pioneer*, 3 January 1895.
78 *Leicester Daily Post*, 30 August 1894.
79 *Labour Leader*, 8 September 1894.
80 As no list of membership is available, this survey of leading ILP members in Leicester is, to say the least, provisional. Information contained in this paragraph has been gleaned from the local press, particularly during local election activity, the *Leicester Trades Council, Trade Union Congress Leicester 1903. Official Souvenir* (1903) to commemorate the 1903 Leicester congress which contains valuable biographical information on early Leicester socialists.
81 By March 1898 membership had grown to 225 and in July 1899 it was stated that only the Bradford, Halifax, Keighley and Leicester branches had adequate resources to fight elections. *I.L.P. News*, March 1898, July 1899.
82 Reid, *op. cit.*, ch. 2.
83 T. Mann, *Trades Unionism and Co-operation in Forecasts for the Coming Century* (1897), esp. 33–7.
84 Rules of the Leicester Labour Club (1896), 15. *Pioneer*, 3 January 1895, contains an article by Mrs Saunderson, the secretary of the women's auxiliary, attacking the local leadership of the party for allotting women a marginal position.
85 Taylor's politics were singled out for note in the Anchor Cooperative's Jubilee history, whose writer proudly recorded that Taylor 'believed that the principles which Christ taught, ought to more largely influence industrial life … and would cause the wealth of the country to be more evenly distributed'. A. Mann, *Democracy in Industry* (1914), 47.
86 Bent was one of the few anarchists who joined the ILP. After being fired for his anarchist activities he was advised by Curley 'to follow the policies of the I.L.P.'. *Midland Free Press*, 6 October 1894. Three weeks later he was elected to the branch's first executive committee. *Ibid.*, 21 October 1894.
87 Barclay, *op. cit.*, 76.
88 *Midland Free Press*, 27 October 1894. *Clarion* readers often formed local social and sporting groups; cycling was a favourite activity.
89 *Ibid.*, 13, 27 October 1894.
90 *Ibid.*, 20 October 1894. Perhaps Hardie's claim mentioned above that the Leicester branch recruited 700 members after the by-election did contain an element of accuracy.
91 Francks of the Braid Hands Society and Woolley of NUBSO were the two major Lib-Labers on the council, while Green of the Railway Servants sat on the local bench thanks to Liberal patronage.
92 *Midland Free Press*, 20 October 1894.
93 *Ibid.*, 27 October 1894. Barclay was punished by the local anarchists, who were also upset by the defection of Bent to the ILP. The following Sunday they wheeled away the dray from which he was addressing his regular meeting in the market place with Barclay still on it. *Ibid.*, 24 November 1892.
94 *Ibid.*, 13 October 1894.
95 B. and S. Webb, *op. cit.*, 384–6.
96 *Midland Free Press*, 27 October 1894. See also the Leicester Trades Council Annual Report for 1895, which contains the ILP municipal programme having been adopted by the Trades Council in October.
97 The figures for the by-election were: ILP 936, Liberal 855. At the previous poll they had been Liberal 1,037, ILP 718.
98 *Midland Free Press*, 22 December 1894.
99 *Ibid.*, 27 October 1894.
100 *Ibid.*, 18 March 1893.
101 *Leicester Trades Council, Trade Union Congress Leicester 1903 Official Souvenir*, (1903), 48. Mann was in this period a Lib-Lab town councillor.
102 *Midland Free Press*, 6 May 1893.
103 *Ibid.*, 6 October 1894. See also J. F. C. Harrison, 'The portrait', *History Workshop Journal, 10* (1980) for a fascinating insight on the continuity of Leicester's Chartist tradition.
104 Broadhurst, 9,792; Hazell, 7,753; Rolleston, 7,654; Burgess, 4,009.
105 *Leicester Chronicle and Leicestershire Mercury*, 20 July 1895.

Chapter 10

1 A. T. Patterson, *Radical Leicester. A History of Leicester, 1780–1850* (1954), 121.
2 *Ibid.*, 288.
3 S. A. Gimson, 'Random recollections', I, 2. Unpublished typescript Leicestershire Record Office.
4 J. T. Stephens, *Social Redemption* (1911), 114–15.

5 *Ibid.*, 22. RC on Framework Knitters (1845), Appendix I, 100, 121.
6 B. Potter, *The Cooperative Movement in Great Britain* (1893), 224–6. Factories Acts returns, 1867–8, 821.
7 Minutes of the General Council of the First International, 13 December 1870, 92–4 of the published volume.
8 B. Jones, *Cooperative Production* (1894), 381.
9 T. Blandford and G. Newell, *A History of the Leicester Cooperative Hosiery Manufacturing Society Ltd. (1898)*, 11, 22.
10 Jones, *op. cit.*, 222, 381.
11 What follows is largely gathered from the entry on Butcher in J. M. Bellamy and J. Saville (eds), *Dictionary of Labour Biography*, I (1972).
12 Jones, *op. cit.*, 381. Butcher's position as manager of the West End works was to be crucial in the survival of the elastic web society as the CWS works became their main customer, thus assuring a secure market.
13 Blandford and Newell, *op. cit.*, 11.
14 Stephens, *op. cit.*, 105.
15 *Ibid.*, 22.
16 G. D. H. Cole, *A Century of Cooperation* (1944), 213.
17 Blandford and Newell, *op. cit.*, 25.
18 *Ibid.*, 14, 15.
19 *Ibid.*, 26. P. N. Backstrom, *Christian Socialism and Cooperation in Victorian England* (1974) for a useful account of E. V. Neale and his colleagues during this period.
20 *Ibid.*, 66. See B. Webb, *op. cit.*, Appendix I, Class IV, Class III.
21 What follows is taken from H. D. Lloyd, *Labour Co-Partnership* (1898), 178–83.
22 Quoted in Jones, *op. cit.*, 378.
23 *Workman's Times*, 14 November 1890.
24 Jones, *op. cit.*, 401–21. Most of these societies were located in Northampton and Northamptonshire villages.
25 E. O. Greening, *A Pioneer Co-Partnership* (1923), 10. Greening also noted that 'all their hopes were centred on uplifting the workers, as workers, on to a higher level for the enjoyment of happier lives.'
26 Lloyd, *op. cit.*, 103.
27 See his biography *Edward Owen Greening* by T. Crimes (1924). Lloyd, *op. cit.*, 105 and for much of what follows.
28 Jones, *op. cit.*, 228.
29 NUBSO monthly reports, April 1879, July 1880, April 1883.

30 Reports from Commissioners, Inspectors and Others on the Factories and Workshops Acts, 1876, minutes of evidence, qq. 7,560–75.
31 So much that he left the CWS in the early 1880s to become a partner in a local private boot business. Jones, *op. cit.*, 227.
32 *Ibid.*, 227.
33 See above, p.101.
34 Greening, *op. cit.*, 13.
35 *Ibid.*, 31. Greening had also been an early advocate of the CWS commencing production in Leicester.
36 The rules of the new society were in fact compiled by the Labour Association of which Greening, along with Neale, were the major figures.
37 B. Webb, *op. cit.*, 139.
38 *Ibid.*, Appendix I, Class I.
39 Greening, *op. cit.*, 24–5.
40 Jones, *op. cit.*, 421–2.
41 Lloyd, *op. cit.*, 110.
42 *Ibid.*, 106–7. The street is still standing, as is the Bede Street factory.
43 Lloyd, *op. cit.*, 112.
44 A. Mann, *Democracy in Industry* (1914), 5.
45 R. Halstead, *The Story of a Village Industrial Democracy, being Twenty One Years' History of the Glenfield 'Progress' Cooperative Boot and Shoe Manufacturing Society Limited (1914?)*, 13.
46 RC on Labour (1892), minutes of evidence, Part II, qq. 16,084–6.
47 Reports of the proceedings of the National Conference, 1893, contained in NUBSO's April 1893 monthly report, 52.
48 Cole, *op. cit.*, 204.
49 Both B. Webb's and B. Jones's books which appeared in the early 1890s were largely prompted by this debate. Webb and Jones were, of course, attacking the producers' movement.
50 Greening, *op. cit.*, 47. Schloss was described as 'a friend of the works [Equity] during this period'.
51 Cole, *op. cit.*, 204.
52 J. Burgess, 'The boot war. How to secure a permanent peace', *Clarion*, 13 April 1895.
53 Leicester Trades Council Annual Report, 1895. See Tom Mann's questions to J. T. W. Mitchel of the CWS at the Royal Commission on Labour (1892), qq. 387–90.
54 Lloyd, *op. cit.*, 104–6.
55 Jones, *op. cit.*, 427 noted that 'in 1889,

Mr. Butcher visited America to inspect all the newest inventions in shoe making machinery'.

56 *Commonweal*, 21 December 1889.
57 Greening, *op. cit.*, 60.
58 NUBSO monthly report, July 1893.
59 1894 Conference Report, 90–1.
60 Greening, *op. cit.*, 101–4.
61 Mann, *op. cit.*, 19.
62 Greening, *op. cit.*, 134–6.
63 Mann, *op. cit.*, 24.
64 Blandford and Newell, *op. cit.*, 54, 66.
65 *Leicester Trades Council, Trade Union Congress Leicester 1903. Official Souvenir* (1903), 21.
66 Lloyd, *op. cit.*, 118.
67 NUBSO Conference Report, 1894, 95–6.
68 *Ibid.*, 111.
69 A. E. Musson, *The Typographical Association. Origins and History up to 1949* (1954), 351.
70 Greening, *op. cit.*, 130.
71 Though in future years the national cooperative movement could successfully curtail the political activities of Amos Mann. Mann had to turn down the offer of the Labour Party parliamentary candidature because of pressure from the cooperative movement. See Mann's entry in Bellamy and Saville, *op. cit.*
72 Greening, *op. cit.*, 88.
73 E. O. Greening, *A Democratic Co-Partnership Successfully Established by Wigston Hosiers Ltd.* (1921), 33–4.
74 *Leicester Trades Council, Trades Union Congress Leicester 1903. Official Souvenir* (1903), 28.
75 Cole, *op. cit.*, 205.
76 Diary of Beatrice Webb, vol. 14, part 1, 6 December 1890, 1210 of typescript.

Chapter 11

1 A. Fox, *A History of the National Union of Boot and Shoe Operatives* (1958).
2 P. Head, 'Industrial organization in Leicester 1844–1914' (Ph.D. thesis, University of Leicester, 1960), 6 notes that imports of foreign footwear did not peak until 1901.
3 See W. R. Garside, *The Measurement of Unemployment in Great Britain 1850–1979* (1980), ch. I on the difficulties of accurate measurement prior to the 1911 Insurance Act.
4 Fox, *op. cit.*, 242–3.

5 NUBSO Annual Register, 1895, 1900.
6 *Leicester Daily Post*, 25 October 1904.
7 Census reports 1891, 1901.
8 Day, in H. Cox (ed.), *British Industries under Free Trade* (1902).
9 Fox, *op. cit.*, 241.
10 Census reports 1891, 1901.
11 Day, *op. cit.*, 249.
12 Fox, *op. cit*, 261.
13 NUBSO monthly report, July 1898.
14 Fox, *op. cit.*, 276.
15 NUBSO monthly report, December 1896.
16 Leicester Trades Council Annual Report, 1896.
17 NUBSO Conference Report, 1892, 37.
18 *Pioneer*, 19 January 1895.
19 No ILP archive material has survived from this period.
20 Minutes of the Leicester Liberal Association, 23 July 1901.
21 *Labour Leader*, 3 December 1898.
22 Leicester Trades Council Annual Report, 1898.
23 *Labour Leader*, 18 March 1899.
24 *I.L.P. News*, March 1899.
25 ILP Conference Report (1897), 19.
26 See the correspondence cited in D. Marquand, *Ramsay MacDonald* (1977), 82.
27 See the acid comments on Richard's campaign for the post of NUBSO general president in *Justice*, 1 July 1899.
28 Banton undertook the delicate task of negotiating with local Liberals MacDonald's status as candidate during the 1903 Gladstone–MacDonald discussions. See Marquand, *op. cit.*, 82.
29 *Leicester Daily Post*, 7 June 1899.
30 *Ibid.*, 50–1
31 Francis Johnson Collection, ILP correspondence file, 1894/187, Mann to Lister; 1895/110, Burgess to Mann.
32 *I.L.P. News*, February 1900.
33 A.C.B., *A Rhymester's Recollections* (n.d., 1903?). There were two more verses in a similar vein.
34 MacDonald claimed in June that he was still committed to the Southampton party as parliamentary candidate and gave no firm indication of his intentions to the Leicester branch until October. See *Leicester Daily Post*, 7 June 1899.
35 *I.L.P. News*, February 1900.
36 R. H. Evans, 'The Biggs family of

Leicester', *Transactions* of the Leicester Archaeological Society, *27* (1972), 229. Some local Liberals, most notably Thomas Wright, did, however, join the Liberal Unionists.

37 *Midland Free Press*, 29 September 1900.

38 Marquand, *op. cit.*, 9, 15.

39 D. Freer, 'Business families in Victorian Leicester' (M.Phil. thesis, University of Leicester, 1975), 265.

40 *Midland Free Press*, 3 March, 26 May 1900. The relief of Ladysmith and Mafeking were celebrated with gusto in Leicester and even the Trades Council was split over the war.

41 Quoted in Marquand, *op. cit.*, 73.

42 *Leicester Daily Post*, 27 September 1900.

43 Wood's address appears in MacDonald's address book of friends and colleagues, contained in the MacDonald Collection at The London School of Economics. Marquand, *op. cit.*, 81.

44 Wood also assisted with the joint administration of the 1896 distress fund with Trades Council officers. See Leicester Trades Council Annual Reports 1896, 1903.

45 NUBSO were the third largest of the trade unions who gave immediate support to the LRC, while Leicester Trades Council, who also affiliated, were the third largest Trades Council. See H. Pelling, *The Origins of the Labour Party* (1976), Appendix B.

46 NUBSO monthly report, June 1900.

47 1900 Union Conference Report, 50.

48 NUBSO monthly report, March 1900.

49 LRC archive, correspondence file, L/97 for LAHU affiliation, 5/243 for elastic web weavers.

50 Leicester Trades Council Annual Report, 1898.

51 LRC archive, correspondence file, 7/303; see also A. Henderson and J. Ramsay Macdonald, *Notes on Organization and the Law of Registration and Elections* (1904), 2–4.

52 See NUBSO monthly report, November 1880. 'We have divided the town into districts and have real earnest workers who are doing house to house calls.'

53 Which indeed he did. The Leicester LRC was held up as a model for other local groups to follow. See Henderson and MacDonald, *op. cit.*, 10–11.

54 Rules of the Leicester LRC contained in the LRC archive, correspondence file, 10/199.

55 Leicester Trades Council Annual Report, 1903 lists those organizations which sent delegates to the first Leicester LRC.

56 A poignant setting! The hospital was a product of an older Labour–Radical Liberal alliance, the anti-vaccination campaign.

57 Minutes of the Leicester Liberal Association, 21 March 1902.

58 *Ibid.*, 23 April 1901, 6 October 1902, 12 January 1903.

59 *Ibid.*, 21 April 1902; *Leicester Daily Post*, 16 March 1901.

60 *Ibid.*, 26 June 1903.

61 Marquand, *op. cit.*, 82. Gladstone was in contact with Wood and between them they managed to persuade the *Leicester Daily Post* to back the Broadhurst–MacDonald combination.

62 *Leicester Daily Post*, 30 June 1903. Leicester Liberals were not unaware of the recent triumphs of 'progressivism' in London. See P. Thompson, *Socialists, Liberals and Labour: The Struggle for London, 1885–1914* (1967), ch. VIII.

63 Leicester Liberal Association Minutes, 4 September 1903, 24 July 1903.

64 *Leicester Daily Post*, 4 September 1903.

65 NUBSO monthly report, June 1903, quoting the *Wolverhampton Express and Star*, 15 June 1903.

66 *Leicester Daily Post*, 31 October 1903.

67 *Ibid.*

68 *Ibid.*

69 *Ibid.*, 3 November 1903.

70 *Leicester Chronicle*, 20 April 1895.

71 *Leicester Daily Post*, 10 June 1905.

72 *Ibid.*, 16, 23, 26 March 1901, 3 November 1902, 31 October 1903.

73 Leicester Council Minutes, 28 October 1902.

74 *The Pioneer*, 17 October 1903.

75 *Leicester Daily Post*, 10, 23 March 1904.

76 Leicester Guardian Workhouse Admission Books, 1900–5. In 1905, 227 footwear workers were admitted to the workhouse, 141 in 1901.

77 *Pioneer*, 27 February 1904.

78 See the letter from George White, the 'test yard' men's spokesman, in *Leicester Daily Post*, 28 March 1904.

79 *Pioneer*, 30 January 1904.

80 *Leicester Daily Post*, 10 March 1904. NUBSO faced legal action against their recent attempts to restrict output, the traditional method of defending jobs

threatened by mechanization.
Furthermore, the union had been
seriously weakened by having to spend
more than £3,000 on unemployment
relief in Leicester between 1903 and
1905. *Labour Leader*, 2 June 1905.

81 *Leicester Daily Post*, 5 March 1904.
Indeed profits were so high in the
Leicester trade that even American
manufacturers opened factories in the
town. See *ibid.*, 23 June 1905.

82 *Ibid.*, 8 March 1904.

83 *Ibid.*, 3 March 1904.

84 *Ibid.*, 4, 23 March 1904.

85 *Ibid.*, 5, 23 March 1904.

86 Pelling, *op. cit.*, 222. See also his *Social
Geography of British Elections 1885–1910*
(1967), 434. David Howell's recent
thorough and penetrating survey of the
rise of the ILP offers a greatly revised
account of the party's formative years.
The conclusions of this chapter
generally accord with Howell's work.
D. Howell, *British Workers and the
Independent Labour Party 1888–1906*
(1982).

87 *Leicester Daily Post*, 17 March 1904.

88 See Amos Mann's (the Lib-Lab
councillor for West Humberstone)
attack on his erstwhile colleague
George Banton, for making
'irresponsible statements' on the
subject. *Ibid.*, 26 March 1904.

89 *Pioneer*, 30 January 1904.

90 Guardian Minutes, 30 May 1905.

91 *Leicester Daily Post*, 18 May 1905.

92 Amos Sherriff, one of the leaders of the
1905 Leicester unemployment march,
used a small part of the money
gathered by the marchers to fund a
local land colony which continued in
existence up until the Second World
War. See his obituary in the *Leicester
Evening Mail*, 19 May 1945.

93 *Leicester Daily Post*, 23 March 1907.

94 *Pioneer*, 30 January 1904.

95 *Leicester Daily Post*, 26 June 1905. The
marchers demanded that the majority
of the cash should be divided between
those who completed the march.

96 The MacDonald Collection (London
School of Economics), vol. 2, reply by
T. F. Richards to a questionnaire
compiled by Mrs M. E. MacDonald.

97 *Leicester Daily Post*, 5 March 1904.
It was reported in June 1905 that
one CAS ward committee had
only £9 to distribute to 160 families.
Leicester Daily Mercury, 26 June
1905.

98 *Ibid.*, 25 October 1902. *Leicester Daily
Post*, November 1904, *passim*.

99 *Pioneer*, 27 February 1904.

100 *Leicester Daily Post*, 26 March 1904.

101 *Ibid.*, 25 October 1904.

102 *Ibid.*, 2 November 1904.

103 Leicester Liberal Association Minutes,
8 February 1904.

104 *Ibid.*, 12 April 1904.

105 *Ibid.*, 12 October 1904.

106 Leicester Liberal Association Annual
Report, 1892.

107 *Leicester Daily Post*, 31 October 1903.

108 Leicester Liberal Association Minutes,
10 October 1904.

109 *Ibid.*, 5 March, 1 October 1907.

110 *Ibid.*, 9 December 1907.

111 *Ibid.*, 28 July 1908.

112 *Ibid.*, 11 December 1905.

113 *Ibid.*, 11 May 1908.

114 For this campaign and the events
leading up to the June 1905 march see
the *Leicester Daily Post*, May, June 1905
passim. Unfortunately no extant issues
of *Pioneer* for these months have
survived.

115 F. J. Gould, *The Life Story of a
Humanist* (1923), 91.

116 Guardian Minutes, 13 December
1904. The allegations concerned the
sale of a pig from the Guardians'
allotments to a member of the Board.

117 His weekly column was entitled 'From
Green Benches'. For his financial
commitment see Marquand, *op. cit.*,
81. In later years MacDonald
employed H. Reynolds, the manager of
Pioneer, as his parliamentary agent. See
the Barrett Collection, MSS 83/LE1/
111, which is deposited in the Modern
Records Centre, University of
Warwick.

118 Leicester Trades Council Annual
Report, 1903.

119 Minutes of the Leicester Liberal
Association, 9 December 1907.

120 It was during the Guardian and local
government elections of 1904 that the
local press first mentioned the existence
of ward committees in every area where
Labour fielded a candidate.

121 *Pioneer*, 27 February 1904, 11
November 1905.

122 *Ibid.*, 23 December 1905.

123 A phenomenon not unique to
Leicester. See S. Pierson, *Marxism and
the Origins of British Socialism* (Ithaca,
NY, 1973), 239.

124 *Leicester Daily Post*, 22 October 1904.
K. D. Brown's *Labour and*

Unemployment 1900–14 (1971) is the best national survey of the unemployment agitation during these years.

125 *Leicester Daily Post*, 22 October 1904. It was reported that 'those employed in the shoe trade were there in good force'.

126 Guardian Minutes, 1 November 1904.

127 *Leicester Daily Post*, 10 May 1905.

128 *Ibid.*, 15 May 1905.

129 See *The Times*, 15 May 1905 and K. Brooker, 'James Gribble and the Raunds strike of 1905', *Northamptonshire Past and Present*, 65 (1981–2), *passim*.

130 Fox, *op. cit.*, 337.

131 *Leicester Daily Post*, 6 May 1905.

132 *Ibid.*, 11 May 1905.

133 *Ibid.*, 30 May 1905. *Labour Leader*, 9, 16, 23 June 1905 contain reports by Pepper of the *Pioneer* which emphasize the importance of the Russian precedent to the leaders of the Leicester march.

134 *Leicester Daily Post*, 30 May 1905.

135 *Ibid.*, 31 May 1905.

136 *Ibid.*, 5 June 1905.

137 *Ibid.*, 1 June 1905.

138 *Labour Leader*, 9 June 1905.

139 *Leicester Daily Post*, 8 June 1905.

140 *The Times*, 12 June 1905.

141 *Labour Leader*, 26 May 1905.

142 *Ibid.*, 16 June 1905.

143 Brown, *op. cit.*, 59–61.

144 In November 1904 Chaplin, in his questionnaire to M. E. MacDonald, noted that Leicester hosiery manufacturers had more or less ceased to lay off adult male skilled operatives as they, the employers, were reluctant to use 'green labour' on the new generation of expensive machines. MacDonald Collection, vol. 2, J. Chaplin to M. E. MacDonald. *Labour Gazette*, December 1905.

145 *Ibid.*, January 1906.

146 *Leicester Daily Post*, 2 November 1905.

147 *Ibid.*, 2 January 1906.

148 *Ibid.*, 3 January 1906.

149 *Ibid.* For the national picture see A. Briggs's lucid discussion 'The political scene' in S. Nowell-Smith (ed.), *Edwardian England 1901–1914* (1964).

150 *Leicester Daily Post*, 3, 6 January 1906.

151 LAHU monthly report, May 1889.

152 *Leicester Daily Post*, 6 January 1906.

153 *Ibid.*, 9 January 1906.

154 *Ibid.*, 11, 12 Janauary 1906.

155 Broadhurst, 14,475; MacDonald, 14,685; Rolleston, 7,504.

156 Quoted in Marquand, *op. cit.*, 95.

157 *Ibid.*, 92–3.

158 *Leicester Daily Post*, 6 January 1906.

159 *Ibid.*

160 H. A. Clegg *et al.*, *A History of British Trade Unions since 1889*, I (1964), 413–22 contains a useful summary of this episode.

161 W. Lancaster, 'The tradition of militancy in the Leicester I.L.P.' (M. A. dissertation, University of Warwick, 1979), 57–60.

Conclusion

1 See the article 'The victory of British boots' in *The Economist*, 3 May 1913.

2 H. Pelling, *The Origins of the Labour Party* (1976); D. Howell, *British Workers and the Independent Labour Party 1888–1906* (1982); R. McKibbin, *The Evolution of the Labour Party 1910–24* (1974); D. Clark, *Colne Valley: Radicalism to Socialism* (1981); J. Hill, 'Manchester and Salford politics and the early development of the Independent Labour Party', *International Review of Social History, 26* (1981), part 1; J. Reynolds and K. Leybourn, 'The emergence of the Independent Labour Party in Bradford', *International Review of Social History, 20* (1975), part 3; T. Woodhouse, 'The working class; in D. Fraser (ed.), *A History of Modern Leeds* (1980).

3 K. O. Morgan, 'The New Liberalism and the challenge of the Labour Party: the Welsh experience 1885–1929', *Welsh History Review, 6* (1973); P. F. Clarke, *Lancashire and the New Liberalism* (1971); A. W. Purdue, 'The Liberal and Labour Party in north east politics', *International Review of Social History, 26* (1981), part 1.

Bibliography

Manuscript Primary Sources

The Rowland Barrett Collection; Modern Records Centre, University of Warwick.
H. Broadhurst Collection; London School of Economics.
Francis Johnson collection; The Archive of the Independent Labour Party, London School
of Economics.
Jung Collection; Archive of First International, International Institute of Social History,
Amsterdam.
The Labour Representation Committee, correspondence file; Harvester Press, Microfilm,
Brighton, 1978.
Leicester Board of Guardians Minute Books, Workhouse Admissions Books; Leicestershire
Records Office.
Leicester Liberal Association Minute Books; Leicestershire Records Office.
Leicester Secular Society Archive, including: minute book, membership book, list of
shareholders of the Leicester Secular Hall Company Ltd, book of newspaper cuttings,
and S. A. Gimson's unpublished typescript 'Random Recollections', vols I and II;
Leicestershire Records Office.
MacDonald Collection 1895–1923; London School of Economics.
National Union of Boot and Shoe Operatives, Minutes of the General Council; National
Union of Footwear, Leather and Allied Trades Head Office, Earls Barton,
Northampton.
Socialist League Archive; International Institute of Social History, Amsterdam.
B. Webb, Diaries; London School of Economics.
Webb Trade Union Collection; London School of Economics.

Printed Primary Sources

British Labour History Ephemera, compiled by M. Katanka and E. Frow; World Microfilms
Publications, London, 1978.
Independent Labour Party Conference Reports.
Leicester Amalgamated Hosiery Union, Monthly Reports.
Leicester Chamber of Commerce, Reports and Yearbooks.
Leicester Council Minutes.
Leicester Footwear Manufacturers' Association, Annual Reports.
Leicester Liberal Association, Annual Reports.
Leicester Poll Books.
Leicester Trades Council, Annual Reports.
Minutes of the General Council of the First International 1870–71, reprinted by Progress
Publishers, Moscow, 1964.
National Union of Boot and Shoe Operatives, Conference Reports, Monthly Reports.

J. Dare, Reports of the Leicester Domestic Mission Society.
Rules of the Leicester Labour Club, 1896.

Parliamentary Publications

Select Committee on Framework Knitters Petitions (1812), Cmd 34.
Report of the Factory Commissioners (1833), Cmd 450.
Royal Commission on Framework Knitters, Commissioner's Report (1845), Cmd 609.
Royal Commission on Framework Knitters, Part 1 (1845), Cmd 618.
Census of Great Britain, 1851; Religious Worship, England and Wales, 1852–3, Cmd 1690.
Census of Great Britain, 1851; 1852–3; Cmd 1691.
Report from the Select Committee on Stoppage of Wages (Hosiery) (1854–5); PP 421.
Report from the Select Committee on Irremovable Poor (1860); PP 520.
Returns of Factories under Inspection: Steam and Water Power; Persons Employed (1862); PP 23.
Census of Great Britain, 1861; 1863; Cmd 3221.
Children's Employment Commission 1862; First Report of the Commissioners (1863), Cmd 3180.
Factory Inspectors' Reports (1863); Cmd 3076.
Children's Employment Commission, Second Report (1864), Cmd 3414.
Children's Employment Commission, Third Report (1864); Cmd 3414–1.
Children's Employment Commission, Fourth Report (1865); Cmd 3548.
Tenth Report of the Commissioner, Royal Commission on Trades Unions, 1867–8; Cmd 3980–VI.
Returns of the Number of Cotton, Woollen, Shoddy, Worsted, Flax, Hemp, Jute, Rope, Horsehair, Elastic, Hosiery, Lace and Silk Factories, subject to the Factories Act (1867–8); PP 453.
Return Showing the Boroughs and Districts in which the Workshops Regulation Act has been enforced by the Local Authorities (1870); PP 425.
Return of the Number of Manufacturing Establishments in which the Hours of Work are Regulated by any Act of Parliament . . . of the Amount of Steam and Water Power in each, etc. (1871); PP 440.
Report from the Commissioners on the Truck System, with Minutes of Evidence and Appendices (1871); Cmd 326; Cmd 327.
Census of England and Wales 1871; 1872; Cmd 767–I–III.
Reports of the Inspectors of Factories (1872); Cmd 602.
Report to the Local Government Board on Proposed Changes in Hours and Ages of Employment in Textile Factories (1873); Cmd 754.
Return of the Number of Factories and Workshops Authorised to be Inspected under the Factories and Workshops Acts (1875); Cmd 754.
Reports from Commissioners, Inspectors and Others on the Factories and Workshops Acts (1876); Cmd 1443 and Cmd 1443–I.
Return of the Number of Factories Authorised to be Inspected under the Factories and Workshops Acts, 1878–9; PP 324.
Official Statistics Committee (1881); Cmd 39.
Census of England and Wales, 1883; 1883; Cmd 3797.
First Report of the Commissioners for Inquiring into the Housing of the Working Classes (1885); Cmd 4402.
Royal Commission on Depression of Trade and Industry (1886); Cmd 4797.
Inspectors of Factories Return showing Names, Dates of Apppointment and Present Salaries of Her Majesty's Inspectors of Factories, etc. (1887); PP 305.
Return Relating to Trades (Hours of Work), 1890; PP 375.
Report of the Board of Trade on Profit-Sharing (1891); Cmd 6267.

Royal Commission on Labour: Minutes of Evidence (1892); Cmd 6795.

Census of England and Wales, 1893–4; Cmd 7058.

Report on the Work of the Labour Department of the Board of Trade, 1893–4; Cmd 7565.

Board of Trade: Profit-Sharing (Labour Department); Report by D. F. Schloss on Profit-Sharing (1894); Cmd 7458.

First and Second Reports of the Select Committee on Distress from Want of Employment (1895); First Report, Cmd 111; Second Report, Cmd 253.

Census of England and Wales 1901, 1902; Cmd 1346.

Report of an Enquiry by the Board of Trade into the Hours of Labour of Workpeople of the U.K.; vol. II: Clothing Trades in 1906, 1909; Cmd 4844.

Miscellaneous Statistics, 1862, 1866, 1879, 1883.

The Labour Gazette: The Journal of the Labour Department of the Board of Trade 1893–1914, monthly.

Newspapers and Periodicals

British Millennial Harbinger
British Shoe Trades Journal
Church Times
Commonweal
The Countryman
Freedom
I.L.P. News
Justice
Labour Leader
Labour Standard
Leicester Advertiser
The Leicester Chronicle and Leicestershire Mercury
Leicester Daily Post

Leicester Journal
The Leicester Reasoner
Medium and Daybreak
Midland Free Press
Midland Workman and General Advertiser
The Nonconformist
Pearson's Weekly
The Pioneer
Shoe and Leather Record
The Spiritualist
The Times
The Two Worlds
Women's Union Journal
The Workman's Times

Local Directories

Drake's *Directory of Leicestershire* (1861).

Harrod's *Directory of Leicestershire and Rutland* (1876).

Spencer's *New Guide to Leicester* (1888).

White's *Directory of Leicester* (1863, 1877).

Wright's *Directory of Leicester* (1860, 1877, 1880, 1882, 1889).

Wright's *Midland Directory* (1864).

Contemporary Printed Works

A.C.B., *A Rhymester's Recollections* (n.d., 1903?).

Atkin, E., *The Vaughan Working Men's College 1862–1912* (1912).

Barclay, Thomas, *The Rights of Labour According to Ruskin* (n.d.).

Bernstein, F. *Lassalle as a Social Reformer* (1893).

Blandford, T. and Newell, G., *A History of the Leicester Cooperative Hosiery Manufacturing Society Ltd.* (1898).

British Boot Machinery Manufacturers' Association, *The History of the Shoe Machinery Monopoly, 1899–1918* (n.d.).

British United Shoe Machinery Co. Ltd., *Historical Survey of Shoemaking in Leicester* (n.d.).

Broadhurst, Henry, *Henry Broadhurst, M.P. The Story of his life from a Stonemason's Bench to the Treasury Bench* (1901).

Burgess, J., *John Burns* (1911).

Cooper, Thomas, *The Life of Thomas Cooper by Himself* (1872).

Cox, H. (ed.), *British Industries under Free Trade* (1902).

Creighton, Louise, *The Life and Letters of Mandell Creighton* (2 vols, 1904).

Felkin, W., *An Account of the Machine Wrought Hosiery Trade: Its Extent and the Condition of the Framework Knitters; being a paper read to the Statistical Section, at the Second York Meeting of the British Association 1845* (1845).

— *History of the Machine Wrought Hosiery and Lace Manufactures* (Centenary edition, 1967).

Galton, F. W. (ed.), *Workers on their Industries* (1896).

Gardiner, *Music and Friends, or Pleasant Recollections of a Dillettante* (1838).

Gould, F.J., *History of the Leicester Secular Society* (1900).

Hall, R., *An Appeal to the Public, on the Subject of the Framework Knitters Fund* (1820).

— *A Reply to the Principal Objections Advanced by Cobbett and Others against the Framework Knitters' Friendly Relief Society. By the Author of 'The Appeal'* (1821).

Halstead, R., *The Story of a Village Industrial Democracy, being Twenty One Years' History of the Glenfield 'Progress' Cooperative Boot and Shoe Manufacturing Society Limited* (n.d., 1914?).

Henderson, A. and MacDonald, J. R., *Notes on Organisation and the Law of Registration and Elections* (1904).

Henson, G., *The Civil, Political, and Mechanical History of the Framework Knitters* (1831).

Holt, R.G., *A Complete Exposure of the Abuses of the Leicester Mechanics Institute* (1835).

Holyoake, G. J., *Secular Prospects in Death, on address at the Funeral of J. Gimson* (1883).

Hunt, W. H. (ed.), *Churchmanship and Labour. Sermons on Social Subjects* (1906).

Hutchins, B. L. and Harrison, A., *A History of Factory Legislation* (1903).

Industrial Remuneration Conference, *The Report of Proceedings and Papers* (1885).

Jackson, W., *An Address to the Framework Knitters of the Town and Country of Leicester* (1833).

Jones, B., *Cooperative Production* (1894).

Jones, W. G., *Leicester Stockingers 1680–1890* (1890).

Illustrated Leicester: Its History and Commerce (1895).

Lassalle, F., *The Working Man's Programme* (1884).

Leicester Cooperative Congress, 1915, Souvenir (1915).

Leicester Illustrated (1891).

Leicester Trades Council, Trade Union Congress Leicester 1903. Official Souvenir (1903).

Lloyd, H. D., *Labour Co-Partnership* (1898).

Lomas, T., *Memoir of the Late Richard Harris* (1855).

Mann, Amos, *Democracy in Industry* (1914).

Mann, T., *The Duties of Co-operators in Regard to the Hours and Conditions of Labour* (1892).

— *Trades Unionism and Co-operation in Forecasts for the Coming Century* (1897).

Marx, K. *Capital*, I (Moscow, 1970).

Mearns, A., *Statistics of Attendance at Public Worship, 1882* (1882).

Merrick, D., *The Warp of Life* (1876).

Miall, A., *Life of Edward Miall* (1884).

Mudie-Smith, R., *Sweated Industries* (1906).

Potter, B., *The Cooperative Movement in Great Britain* (1893).

Read, R., *Modern Leicester* (1881).

Redfern, P., *The Story of the C.W.S.* (1913).

Schloss, D. F., *Bootmaking: Life and Labour* (1889).

— *Methods of Industrial Remuneration* (1892).

Socialist Group of the London Society of Compositors, *Socialism and Trade Unionism* (1896).

Stephens, J. T., *Social Redemption* (1911).

Thomas, A. H., *A History of the Great Meeting, Leicester, and Its Congregation* (1908).

Thompson, J., *History of Leicester in the Eighteenth Century* (1871).

Villiers, Brougham, *The Socialist Movement in England* (1908).

Webb, B. and S., *Industrial Democracy* (1898).

— *History of Trade Unionism* (1919).

Webb, C., *Industrial Co-operation* (1904).

Webb, S. and Freeman, A. (eds), *Seasonal Trades* (1912).

Willkomm, Gustav, *Technology of Frame-Work Knitting for Technical Schools and Self-Instruction* (trans. W. T. Rowlett, 2 vols, 1885).

Works of Reference

Bellamy, J.M. and Saville, J. (eds), *Dictionary of Labour Biography* (6 vols, 1972–82).

Dictionary of National Biography.

Harrison, R., Woolven, G. and Duncan, R. (eds), *The Warwick Guide to British Labour Periodicals, 1790–1970* (1977).

McCabe, J., *A Biographical Dictionary of Modern Rationalists* (1920).

Norton, J. E., *A Guide to the National and Provincial Directories of England and Wales* (1950).

Smethurst, J. B., *A Bibliography of Cooperative Societies' Histories* (1973).

Secondary Sources

Aldcroft, D. H. (ed.), *The Development of British Industry and Foreign Competition 1875–1914* (1968).

Alexander, D., *Retailing in England during the Industrial Revolution* (1970).

Allaway, A. J. *Vaughan College Leicester 1862–1962* (1962).

Backstrom, P. N., *Christian Socialism and Cooperation in Victorian England* (1974).

Bailey, P., *Leisure and Class in Victorian England* (1978).

Barclay, T., *Memoirs and Medleys. The Autobiography of a Bottlewasher* (1934).

Bealey, F. and Pelling, H., *Labour and Politics, 1900–1906* (1958).

Blewett, Neal, *The Peers, the Parties and the People: The General Election of 1910* (1972).

Bowen, Desmond, *The Idea of the Victorian Church: A Study of the Church of England 1833–1889* (Montreal, 1968).

Briggs, A., *The History of Birmingham* (2 vols, 1952).

— (ed.), *Chartist Studies* (1959).

— *Victorian Cities* (1968).

— *Essays in Labour History, vol. II, 1886–1923* (1971).

— and Saville, J. (eds), *Essays in Labour History*, vol. I (1960).

Brockway, F., *Inside the Left* (1942).

Brown, K. D., *Labour and Unemployment 1900–1914* (1971).

Burgess, J., *Will Lloyd George Supplant Ramsay MacDonald?* (n.d., 1926?).

— *A Potential Poet? His Autobiography and Verse* (1927).

Burgess, K., *The Challenge of Labour, Shaping British Society 1850–1930* (1980).

Butler, D. and Stokes, D., *Political Change in Britain. The Evolution of Electoral Choice* (1974).

Bythall, D., *The Sweated Trades. Outwork in Nineteenth Century Britain* (1978).

Chadwick, Owen, *The Secularization of the European Mind in the 19th Century* (1975).

— *The Victorian Church* (2 vols, 1966).

Church, R. A., *Economic and Social Change in a Midland Town: Victorian Nottingham* (1966).

— *The Great Victorian Boom 1850–1873* (1975).

Clapham, J. H., *An Economic History of Great Britain* (3 vols, 1963 edn).

Clark, D., *Colne Valley: Radicalism to Socialism* (1981).

Clarke, P. F., *Lancashire and the New Liberalism* (1971).

Clayton, J., *The Rise and Decline of Socialism in Great Britain 1884–1924* (1926).

219

Clegg, H. A., Fox, A. and Thompson, A. F., *A History of British Trade Unions since 1889*, vol. I. *1889–1910* (1964).

Clinton, A., *The Trade Union Rank and File. Trade Councils in Britain 1900–40* (1977).

Cohen, G., *Karl Marx's Theory of History. A Defence* (1978).

Cole, G. D. H., *A Century of Cooperation* (1944).

— *A History of Socialist Thought* (3 vols, 1956).

Crimes, T., *Edward Owen Greening* (1924).

Crossick, G. (ed.), *The Lower-Middle Class in Britain 1870–1914* (1977).

Cumbler, J. T., *Working-Class Community in Industrial America* (Westport, Conn., 1979).

Cunnington, C. W. and P., *The History of Underclothes* (1951).

Dangerfield, G., *The Strange Death of Liberal England* (1936).

Daunton, M. J., *Coal Metropolis, Cardiff, 1870–1914* (1977).

Davies, H., *Worship and Theology in England*, vol. IV (Princeton, NJ, 1968).

Drake, Barbara, *Women in Trade Unions* (1920).

Dyos, H. J. (ed.), *The Study of Urban History* (1968).

— and Wolff, M., *The Victorian City, Images and Realities* (2 vols, 1973).

Elliott, Malcolm, *Victorian Leicester* (1979).

Ellis, C. D. B., *History in Leicester* (1948).

Lord Elton, *James Ramsay MacDonald* (1939).

Erickson, C., *British Industrialists. Steel and Hosiery, 1850–1950* (1959).

Ervine, St J., *God's Soldier: General William Booth* (2 vols, 1934).

Floud, R., *An Introduction to Quantitative Methods for Historians* (1973).

Foster, J., *Class Struggle and the Industrial Revolution: Early Industrial Capitalism in Three English Towns* (1974).

Fox, A., *A History of the National Union of Boot and Shoe Operatives, 1870–1957* (1958).

— *Beyond Contract: Work, Power and Trust Relations* (1974).

Fraser, D. (ed.), *A History of Modern Leeds* (1980).

Fraser, W. H., *The Coming of the Mass Market 1850–1914* (1981).

Friedman, A. L., *Industry and Labour. Class Struggle at Work and Monopoly Capitalism* (1977).

Garside, W. R., *The Measurement of Unemployment in Great Britain 1850–1979* (1980).

Gould, F. J., *The Life Story of a Humanist* (1923).

Gradidge, R., *Dream Houses. The Edwardian Ideal* (1980).

Gray, R. Q., *The Labour Aristocracy in Victorian Edinburgh* (1976).

Greening, E. O., *A Democratic Co-Partnership Successfully Established by Wigston Hosiery Ltd.* (1921).

— *A Pioneer Co-Partnership* (1923).

Gurnham, R., *The Hosiery Unions 1776–1976* (1976).

Habakkuk, H. J., *American and British Technology in the Nineteenth Century: The Search for Labour Saving Inventions* (1962).

Harrison, J. F. C., *The Second Coming. Popular Millenarianism 1780–1850* (1979).

Harrison, R. J., *Before the Socialists* (1965).

Hartopp, H., *Roll of the Mayors of the Borough and Lord Mayors of the City of Leicester, 1209–1935* (1935).

Hawtin, G., *A Century of Progressive Thought: The Story of the Leicester Secular Society* (1974).

Henriques, U. R. Q., *The Early Factory Acts and Their Enforcement* (1971).

Hextall, J. E. and Brightman, A. L., *Fifty Years of Church, Men, and Things at St. Paul's Leicester* (1921).

Hilton's 1869–1969: S. Hilton & Sons Ltd (private publication, 1969).

Hinton, J. *The First Shop Stewards Movement* (1973).

Hobsbawm, E. J., *Primitive Rebels* (1959).

— *Labouring Men* (1964).

— *Labour's Turning Point 1880–1900* (1974).

Hobson, S. G., *Pilgrim to the Left. Memoirs of a Modern Revolutionary* (1938).

Hollis, P. (ed.), *Pressure from Without in Early Victorian England* (1974).

Holt, Raymond V., *The Unitarian Contribution to Social Progress in England* (1938).

Holton, R. J., *British Syndicalism, 1900–1914* (1976).

Hoskins, W. G., *The Midland Peasant. The Economic and Social History of a Leicestershire Village* (1965).

Howell, D., *British Workers and the Independent Labour Party 1888–1906* (1982).

Hunt, E. H., *Regional Wage Variations in Britain 1850–1914* (1973).

Inglis, K. S., *Churches and the Working Classes in Victorian England* (1963).

Jefferys, J. B., *Retail Trading in Britain 1850–1950* (1954).

Jones, P. d'A., *The Christian Socialist Revival 1877–1914* (Princeton, NJ, 1968).

Jowitt, J. A. and Taylor, R. K. S., *Bradford 1890–1914: The Cradle of the Independent Labour Party* (University of Leeds, Dept of Adult Education, Bradford Centre Occasional Papers No. 2, 1980).

Joyce, Patrick, *Work, Society and Politics: The Culture of the Factory in Late Victorian England* (1980).

Judd, Dennis, *Radical Joe. A Life of Joseph Chamberlain* (1977).

Kapp, Y., *Eleanor Marx* (2 vols, 1979).

Kirk, N., *The Growth of Working Class Reformism in Mid-Victorian England* (1985).

Kitson Clark, G., *The Making of Victorian England* (1962).

Lee, A. J., *The Origins of the Popular Press 1855–1914* (1976).

Levine, D., *Family Formation in an Age of Nascent Capitalism* (1977).

Lott, F. B., *Story of the Leicester Mechanics Institute* (1935).

Mann, Tom, *Memoirs* (1967 edn).

Marquand, D., *Ramsay MacDonald* (1977).

Mayor, Stephen, *The Churches and the Labour Movement* (1967).

McGee, J. E., *A History of the British Secular Movement* (Kansas, 1948).

McKendrick, N. (ed.), *Historical Perspectives: Studies in English Thought and Society* (1974).

McKibbin, R., *The Evolution of the Labour Party 1910–24* (1974).

McLeod, H., *Class and Religion in the Victorian City* (1974).

Mellor, H. E., *Leisure and the Changing City 1870–1914* (1976).

Miliband, R., *Parliamentary Socialism* (1973).

Mills, D. R., *Lord and Peasant in Nineteenth Century Britain* (1980).

Moore, R., *Pit-men, Preachers, and Politics. The Effects of Methodism in a Durham Mining Community* (1974).

Moore, R. F., *The Emergence of the Labour Party 1880–1924* (1978).

More, C., *Skill and the English Working Class 1870–1914* (1980).

Morgan, K. O., *Keir Hardie* (1975).

Morris, M., *William Morris, Artist, Writer, Socialist* (1966).

Musson, A. E., *The Typographical Association. Origins and History up to 1949* (1954).

— *British Trade Unions 1800–1875* (1972).

— *The Growth of British Industry* (1978).

— and Robinson, E., *Science and Technology in the Industrial Revolution* (1969).

Nowell-Smith, S. (ed.), *Edwardian England 1901–1914* (1964).

Obelkevich, J. *Religion and Rural Society.* (1976).

O'Day, A. (ed.), *The Edwardian Age. Conflict and Stability 1900–1914* (1979).

Olivers 1860–1950 (private publication, 1950).

Patterson, A. T., *Radical Leicester. A History of Leicester, 1780–1850* (1954).

Pelling, H., *A History of British Trade Unions* (1963).

— *Social Geography of British Elections 1885–1910* (1967).

— *Popular Politics and Society in Late Victorian Britain* (1968).

— *The Origins of the Labour Party* (1976).

Pierson, S., *Marxism and the Origins of British Socialism* (Ithaca, NY, 1973).

Pochin, R. E., *Over My Shoulder and Beyond* (1954).

Pollard, S., *The Genesis of Modern Management* (1965).

Pressnell, L. S., *Country Banking in the Industrial Revolution* (1956).

Pye, N., *Leicester and Its Region* (1972).

Quail, J., *The Slow Burning Fuse: The Lost History of British Anarchism* (1978).

Quin, M., *Memoirs of a Positivist* (1924).

Redfern, P., *Journey to Understanding* (1946).

Reid, F., *Keir Hardie. The Making of a Socialist* (1978).

Royle, E., *Radical Politics 1790–1900. Religion and Unbelief* (1971).

— *Victorian Infidels. The Origins of the British Secularist Movement 1791–1866* (1974).

— (ed.), *The Infidel Tradition from Paine to Bradlaugh* (1976).

— *Radicals, Secularists and Republicans. Popular Freethought in Britain 1866–1915* (1980).

Sacks, B., *J. Ramsay MacDonald in Thought and Action* (Albuquerque, 1952).

Saul, S. B., *The Myth of the Great Depression 1873–1896* (1969).

Schumpeter, J., *Business Cycles*, vols. I and II (1939).

Silverman, H. A., *Studies in Industrial Organisation* (1946).

Simmons, J., *Leicester Past and Present* (2 vols, 1974).

Snell, Harry, *Men, Movements and Myself* (1936).

Stacey, M., *Tradition and Change. A Study of Banbury* (1960).

Stead and Simpson Centenary, 1834–1934 (private publication, n.d.).

Sutherland, G. (ed.), *Studies in the Growth of the Nineteenth Century Government* (1972).

Sutton, G.B. *C. and J. Clark 1833–1903. A History of Shoemaking in Street, Somerset* (1979).

Taylor, P. A. M., *'Expectations Westward': The Mormons and the Emigration of Their British Converts in the Nineteenth Century* (1965).

Thernstrom, S., *Poverty and Progress. Social Mobility in a Nineteenth Century City* (Cambridge, Mass., 1964).

Thomis, M. I., *The Luddites. Machine Breaking in Regency England* (1970).

Thompson, A. M., *Here I Lie. The Memorial of an Old Journalist* (1937).

Thompson, E.P., *The Making of the English Working Class* (1968).

— *William Morris. Romantic to Revolutionary* (1977).

Thompson, P., *Socialists, Liberals and Labour: The Struggle for London, 1885–1914* (1967).

— *The Edwardians* (1975).

Thornley, J., *Workers Cooperatives, Jobs and Dreams* (1981).

Tilly, L. A. and Scott, J. W., *Women, Work and Family* (New York, 1978).

Tiltman, H. H., *James Ramsay MacDonald. Labour's Man of Destiny* (1929).

Torr, D., *Tom Mann and His Time*, (1956).

Turner, H. A., *Trade Union Growth, Structure, Policy* (1962).

Victoria History of the Counties of England. A History of the County of Leicester, vol. IV (1958).

Vincent, J., *The Formation of the Liberal Party 1857–1868* (1966).

Webb, B. *Our Partnership*, ed. B. Drake and M. Cole (1948).

Webb, C. W., *Corah's of Leicester* (1948).

Wells, F. A., *The British Hosiery and Knitwear Industry: Its History and Organisation* (1972).

Wigley, J., *The Rise and Fall of the Victorian Sunday* (1980).

Williams, D. (ed.), *The Adaptation of Change. Essays upon the History of 19th Century Leicester and Leicestershire* (1980).

Wolfe, W., *From Radicalism to Socialism: Men and Ideas in the Formation of Fabian Socialist Doctrines 1881–1889* (New Haven, Conn., 1975).

Yeo, S., *Religion and Voluntary Organisations in Crisis* (1976).

Articles

Barke, M., 'Census enumeration books and the local historian', *The Local Historian*, 10, 5 (1973).

Barrow, L., 'Socialism in eternity. The ideology of plebein spiritualists, 1853–1913', *History Workshop Journal*, 9 (1980).

Blewett, Mary H., 'The union of sex and craft in the Haverhill shoe strike of 1895', *Labour History*, 20, 3 (1979).

222

Brooker, K., 'The Northampton shoemakers' reaction to industrialisation: some thoughts', *Northamptonshire Past and Present*, 6, 3 (1980).

— 'James Gribble and the Raunds strike of 1905', *Northamptonshire Past and Present*, 6, 5 (1981–2).

Brown, K. D., 'The Labour Party and the unemployment question 1906–10', *Historical Journal*, 14 (1971).

Brunner, E., 'The origins of industrial peace: the case of the British boot and shoe industry', *Oxford Economic Papers*, nos. 1, 2 (June 1949).

Chandler, T. J., 'The Leicestershire hosiery trade 1844–1954', *Hosiery Trade Journal*, April 1955.

Chapman, S. D., 'The genesis of the British hosiery industry 1600–1750', *Textile History*, 3 (1972).

— 'Enterprise and innovation in the British hosiery industry, 1750–1850', *Textile History*, 5 (1974).

Church, R. A., 'Labour supply and innovation, 1800–1860: the boot and shoe industry', *Business History*, 12 (1970).

Davies, D. J., 'Aspects of Latter Day Saint eschatology', *A Sociological Yearbook of Religion in Britain*, 6 (1973).

Dingle, A. E., 'Drink and working class living standards in Britain 1870–1914', *Economic History Review*, 4 (1972).

Dodd, M. H., 'Marlboro, Massachusetts and the shoe workers strike of 1898–1899', *Labor History*, 20, 3 (1979).

Dunbabin, P. D., 'Parliamentary elections in Great Britain, 1868–1900: a psephological note', *English Historical Review*, 81 (1966).

Evans, R. H., 'The Biggs family of Leicester', *Transactions* of the Leicester Archaeological Society, 27 (1972).

Fraser, S. M., 'Leicester and smallpox: the Leicester method', *Medical History*, 24 (1980).

Granger, A., 'History of the boot and shoe industry in Leicester', British Boot and Shoe Institute *Journal* (1965).

Greaves, R. W., 'Roman Catholic relief and the Leicester election of 1826', *Transactions* of the Royal Historical Society (1946).

Harrison, Brian and Hollis, Patricia, 'Chartism, liberalism and the life of Robert Lowery', *English Historical Review*, 82 (1967).

Harrison, J. F. C., 'The Portrait', *History Workshop Journal*, 10 (1980).

Hartley V. A., 'Monsters in Campbell Square. The early history of two industrial premises in Northampton', *Northamptonshire Past and Present*.

Hill J., 'Manchester and Salford politics and the early development of the Independent Labour Party', *International Review of Social History*, 26 (1981).

Hillman H. C., 'The size of firms in the boot and shoe industry', *Economic Journal*, 49 (1939).

Hobsbawm, E. J. and Scott, J. W., 'Political shoemakers', *Past and Present*, 89 (1980).

Hopkin, D., 'The membership of the I.L.P. 1904–1910', *International Review of Social History*, 20 (1975).

Kirk, N., 'Cotton workers and deference', *Bulletin* for the Society for the Study of Labour History, 42 (1982).

Stedman Jones , G., 'Class struggle and the industrial revolution', *New Left Review*, 90 (1975).

— 'Working class culture and working class politics in London, 1870–1900', *Journal of Social History*, 7 (1971).

Lloyd, T. O., 'Lib-Labs and unforgiveable electoral generosity', *Bulletin* of the Institute of Historical Research, 48 (1975).

Mathew, H. C. G., McKibbin, R. I. and Kay, J. A., 'The franchise factor in the rise of the Labour Party', *English Historical Review*, 91 (1976).

McKibbin, R., 'James Ramsay MacDonald and the problem of the independence of the Labour Party', *Journal of Modern History*, 42 (1970).

Mcleod , R. M., 'Law, medicine and public opinion, the resistance to compulsory health legislation 1870–1907' *Public Law*, 1967.

Mendels, F. F., 'Protoindustrialisation: the first phase of the industrialisation process', *Journal of Economic History*, 32 (1972).

Moorhouse, H. F., 'The Marxist theory of the labour aristocracy', *Social History*, 3, 1 (1978).

Morgan, K. O., 'The New Liberalism and the challenge of the Labour Party: the Welsh experience 1885–1929', *Welsh History Review*, 6 (1973).

Musson, A. E., 'Industrial motive power in the United Kingdom, 1800–1870', *Economic History Review*, 29 (1976).

Pickering, W. S. F., 'The 1851 religious census – a useless experiment?', *British Journal of Sociology*, 18 (1967).

Porter, J. H., 'Wage bargaining and conciliation agreements, 1860–1914', *Economic History Review*, 33, 3 (1970)

Potter, M., 'The progressive alliance', *History*, 58 (1973).

Price, R. N., 'The Working Men's Club movement and Victorian social reform ideology', *Victorian Studies*, 15 (1971).

Purdue, A. W., 'The Liberal and Labour Party in north east politics', *International Review of Social History*, 26 (1981).

Reid, D. A., 'The decline of St. Monday 1766–1876', *Past and Present*, 71 (1976).

Reynolds, J. and Leybourn, K., 'The emergence of the Independent Labour Party in Bradford', *International Review of Social History*, 20 (1975).

Ripley, Jane, 'Handframe knitting: the development of patterning and shaping', *Textile History*, 6 (1975).

Samuel, R., 'The workshop of the world. Steam power and hand technology in mid–Victorian Britain', *History Workshop Journal*, 3 (1977).

Sewell, W. H., 'Social mobility in a nineteenth-century European city: some findings and implications', *Journal of Interdisciplinary History*, 7 (1976).

Simmons, J., 'A Victorian social worker: Joseph Dare and the Leicester Domestic Mission', *Transactions* of the Leicester Archaeological and Historical Society, 26 (1971).

Smith D. M., 'The British hosiery industry at the middle of the 19th century', *Transactions* of the Institute of British Geographers, 32 (1963).

Thompson, D. M., 'The 1851 religious census: problems and possibilities', *Victorian Studies*, 11, 1 (1967).

Thompson, E. P. 'Time, work discipline, and industrial capitalism', *Past and Present*, 38 (1967).

Thorn, G. 'The early history of the 'Amalgamated Society of Boot and Shoe Makers (Cordwainers)', *Bulletin* of the Society for the Study of Labour History, 39 (1939).

Tillott, P. M., 'The analysis of census returns', *Local Historian*, 8, 1 (1968).

Watmough, P. A., 'The membership of the Social Democratic Federation 1885–1902', *Bulletin* of the Society for the Study of Labour History, 34 (1977).

Yeo, S., 'A new life: the religion of socialism in Britain 1883–1896', *History Workshop Journal*, 4 (1977).

Unpublished theses

Atkinson, B. J., 'The Bristol Labour movement, 1868–1906' (D.Phil. thesis, University of Oxford, 1969).

Butler, B. J., 'Frederick Lewis Donaldson and the Christian Socialist movement' (M.Phil. thesis, University of Leeds, 1970).

Church, R. A., 'The social and economic development of Nottingham in the nineteenth century' (Ph.D. thesis, University of Nottingham, 1960).

Cox, D., 'The rise of the Labour Party in Leicester' (M.A. dissertation, University of Leicester, 1959).

224

Cunningham, T. M., 'The Growth of Peterborough 1850–1900' (Ph.D. thesis, University of Cambridge, 1972).

Elliott, M., 'The Leicester Board of Health 1849 to 1872: a study of progress in the development of local government' (M. Phil. thesis, University of Nottingham, 1971).

Fincher, J. A., 'The Clarion movement: a study of a socialist attempt to implement the co-operative commonwealth in England, 1891–1914' (M.A. dissertation, University of Manchester, 1967).

Ford, C. F., 'The political behaviour of the working-class in Coventry 1870–1900' (M.A. dissertation, University of Warwick, 1973).

Fraser, W. H., 'Trades Councils in England and Scotland 1858–1897' (Ph.D. thesis, University of Sussex, 1967).

Freer, D., 'Business families in Victorian Leicester' (M. Phil. thesis, University of Leicester, 1975).

Head, P., 'Industrial organisation in Leicester 1844–1914' (Ph.D. thesis, University of Leicester, 1960).

Hendricks, J. B. 'The tailoresses in the ready made clothing industry in Leeds, 1889–1899: a study in labour failure' (M.A. dissertation, University of Warwick, 1970).

Higgins, D. W. S., 'For the socialist cause: Rowland Barrett, 1877–1950: a biography' (M.A. dissertation, University of Warwick, 1980).

Hill, J., 'Working-class politics in Lancashire 1885–1906. A regional study in the origins of the Labour Party' (Ph.D. thesis, University of Keele, 1971).

Jones, R. L., 'The sociological context of trade union activity in the East Midlands boot and shoe industry in the late Victorian era' (M.Sc. dissertation, University of Loughborough, 1969).

Lancaster, W., 'The tradition of militancy in the Leicester I.L.P.' (M.A. dissertation, University of Warwick, 1979).

— Radicalism to socialism: the Leicester working class 1860–1906 (Ph.D. thesis, University of Warwick, 1982).

Mountfield, P. R., 'The location of footwear manufacture in England and Wales' (Ph.D. thesis, University of Nottingham, 1962).

Newton, R., 'Victorian Exeter 1837–1914' (Ph.D. thesis, University of Exeter, 1966).

Ross, J. S., 'English freethought 1875–1893. Secularism and connected movements in late Victorian England' (M.A. dissertation, University of Exeter, 1978).

Sutton, G. B., 'Shoemakers of Somerset. A history of C. & J. Clark 1833–1903'. (M.A. dissertation, University of Nottingham, 1959).

Thompson, D. M., 'The churches and society in Leicestershire 1851–1881' (Ph.D. thesis, University of Cambridge, 1969).

Tiller, K., 'Working class attitudes and organisation in three industrial towns, 1850–1875' (Ph.D. thesis, University of Birmingham, 1975).

Todd, N., 'A history of Labour in Lancaster and Barrow-in-Furness' (M.Litt. thesis, University of Lancaster, 1976).

Watmough, P., 'The politics of unemployment in London, 1892–1895' (M.A. dissertation, University of Warwick, 1975).

Index